JEKKA'S HERB
COOKBOOK

JEKKA'S HERB COOKBOOK

Jekka McVicar

10 9 8 7 6 5 4 3 2

Published in 2010 by Ebury Press, an imprint of Ebury Publishing

A Random House Group Company

Text copyright © Jekka McVicar 2010
Illustrations copyright © Hannah McVicar 2010

The Random House Group Limited Reg. No. 954009

Addresses for companies within the Random House Group can be found at
www.randomhouse.co.uk

A CIP catalogue record for this book is available from the British Library

The Random House Group Limited supports The Forest Stewardship Council® (FSC®),
the leading international forest certification organisation. Our books carrying the FSC
label are printed on FSC® certified paper. FSC is the only forest certification scheme
endorsed by the leading environmental organisations, including Greenpeace. Our paper
procurement policy can be found at www.randomhouse.co.uk/environment

To buy books by your favourite authors and register for offers visit
www.randomhouse.co.uk

Design: Will Webb
Illustrations: Hannah McVicar

Printed and bound in China by C & C Offset Printing Co., Ltd

ISBN 9780091930417

This book is not a medical reference book nor is it a substitute or to be relied on for
medical, healthcare, or pharmaceutical advice. Please consult your GP before changing,
stopping or starting any medical treatment. The author and the publisher disclaim as far
as the law allows any liability arising directly or indirectly from the use, or misuse, of the
information and suggestions contained in this book.

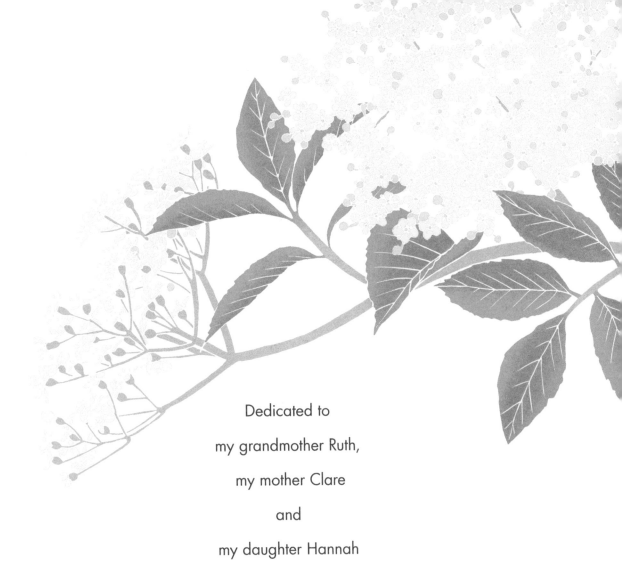

Dedicated to

my grandmother Ruth,

my mother Clare

and

my daughter Hannah

CONTENTS

FOREWORD

I've known the lovely Jekka for many years now and she is passionate about many things in life, but especially herbs. Without fail, each time I see her I learn something new about these wonderful plants. Jekka believes herbs are one of the best things in the world and after listening to her rave about their many benefits you can't help but agree with her.

Not only does she know loads about growing, cooking and storing herbs, she is also full of good information about how they can make you feel. I have no doubt that if more people were into growing and cooking their own herbs on a regular basis we'd be well on our way to having a happier and healthier country.

Jekka really is the herb queen of England in my books, yet she doesn't just know about the herbs we commonly enjoy in this country, she also knows about herbs from all around the world. If you're a foodie geek like me, you'll always find yourself ordering the newcomers to the ever-increasing collection at her farm.

In this day and age, varieties of herbs we used to think of as quite exotic are readily available in our local supermarkets. What's exciting and clever about what Jekka has done with this book is that she's focused on a 'hit-list': her top 50 cooking herbs of all time, and gives you delicious and exciting ways of using them. If you use herbs on a regular basis, you'll have tastier food and be a healthier person and I have no doubt you'll enjoy them and find Jekka's many practical hints and tips incredibly useful, as I have done over the years. Her book is a great start to finding serious solutions to good, exciting eating.

Jamie Oliver

INTRODUCTION

My passion for herbs has evolved over 50 years – it started before I went to school. My mother, who was a keen grower of herbs and vegetables, to the extent that we were self-sufficient, had a herb bed that contained over 25 different herbs. There was lemon thyme, French tarragon, dill, horseradish and spearmint, to name but a few. She was always bottling, preserving and baking. She taught me which mint to pick to make mint sauce and then how to prepare it, and for a number of years this was my special contribution to the Sunday meal. When I was at school I had what was called a garden plot, now known as an allotment, where I grew salads, including purslane and rather awful radishes, which I proudly brought home for the family to eat.

When I started work, I was working in television – often on short contracts – and in-between jobs I ended up working at 'Tumbler's Bottom Herb Farm'. I thought I knew a lot about herbs, thanks to my mother's garden, but soon realised I knew nothing. I became fascinated by the different varieties of herb at the farm and with this burgeoning knowledge and access to new plants my personal herb garden in Bristol expanded rapidly. It was from this garden that the idea for Jekka's Herb Farm originated. I was at home with my two small children one day when a girlfriend came round and asked if she could have some French tarragon. I told her to help herself and it dawned on me that she could not buy it anywhere yet I could grow it. Within a few months my husband and I had converted our small back garden into a mini organic herb farm and had started to supply local greengrocers and a garden centre with organic culinary pot herbs. Within a year I needed more space as it was becoming difficult to keep up with demand so we moved the farm to our present site in South Gloucestershire. The business has grown from there and in the early 1990s we started exhibiting organic culinary and medicinal herbs at the Royal Horticultural Society (RHS) flower shows where we have now been awarded over 60 RHS gold medals. There are currently over 650 different species of herb being grown at the farm, which we supply to our customers throughout the UK, mainly via mail order.

My interest in herbs is ever increasing and I am particularly fascinated by their incredible versatility. Herbs have long been a part of our history, yet we often remain wary of utilising them to their full potential. Not only do herbs impart flavour, aroma and texture to cooking, they are also beneficial to our diet and have medicinal and even household uses. It is well documented, for example, that thyme contains antiseptic oils, which counteract decay and contamination, sage contains a natural preservative, which prolongs the shelf life of food, and aniseed-flavoured herbs, such as French tarragon, help the digestion of fatty foods.

In this book I have limited myself to talking about my top 50 culinary herbs. These range from the well loved and well known parsley and rosemary to the more exotic curry leaf and Vietnamese coriander. All the herbs chosen are ones that I grow on my herb farm and have used for many years in the kitchen. There is a chapter devoted to each herb and within it you will learn how that herb is grown, its culinary benefits and what different varieties are available, before discovering the recipes that I hope will entice you to cook with it. I have also included a section entitled 'Excess Bay/Dill etc.' because there are times of the year when one has a glut of a specific herb and no idea how to preserve or harvest it for the winter months. My aim is to illustrate the wide range of herbs now available, how you can combine different herbs, and how they can be used, not only in savoury dishes but to make delightful desserts.

The recipes in this book are inspired by my love and enjoyment of food. I am a passionate cook and am always experimenting with how to incorporate new herbs and flavours into my dishes. Over the years I have discovered that one of the enormous benefits of cooking with herbs is their amazing ability to enhance dishes: they can transform a cheap cut of meat, stretch a sauce for pasta and add a new dimension to vegetables, eggs or just about anything! I have also drawn inspiration from friends and, above all, my family. I grew up surrounded by marvellous home cooks and as a result this book is infused with four generations of passion and talent. My grandmother, Ruth Lowinsky, wrote cookery books from 1930– 1950 and she inspired me to write my own; my mother, Clare, kept detailed handwritten notes of her recipes and encouraged my love of cooking; and my daughter, Hannah, whom I am proud to say has also inherited my love of food and cooking, has filled this book with her beautiful illustrations. (In doing so she is also following a family tradition as my grandfather, Thomas Lowinsky, illustrated my grandmother's original cookery books.) And finally, a number of professional chefs – Jamie Oliver, Heston Blumenthal, Michael Caines and Rick Stein, to name a few – have also found their way to the farm over the years and have been enthused by the herbs we grow. They, too, have motivated me to try new ways of cooking with herbs.

I hope that this book will inspire you both to grow and cook with herbs and to enjoy the pleasure of these remarkable plants.

General Recipe Notes

Produce
Having been an organic herb farmer for over 25 years, it goes without saying that I prefer to use organic and locally grown or raised produce in all my recipes, but I leave the choice up to you.

Herbs – in all the recipes I use fresh herbs; if you are using dried, please halve the quantities I have given as dried herbs have a stronger and more intense flavour.

Eggs – unless otherwise stated, eggs are medium. Where possible, use organic free-range eggs.

Milk – I use semi-skimmed milk.

Butter – I always use unsalted butter, and organic where possible. One can always add salt, but you can never take it away.

Sugar – sugar is granulated unless otherwise specified.

Fish – during my lifetime the depletion in fish stocks has been staggering. I try, where possible, to source fish that has been ethically farmed or caught, and such fish is now becoming more easily available.

Making preserves, jams, jellies or chutneys
Making preserves is a wonderful way of conserving the harvest for use throughout the winter months, however it is important to follow a few simple rules when preserving foods because botulism (a bacterial infection) can be very dangerous. Botulism can be difficult to detect as the bacteria are often found in minute quantities. Home-made preserves that are made without vinegar, salt or preservatives are more susceptible to bacteria as they lack the acidity which stops the bacteria's development.

So, to avoid complications:

* Choose only fresh unblemished fruit, vegetables and/or herbs.
* Storage jars or bottles must be thoroughly cleaned, sterilised (see page 12) and dried.
* The lids or tops of the storage jars should be new or lined with greaseproof paper and fit tightly.
* Clean cutlery should always be used when extracting the contents from the jars.
* Once opened the jars should be kept in a cool dark place or stored in a fridge and consumed fairly quickly. If at any time the contents of the jar look or smell suspicious, bin or compost them.

How to sterilise jars and bottles

While, there are a number of methods you can use to do this, I prefer to use either of the following:

❀ Pre-heat the oven to its lowest setting. Wash the jars and bottles and their tops well in hot soapy water, rinse then place them in the oven for at least 15–20 minutes prior to use. Remove the jars or bottles from the oven and fill, cover, or cool them, according to your recipe.

❀ Wash the jars or bottles in hot soapy water, rinse and leave to drain. Fill a large pan with cold water, immerse the jars or bottles in the water, bring to the boil, and simmer for 10–15 minutes. Remove the jars or bottles from the water using clean tongs, drain until fully dry, then fill.

How to skin tomatoes

Place the washed tomatoes in a bowl. Bring a kettle to the boil, pour the boiling water over the tomatoes, covering them completely, and leave for 3–4 minutes. Gently tip the tomatoes into a colander to drain. Taking care, as the tomatoes are hot, use a sharp-tipped knife to make a small nick in the skin, then it should peel off easily.

The sauce below can be enhanced by adding the herb of your choice, according to what best suits the dish you are serving it with. It can be sieved if you want a smooth sauce.

Some useful basic recipes

BASIC TOMATO SAUCE

Serves 2

25 g unsalted butter
1 tbsp olive oil
1 small onion, finely sliced
1 garlic clove, crushed
250g fresh tomatoes, skinned (see above) and finely sliced, or 400 g can of chopped Italian tomatoes
½ tsp soft brown sugar
salt and freshly ground black pepper

In a pan or frying pan, melt the butter and the oil. When just bubbling, add the onion and cook it gently until its flesh is translucent. Add the garlic and cook for a further minute, then add the tomatoes, sugar and salt and black pepper to taste.

CHICKEN STOCK

Makes 1 litre

1 chicken carcass (raw or cooked)
with giblets, washed
1 large onion, quartered
1 large carrot, scraped and cut into 4
1 tsp salt
bouquet garni (see page 40)
2 litres cold water (or 1 litre if
using a pressure cooker)

Break up the carcass and put it in a large pan or a pressure cooker (this is not only a great eco way to cook, as it uses less power and half the amount of water, it is also so much faster than simmering in a pan for hours). Add all the other ingredients and bring to the boil, uncovered. Using a slotted spoon, remove any scum that rises to the surface.

Put on the lid, reduce the heat and simmer very slowly for 1½ hours, or if using a pressure cooker, follow the manufacturer's instructions to bring the cooker to high pressure (15lb) for 45 minutes, then reduce the pressure slowly.

Strain the stock into a large bowl and leave to cool. When cold, remove the fat. Keep in the fridge and use within 3 days.

VEGETABLE STOCK

Makes 1.5 litres

2 large onions, sliced
4 large carrots, scraped and sliced
50 g swede or turnip,
peeled and sliced
1 leek, sliced and washed
bouquet garni (see page 40)
1 tsp salt
4 peppercorns
2.8 litres cold water (or 1.4 litres if
using a pressure cooker)

Put all the ingredients into a large pan and bring to the boil, uncovered. Using a slotted spoon, remove any scum that rises to the surface.

Put on the lid, reduce the heat and simmer for 1 hour. If using a pressure cooker, follow the manufacturer's instructions to bring the cooker to high pressure (15lb) for 15 minutes, then reduce the pressure slowly.

Strain the stock into a large bowl and leave to cool. Once cold, refrigerate and use within 3 days.

ANGELICA

(also known as Root of the Holy Ghost, European Angelica)
Angelica archangelica

My earliest memory of this herb is picking off the translucent green sugary pieces from my birthday trifle and reserving them for eating last. These were the candied stems of angelica that were traditionally used to decorate cakes and, on very special occasions, trifles. (Trifles just have to be the best 'left over pudding', so I have included a favourite version of this typically English dish on page 18.) Stems of angelica are not the only part worth eating; the leaves have a unique flavour which combines well with many fruit and vegetable dishes.

Description

Once angelica goes to flower it is absolutely stunning; it is one of the best architectural plants you can grow, giving great structure to a herb garden. The sweet honey scent of the flowers is lovely, too, especially when it catches an early summer's warm breeze. This is an interesting herb because, if it is growing happily, it will not die until it has flowered and set seed (the horticultural name for this is monocarpic), usually living for 2–4 years. Its final height, when in flower, is a magnificent 2.5m. The greenish-white, sweetly scented flowers are formed in large round clusters in the late spring to early summer of the second or third year. The large, deeply divided, bright green leaves around the base of the plant decrease in size around the stem and emit the smell of sweet muscatel when crushed or, if you have a powerful sense of smell, something like gin – as it is one of the main ingredients of the spirit.

Raise this plant from seed sown in the autumn into small pots or modules. In the early stages make sure seedlings and plants do not dry out. Plant out in the following spring into a deep moist soil, as angelica prefers to have its roots in the shade and its flowers in the sun. Being very tall when in flower, though, you should choose your site carefully: place it towards the back of a border or in the centre of the garden. If it is grown in an exposed windy site you may need to stake the plant when it goes into flower to stop the stems breaking. It is not an ideal plant for a pot because of its size.

History in cooking

Throughout history angelica has been used as a vegetable. In Greenland, Sweden and Finland the young shoots are blanched and used in soups and stews. Traditionally it has been used to flavour many drinks including Absinthe and Anisette Vermouth, as well as the aforementioned gin, where it is combined with juniper. If you are an enthusiastic forager please be aware that you do need to know what you are looking for, as angelica has been mistaken for hemlock (Conium maculatum), which is extremely poisonous. Unlike angelica, hemlock has a foul smell when the leaves are crushed, the white flowers form flat clusters and it has purple spots on its stems.

Harvesting and uses

Leaves:

Pick young leaves to use fresh in late spring to early summer while still soft. Their flavour is dry with a slightly bitter tang and a hint of aniseed and should be used sparingly – a little is good, a lot is not. It is ideal in salads, blanched as a spring vegetable, or used as flavouring in soups and stews. When stewed with fruit such as gooseberries or rhubarb, angelica reduces the tartness of the fruit and by so doing cuts down the amount of sugar needed to sweeten a dish. When using the leaves in this way it is a good idea to tie them up with a piece of string, tightly enough so they don't drift off into the fruit and can be easily removed once the fruit is cooked; if you leave the bunch in when serving the dish the flavour of the leaves would overpower the fruit.

Flowers:

Pick the small green flower as soon as you see it opening in late spring to early summer in the second or third year of the plant's life. These sweetly scented flowers also have a warm slightly aniseed flavour. Add to fruit salads, cordials, cream cheese, crème fraîche and fruit sorbets.

Stems:

Cut the stems of second-year growth before the flower head forms in early summer. Young tender stems can be steamed as a vegetable, candied, or used to make jam (see my recipe on page 21).
The stems need to be boiled, peeled, then boiled again before starting the cooking process. Alternatively, they can be peeled then soaked in brine (a solution of 3 tablespoons of salt per 1 litre of boiling water) for 12 hours before steaming.

Seeds:

Harvest seed heads in late summer and early autumn of the second and third year as soon as the seeds turn from pale green to pale brown and start to fall. They have an aromatic musky flavour and are excellent in soups, eggs and custards.

Roots:

Dig up second-year growth in late spring to early summer before the plant runs to flower. The roots can be used medicinally to treat digestive ailments; traditionally, though, these were eaten as a root vegetable. I have tried it and was not enamoured with the flavour or texture – it was rather stringy and tasted of anise and gin.

Properties Angelica leaf and stem are considered appetite stimulants. They are also high in potassium and magnesium.

Different varieties

Wild Angelica

(also known as Ground Ash, Jack Jump About)

Angelica sylvestris

Tall, hardy monocarpic herb with umbels of flowers in summer that are white and often tinged with pink, sitting atop stems that often have a purple tinge. The large lower leaves are narrow and sharply toothed and the roots are thick and grey on the outside. The plant is native throughout Europe, including Britain. It is often found growing in moist fields and hedgerows. Harvesting is carried out in September; young leaves can be used as an aromatic herb in salads and the seeds are used by confectioners in pastry.

American Angelica

(also known as Bellyache Root, High Angelica)

Angelica atropurpurea

Tall, hardy monocarpic herb with white to greenish white flowers from early to mid-summer. The mid-green leaves are large and the roots are purple. The whole plant has a powerful odour when fresh. It is found growing wild in fields and damp places in Canada and north-eastern and the north-central states of the USA. It is used in the same way as *Angelica archangelica*.

Alexanders (also known as Maceron)

Smyrnium olusatrum

Tall, hardy monocarpic herb with large, broad clusters of green–yellow small flowers in late spring and early summer. The mid-green wide oval shaped leaves when crushed are highly aromatic with a pleasant scent. It can be found growing wild in Europe, especially on the coast on cliffs, rocks and damp sand dunes. The young leaves can be used in the same way as angelica. In France it was historically considered an important vegetable.

ANGELICA AND APPLE SNOW TRIFLE

This delicious trifle is made with masses of fruit but is not too heavy at the end of a meal as it is lightened with egg whites. The angelica leaves reduce the tartness of the fruit, making the fruit flavour more predominant, but they should be removed before adding the egg whites otherwise their flavour will overpower the pudding.

My mum always made this trifle as a birthday treat, serving it with candles in the meringues.

Warning There can be an increased risk of salmonella poisoning when eating raw and lightly cooked eggs. Pregnant women, the elderly and young children should take particular care and such dishes are not recommended. If you are concerned, this pudding can be made by omitting the egg whites, but it will be heavier.

Serves 8

750 g Bramley apples, peeled, cored and sliced
100 g young small angelica leaves, left whole and tied with string for easy removal
75 g caster sugar
150 g dates, stoned
100 ml apple juice, plus another 2–4 tbsp for soaking the sponge fingers
6 sponge fingers
2 tbsp Calvados (optional)
3 egg whites
baby meringues
icing sugar, for dusting
pieces of candied angelica, to decorate

Put the apples in a medium-sized pan with the angelica leaves, sugar and 100 ml of water. Bring to the boil, cover, and cook over a low heat for about 10 minutes, stirring halfway, until the apples collapse to a mush.

Remove the angelica leaves. Purée the apples in a liquidiser, transfer to a bowl and leave to cool.

Place the dates and apple juice in the food processor and process until puréed but not too smooth. Cover the base of a 20-cm trifle bowl with the sponge fingers, sugared-side down. Sprinkle over either a mixture of 2 tablespoons of apple juice and 2 tablespoons of calvados, or just 4 tablespoons of apple juice, if you prefer. Spread the date purée on top.

Whisk the egg whites until stiff and fold into the cooled apple purée. Pour this over the trifle base and decorate with meringues. Cover and chill for at least half a day. If you make this a day in advance, decorate with meringues closer to the time.

Dust with icing sugar and scatter over the candied angelica stems before serving.

BRAISED LETTUCE AND ANGELICA FLOWERS

My grandmother often cooked lettuces. This is one of her recipes that I have adapted. The use of angelica flowers, with their lightly sweet aromatic flavour, complements the lettuce and is wonderful against the saltiness of the bacon.

It makes a lovely light supper when served with crusty home-made bread.

Serves 2–4

4 firm round lettuces, either Cos, or Little Gem
butter, for greasing
4 rashers middle back bacon
1 carrot, finely chopped
1 onion, finely sliced
1 tbsp angelica flowers, removed from stalks
300 ml strong chicken or vegetable stock (home-made if possible(see page 13))
1 tbsp chopped parsley, to garnish

Wash the lettuces well and remove any loose or damaged outer leaves before placing them, whole, in a large pan. Cover with cold water and bring to the boil. Immediately remove from the heat, strain, and rinse under cold running water. Shake off as much water as possible and dry on kitchen paper.

Pre-heat the oven to 180°C/350°F/gas mark 4. Grease an ovenproof dish and line the base with the rashers of bacon. Sprinkle over the carrot, the onion and half of the angelica flowers. Fold under the tops of the outer lettuce leaves to make neat parcels and place them on top of the onion and carrot mixture. Pour over the stock and cover with greaseproof paper. Cook in the oven for 45 minutes.

Lift out the lettuces and arrange on plates or a large serving dish. Reduce the stock and bacon and vegetable mixture in which they were cooked and pour over the lettuces. Sprinkle with chopped parsley and the remaining angelica flowers.

ANGELICA AND GOOSEBERRY COMPOTE

When dining at my great aunt's house she always produced a trolley full of puddings; two were always a fruit compote of some sort. One of her great tips was to add a good handful of angelica leaves when cooking gooseberries, not only to reduce the tartness of the fruit but also because the muscatel flavour of the leaves cuts through the acidity of the gooseberries. You can adjust these measurements to meet your needs and personal tastes. Serve with home-made yoghurt or crème fraîche with a little nutmeg grated over.

Serves 6–8

900 g gooseberries, topped and tailed
225 g angelica leaves, tightly tied up with string
juice and pared rind of 1 orange
150 ml cold water
50 g caster sugar

Combine all the ingredients in a large pan and gently cook until the fruit is tender. Once cooked, remove the angelica leaves and orange rind and discard.

Excess angelica

Candied angelica stems

Making candied angelica stems can take time, but it is worth it for they taste delicious. The reason for the many washes is to make the stems tender and palatable. This is a traditional recipe; the candied stems can be used on many puddings and cakes as decoration or as an added crunch, for example, in a fruit fool.

Warning Wear long-sleeved shirts when picking the angelica stems as they contain furanocoumarins, which are toxic chemicals produced by the plant and which may cause skin irritation and allergic reactions.

some second-year stems (use as many as you want, but do not be over-ambitious)
granulated sugar (equal in measure to the cooked angelica stalks, see recipe)
water
1 tsp bicarbonate of soda
caster sugar, for dusting

Choose sturdy, succulent green stems, not pale or weak ones or any that are coloured purple. Remove all leaves, then cut into 8–13-cm lengths. Place them in a pan with just enough water to cover. Simmer the sticks until tender, approximately 25–45 minutes, depending on the thickness of the stems. Drain, return to the pan, cover with cold water, and bring to the boil for 5 minutes. Remove from the heat, drain and peel off the outside skin.

Return the stalks to the pan and add enough water to cover and the bicarbonate of soda. Bring to the boil again and count to 5. Remove from the heat, drain immediately and allow to cool.

When cool, weigh the angelica stalks and add an equal amount of granulated sugar. Place the sugar and angelica in a covered dish, gently mix and leave in a cool place for 2 days. After this time the sugar will have dissolved to make a syrup.

Pre-heat the oven to its lowest setting. Tip the stalks and their syrup into a pan and slowly bring to the boil again. Turn the heat down to a simmer and cook, stirring occasionally, until the angelica stalks have a clear green colour which is rather translucent.

When the clarity and colour have been achieved, drain again, discarding all the liquid. Sprinkle over as much caster sugar as will cling to the angelica. Put the angelica in the cool oven to dry (about 1½–2 hours) – if it is not thoroughly dry it will become mouldy later.

Store the dried candied angelica stems between pieces of greaseproof paper in an airtight container for up to 3 months.

Angelica jam

This is a great way to preserve angelica, especially if you do not have the time or patience to candy the stems. I have often been asked to describe the flavour and the best description I could come up with is 'gin on toast'!

Makes 1.3–1.8 kg

angelica stems (enough to make 900 g cooked weight)
700 g caster/granulated sugar
425 ml water
juice and rind of 1 lemon

Choose young tender stems from 2-year-old plants for this jam. Remove all leaves then cut them into lengths that will fit into your pan. Fill the pan with water, bring to the boil and add the stems. Return to the boil then lower to a simmer. Cook until the stems are tender, about 25–45 minutes depending on the thickness of the stems. Drain.

Fill the pan with fresh cold water and leave the stems to soak overnight (at least 12 hours). Drain, and throw away the water. If you have used mature stems they may need to be peeled, so do so now. Weigh the stems, and for every 900 g of angelica stems you will need 700 g of sugar.

Cut the cooked stems into bite-sized pieces and add them to a large pan. (I use a preserving pan, which is a very worthwhile investment if you often make chutneys, jams and jellies.) Add the sugar and the water and cook over a very low heat, stirring constantly until the sugar is dissolved. Add the lemon juice and rind, bring to the boil and boil rapidly until setting point is reached. To tell when setting point has been reached, either use a sugar thermometer (the setting point being 110°C/200°F), or put a little jam on a chilled saucer – as it cools the jam should begin to set and will wrinkle slightly when you draw your finger across it.

Cool slightly before pouring into warm, sterilised jars (see page 12), cover and seal immediately. This will keep for a year in sealed jars. Once the jar is opened, store in the fridge and use within 4 weeks.

ANISE HYSSOP

(also known as Giant Hyssop, Blue Giant, Hyssop, Fennel Hyssop,
Fragrant Giant Hyssop, Mexican Hyssop)
Agastache foeniculum (Pursh) Kuntze

Interestingly, there are few references in cookbooks or dedicated herb books to this most attractive, under-used herb, other than the fact that it is a native of North America and eastern Asia; where it was originally used in teas to treat fevers and as a food seasoning. Personally, I rate this herb not only for being another useful culinary herb which combines well with many dishes, but also for the fact that it looks wonderful in the garden.

Description

This short-lived eye-catching herb is a delight, with its striking blue–purple spikes that flower throughout the summer and which attract bees and butterflies. It is an herbaceous herb that dies back into the ground in winter and reappears in the spring.

It can be raised from seed sown under protection in spring or from cuttings taken from non-flowering shoots in midsummer. Plant seedlings out in the late spring when the soil has started to warm up and there is no threat of frosts. Ideally, plant anise hyssop in a sunny position in rich moist soil, however it will adapt to most soils, with the exception of those that are very dry. Anise hyssop also happily adapts to being grown in a large container.

History in cooking

Historically *Agastache foeniculum* was used by the Native American Indians, and *Agastache rugosa* has been used for thousands of years in Chinese medicine. The few references to food that I could find are always associated with herbal teas in the USA and with marinades and fish in Asia.

Harvesting and uses

Leaves:
The leaves have a lovely warm minty/anise flavour which works well with fish, chicken, vegetables, puddings, sauces and teas. The young leaves should be picked from early to midsummer for use fresh and for preserving. The leaves can be frozen whole or chopped, or made into oils, vinegars, butters or sauce (see page 27).

Flowers:
The flowers are best used fresh, but this is not a problem as the herb flowers for most of the summer until early autumn, giving plenty of opportunities to gather them as they open. They can be pulled from the flowering spikes without having to remove the whole stem, thereby preserving the look of the plant.

Stems:
Stems are best cut in early summer; left any later they become tough and stringy. Cut them down to 4–6 cm from the ground and the

plant will respond by producing new bushy growth. The stems are great for either using as skewers for barbecuing vegetables or alternatively for placing on top of the rack onto which you can then place the fish.

Properties

Anise hyssop is a member of the mint family and as such has rather similar medicinal and digestive properties; it is reputedly an appetite stimulant and it is also said that the volatile oils in this plant, which give it its minty liquorice flavour, are a beneficial digestive. I have also found over the years that if one wants a slightly more herby/liquorice flavour in a recipe that uses mint, anise hyssop makes an excellent substitute for it.

Different varieties

Korean Mint (also known as Huo Xiang)
Agastache rugosa
Short-lived perennial herb with lovely mauve–purple flower spikes in summer. Distinctly minty-scented, mid-green, oval pointed leaves which can be used in culinary dishes. Makes a good tea for hangovers!

ANISE HYSSOP AND APPLE SALAD

When I first started growing this herb I simply used it in salads. This was one of my first recipes, and one that I have developed and updated over the years. The warm flavour of the anise combined with the sweetness of the apple and the cool, slightly bitter flavour of lettuce really stimulates the taste buds.

Serves 4

1 cucumber
salt
2 Cox's apples, cored then sliced
½ iceberg lettuce, sliced
½ head Chinese leaves, sliced
1 endive/chicon, sliced
1 tbsp finely chopped anise hyssop leaves,
5 anise hyssop flowering spikes, individual flowers removed

For the dressing
3 tbsp basil olive oil (see page 36) (or use a light plain olive oil)
1 tbsp balsamic vinegar

Peel the cucumber (if you want to be fancy, leave alternate stripes of skin). Slice thinly, then sprinkle salt over the cucumber and leave for at least 1 hour. Wash the salt off under cold water and drain.

Core and slice the apples – there is no need to peel them. Mix together the sliced apple, iceberg lettuce, Chinese leaves, endive, cucumber and anise hyssop leaves. Toss in the flowers, reserving a few for scattering over the finished salad.

Make the dressing by mixing together the ingredients. Pour over the salad and then toss. Scatter the remaining flowers over the salad and serve.

ANISE HYSSOP SORBET WITH CRYSTALLISED ANISE HYSSOP LEAVES

As a form of food, sorbet is brilliant. The Romans ate it between each course to clear the palate and also to act as a digestive. The lovely minty anise flavour of the leaves combines well with melon, especially Galia (see opposite). Crystallising the leaves as decoration makes this pudding extra special; the added texture complements both the sorbet and the melon.

This whole pudding can be made a few days in advance, so it is ideal if you are planning a large meal or are very busy.

Warning There can be an increased risk of salmonella poisoning when eating raw and lightly cooked eggs. Pregnant women, the elderly and young children should take particular care, and such dishes are not recommended.

Serves 4–6

425 ml water
225 g granulated sugar
1 lemon
1 large handful of anise hyssop leaves (young ones have a stronger anise flavour)

For the crystallised anise hyssop leaves
12 or 24 even-sized anise hyssop leaves
2 egg whites
1 tbsp caster sugar

First, make the crystallised anise hyssop leaves, as these need to be made the day before serving. Remove any stalks from the leaves and make sure they are clean and patted dry on kitchen paper. Lightly whisk the egg whites and use some of it to brush each leaf on both sides. Reserve the remaining egg white for making the sorbet. Sprinkle each leaf with caster sugar, lay them gently on a baking sheet lined with greaseproof paper and leave in a warm dry place for 12 hours.

Put the water and sugar in a small pan over a low heat, stirring all the time until the sugar is dissolved. Peel a strip of lemon rind and add it to the pan. Bring to the boil, reduce the heat and simmer for 5 minutes. Remove from the heat and allow to cool for a few minutes.

Chop the anise hyssop leaves, place them in a bowl with the juice of the lemon. Pour the hot, but not boiling, sugar syrup onto the leaves and lemon juice. Set aside to allow the flavours to infuse and until the syrup is cold.

Strain the syrup into another bowl and place in the freezer for about 2 hours, until it starts to crystallise and become mushy. Whisk the egg white left over from making the leaves until stiff, fold into the half-frozen syrup and return to the freezer for a minimum of 4 hours before serving.

MELON

Cut the melon into 4–6 pieces (depending on the number of guests you are feeding) and remove the pips. If you wish to be delicate, cut the flesh so that it is easily removed from the skin or, if you are like me, leave it for the guests to attack with gusto.

1 ripe melon, preferably Galia

Place the melon pieces on individual serving plates, put a spoonful of sorbet into the middle of each piece, and decorate with the crystallised leaves.

Excess anise hyssop

It is often said that culinary accidents are sometimes the best. This recipe was one I came across purely by chance. I wanted to make mint sauce to go with lamb chops but for some reason when I went onto the farm I became distracted and I picked anise hyssop instead. On returning to my kitchen I noticed my mistake but thought it would make a nice change. It certainly did, so if you have a glut of this herb this is a wonderful way of preserving and using these leaves.

Anise hyssop sauce
This sauce goes well with cold or hot lamb and cold pork.

1 bunch of anise hyssop
caster sugar (enough to cover the leaves when chopped)
balsamic vinegar

Remove the anise hyssop leaves from the stalks and chop them very finely. Add the sugar and keep chopping – this way the oils and flavours of the anise hyssop are amalgamated into the sugar. Once you are happy that it is all combined, transfer the anise hyssop and sugar to a small bowl. Stir in enough vinegar to just make it runny. Check the sweetness and add extra sugar if required. This will keep in a sealed jar or bottle in a fridge for up to a week. Stir well before use. If the vinegar has started to dry out, add a little more.

BASIL

(also known as Sweet Basil, Genovese Basil)
Ocimum basilicum

I think basil could merit a complete book on its own; it is a herb that never ceases to amaze me, from its culinary appeal to its astounding medicinal properties. When I started herb farming, over 3 decades ago, this was a herb I was told to use sparingly as the flavour could be overpowering; looking back I think we were just unsure how to use basil as it was such a new herb to us. Of course, now it is used prolifically in the kitchen, and I myself use it liberally in many dishes from pasta to custards, to teas, to salads, to sauces. It is one of the must-have culinary delights that can literally transform a meal into a feast.

Description

The most popular basil, Sweet Basil (*Ocimum basilicum*), has clusters of small, white tubular flowers in summer and green, oval, pointed leaves that have a wonderful smell when crushed.

Basil, in the majority of cases, is an annual herb, meaning that it lasts only one year in the garden or in a pot, and for this reason it needs to be raised from seed each season. Sow the seed under protection in early spring and outside direct into the ground in late spring or early summer, when the soil is warm to the touch and risk of frost has passed. Choose a well-drained fertile soil in a sunny warm situation, with a bit of shelter from the midday sun.

This herb is ideal for growing in containers, especially in cool temperate climates, as it gives the flexibility of being able to easily bring it under cover and provide it with protection from inclement weather and slugs. When growing in containers, use a soil-based potting compost.

Basil is a good companion plant; it repels white fly, aphids, tomato hornworms, asparagus beetles and fruit fly, and also, if kept in a pot on your windowsill, flies from the kitchen.

History in cooking

Before becoming king of the kitchen, this herb was steeped in history and folklore. You can find different forms of basil growing throughout the world, and as I researched into its properties I found that each culture uses it differently. Thousands of years ago basil was used by the ancient Egyptians to clear poisons from the body. There is a wonderful folklore story which is said to originate from the ancient Greeks who believed that if you wanted to grow intensely strong, fragrant basil, you should shout and swear as you sowed the seed! In India the use of this herb dates back over 1,000 years; it is considered a sacred herb and is used medicinally as a detoxifier and a heart medicine. In the 17th century, Nicholas Culpeper, the famous herbalist, wrote of basil's uncompromising if unpredictable appeal: 'it either makes enemies or gains lovers, but there is no in-between.'

Harvesting and uses

Leaves:

In cool climates the leaves are available from late spring until late summer; in warm climates they can be available all year round. The leaves have a wonderful spicy, minty flavour which is good with tomatoes, lemons, fish, chicken, pasta, pizza, marinades, salads, dressings and teas. A word of warning, though; the flavour can be ruined if the leaves are cooked for too long, so it is best to add basil to warm dishes at the end of cooking, when the heat will release its flavour and aroma. It is a herb that is favoured in many international cuisines, notably Mediterranean cooking, and in Thailand and other countries the leaves are added to soups and fish dishes. However, the leaves are rarely used in Indian cooking; more often they are used to make herbal teas, usually combined with other herb seeds or simply with tea leaves to make a refreshing drink.

The leaves do not freeze well as they become slimy when thawed, so the best preserving methods for use in the home is either in oils, vinegars, butters or sauces (see pages 35 and 36).

Flowers:

The flowers are best used fresh from the plant throughout the summer months. Gently pull each one away from the flowering spikes before adding to the dish. They are very good with salads, both savoury and sweet, and jellies, especially with fruit such as pears or figs.

Properties

Basil is a member of the renowned mint family which, when used in cooking, stimulates digestion and is a beneficial antioxidant. Medicinally, it is used to treat bronchitis, colds, fevers and stress; the juice of the leaves are used for skin complaints, and the essential oil extracted from it is used to treat ear infections and as an insect repellent. Current research has shown that it has the ability to reduce blood-sugar levels and it is used in the treatment of some types of diabetes.

Different varieties

African Blue Basil

Ocimum 'African Blue'
Lovely dark purple–blue, oval highly scented leaves that have a very fruity flavour. This basil is a perennial in its country of origin.

Cinnamon Basil

Ocimum basilicum 'Cinnamon'
Olive green–brown, oval, pointed, slightly serrated leaves that have a very spicy flavour. Lovely in stir fry dishes.

Dark Opal Basil, Purple Basil

Ocimum basilicum var. *purpurascens* 'Dark Opal'
Dark purple, oval, pointed leaves that have a very spicy warm flavour. Great added to rice and pastas, not only for its clove-scented flavour but also as a stunning colour contrast.

Greek Basil

Ocimum minimum 'Greek'
Small, green, oval, pointed leaves. In Greece pots of basil are placed on gate posts as a sign of welcome, or placed on tables to keep flies away. These small leaves are lovely with tomatoes.

Holy Basil, Tulsi

Ocimum tenuiflorum
Hairy and slightly serrated leaves that have a very pungent scent and flavour. Tulsi is often added to Thai dishes.

Lemon Basil

Ocimum x *citriodorum*
These wonderful lemon-flavoured leaves make the best salad dressing. They are also great for making sorbets and other puddings.

Lettuce Leaf Basil

Ocimum basilicum 'Napolitano'
Large, bright green, textured, crinkled oval leaves. Good for pasta sauces and for making pesto and basil oil (see page 36).

Mrs Burns Basil

Ocimum basilicum 'Mrs Burns'
Green, oval, intensely lemon-scented and flavoured leaves. Great with fish, chicken, rice and pasta, and also for making dressings and sauces.

Thai Basil

Ocimum basilicum 'Horapha'
Attractive oval, mulberry-tinted leaves that have an anise scent and flavour. Essential in Thai cooking.

SWEET BASIL GNOCCHI

To be honest, once you have eaten home-made gnocchi you will not only be inspired by the flavour but also by how easy they are to make. Adding the basil to the gnocchi rather than the sauce means its flavour comes through separately rather than being absorbed or overpowered by other ingredients in the sauce.

Serves 4–6

For the sauce
400 g can chopped tomatoes
1 shallot, finely chopped
2 garlic cloves, finely chopped
1 rosemary sprig, 2 thyme sprigs, or a couple of bay leaves
salt and freshly ground black pepper
pinch of sugar (optional)

For the gnocchi
500 g waxy potatoes (such as Charlotte, Nicola or Maris Peer), peeled and diced
15 g sweet basil leaves, finely chopped
200 g plain flour
salt and freshly ground black pepper
60 g wild rocket, washed, dried and roughly torn, to serve

First make the sauce. Pour the tomatoes into a small pan, then half-fill the can with water and pour this into the pan. Stir in the shallot, garlic, herb sprigs or leaves and add salt and black pepper to taste. (Mum always added a pinch of sugar to enhance the flavour of the tomatoes.) Bring to the boil and simmer gently for at least an hour until thickened and dark red.

As the sauce simmers, boil the potatoes for 10–15 minutes until tender, then drain and mash them well. Try to get the mash as smooth as possible because lumps will be noticeable in the gnocchi. Sprinkle over the basil, flour and plenty of salt and black pepper. Using a wooden spoon or your hands, bring together to make a firm dough. Knead the dough gently for a couple of minutes then roll out into sausages about 1 cm thick. Cut the sausages into pieces 2.5 cm long.

Put a large pan of water on the heat, bring to the boil then turn down to a simmer. Add the gnocchi to the simmering water for 1–2 minutes, until they rise to the surface, then scoop them out as they rise using a slotted spoon. Toss with the tomato sauce, fold in the rocket leaves and serve.

VICKI'S BASIL AND CHILLI PEPPERS WITH PESTO SAUCE

Vicki works with me on the herb farm and, like many who work here, she is a true foodie who loves fresh ingredients. The pesto sauce not only goes really well with the peppers, it is also is a great way of preserving the flavour of the basil leaves for a few days. Any leftover pesto can be mixed with cooked pasta or added to a tomato salad. This is delicious served with a fresh salad, plain boiled rice or poached salmon.

Serves 4

4 red peppers, halved and seeded
olive oil, for greasing and drizzling

Start by making the pesto sauce. Blend the pine nuts, basil leaves, garlic and Parmesan in a blender until smooth. Add the oil slowly and continue to blend the mixture until you have a thick paste. Season with salt to taste. Pour the sauce into a sealed plastic

4 tbsp cream cheese
1 medium-sized red chilli, finely chopped and seeded
1 tbsp chopped sweet marjoram
salt and freshly ground black pepper

For the pesto sauce
1 tbsp pine nuts
4 tbsp chopped basil leaves – sweet, greek or lettuce
2 garlic cloves, sliced
75 g Parmesan
6 tbsp sunflower oil or light olive oil (not virgin)

container and store in the fridge until required. It will keep for up to 1 week as long as the oil does not dry out; if it is looking dry, top up with more oil.

Pre-heat the oven to 200°C/400°F/gas mark 6. Place the pepper halves in a lightly oiled ovenproof dish. To each pepper half add 1 tablespoon of cream cheese, a sprinkling of chopped chilli, followed by 1 tablespoon of the pesto sauce. Sprinkle the sweet marjoram over all the peppers, followed by a drizzle of olive oil, and season with salt and black pepper. Place the dish in the centre of the oven for 20–25 minutes.

BASIL MAYO

This mayonnaise goes well with cold fish or chicken and is brilliant with boiled eggs. I have to admit that I use a food processor to make it, as I find it quicker and more reliable. My mother was transfixed when I demonstrated how easy it was compared to how long it took her to make it by hand. She did, however, consider it cheating and not proper cooking!

Warning There can be an increased risk of salmonella poisoning when eating raw and lightly cooked eggs. Pregnant women, the elderly and young children should take particular care, and such dishes are not recommended.

Makes 300 ml

2 medium egg yolks
1 tbsp lemon juice
1 tsp Dijon mustard
salt and freshly ground black pepper
300 ml light olive oil or vegetable oil, or a mixture of the 2
2–4 tbsp finely chopped basil leaves (lemon basil is especially good here)

Place the egg yolks, 2 teaspoons of the lemon juice, the mustard and a pinch of salt into the bowl of a food processor or blender and process until the mixture just begins to thicken.

Pour the olive oil into a measuring jug and, with the motor running, gradually add the oil to the egg-yolk mixture in a thin steady stream, occasionally stopping to scrape down the side of the bowl, until the mixture is thick, creamy and pale. You need to add the oil slowly, but not too slowly or the mixture might thicken too quickly. (If this happens, add about 2 teaspoons of hot water to thin down the mayonnaise before adding the remaining oil.)

Add the remaining lemon juice, stir in the basil, taste and adjust the seasoning, if necessary. Transfer to a small airtight container. (A good tip is to place a piece of plastic film directly on the surface of the mayonnaise, to prevent a skin forming, before covering with a tightly fitting lid.) Place in the fridge and use as required.

This will keep in the fridge for up to 3 days.

SWEET BASIL AND LEMON SORBET

The combination of the following basil leaves – lettuce, greek or sweet – with the sharpness of lemon is brilliant. This is a simple summer pudding which always finds favour with my family and friends.

Serves 4

150 ml water
150 g caster sugar
zest of 2 lemons
1 large bunch of basil leaves (whichever you wish), reserve some to serve
150 ml lemon juice

Place the water, sugar and lemon zest in a small pan, bring to the boil and simmer for 4 minutes. Remove from the heat and allow to cool for a while.

Remove the basil leaves from the stems (discarding the stems) and purée the leaves in a pestle and mortar or liquidiser. Add the lemon juice and basil purée to the lemon-zest syrup, stir well, then allow to cool for 30 minutes to allow the flavours to infuse. If you wish to be posh, strain the infusion through a sieve or if, like me, you love the leaves, simply pour it straight into a plastic tub or earthenware freezer-proof dish and place it in the freezer.

Generally, sorbet takes 2 hours to set. So that the sorbet is not rock hard, remove the container from the freezer after 30 minutes, beat the sorbet with a fork and return to the freezer. Repeat this 3 more times. You will find that this will make the sorbet crystallise rather than set as a rock of ice.

Serve decorated with some fresh basil leaves.

BASIL PANNACOTTA

When Jamie Oliver first started training the students at his restaurant Fifteen I was most impressed by one of them who, on hearing my talk on herbs and how in India basil is infused in milk and given to children as a bedtime drink, produced a pannacotta infused with basil. It was delicious, and this is my version of what I tasted that day. Serve it with fresh fruit such as figs, redcurrants, peaches or nectarines.

Serves 4
2 big bunches of basil (Purple, Cinnamon, Thai or Lemon – whichever you wish)
70 ml milk
2 vanilla pods, scored and seeds removed
finely grated zest of 1 lemon
375 ml double cream
1½ leaves gelatine, soaked in water
icing sugar

Remove the basil leaves from their stems and chop very finely, leaving a few whole to decorate.

Put the milk, vanilla pods and seeds, lemon zest and half the cream into a small pan, bring gently to the boil and slowly simmer for 10 minutes or until reduced by a third. Remove from the heat and pour into a bowl. Remove the vanilla pods and stir in the finely chopped basil leaves and the soaked gelatine leaves until dissolved.

Allow to cool a little, then place the bowl in the fridge, stirring occasionally until the mixture coats the back of a spoon. Remove from the fridge and either strain the mixture through a fine sieve to remove the basil, or leave them in if, like me, you like the direct flavour of the leaves.

Whip the remaining cream with the icing sugar then mix together the two cream mixtures. Divide among 4 individual serving moulds – I usually use small glasses. Cover and chill for at least 1 hour in the fridge.

When ready to serve, dunk the base and sides of the glasses into hot water and then tip the pannacotta out onto a serving plate. Decorate with a few basil leaves to serve.

BASIL BISCUITS

Baking biscuits has been part of my childhood and my children's. Hours have been spent round the kitchen table creating many different shapes and recipes. This is a reliable and tasty biscuit that can be served with fruit fools, sorbets, or simply on its own.

Makes 15–20

Pre-heat the oven to 180°C/350°F/gas mark 4.

100 g butter
50 g sugar
50 g ground almonds
100 g plain flour
1 large tbsp chopped basil leaves
(sweet, lemon, cinnamon or purple
– whichever you wish)

Cream together the butter and the sugar, add the ground almonds, mix well, then add the flour. Knead together on a lightly floured board to form a dough. Roll the dough in the chopped basil leaves until the leaves are amalgamated into the dough, then roll it into a 5-cm diameter sausage. Slice into 1-cm-thick slices.

Place the slices onto a baking sheet that is well greased or lined with non-stick baking parchment.

Bake for 10–15 minutes until lightly golden. Remove at once and cool the biscuits on a wire rack.

Excess basil

Basil sauce

This sauce goes well with cheeses, tomatoes, lettuce and cold meats and fish. The lemon basil sauce version is particularly good with cold salmon or trout.

1 bunch of basil (sweet, lemon, purple or Greek – whichever you wish)
caster sugar (enough to cover the chopped leaves)
white wine vinegar

Remove the basil leaves from the stalks then chop them very finely. Add the sugar and keep chopping so that the oils and flavours of the basil are amalgamated into the sugar.

Once you are happy that it is all mixed together, transfer the chopped basil and sugar to a small bowl. Stir in just enough white wine vinegar to make the sauce runny but not so much that you have masses of vinegar. Check the sweetness and add extra sugar, if required.

Basil oil

This is a delicious way of using up lots of basil leaves. However, when making oils using fresh produce one has to be extremely careful. Although oil by itself does not pose a risk for botulism, the addition of fresh herbs, in particular garlic, to oils can make this product potentially unsafe. Lemon juice, when added to the oil and herbs, will act as a natural preservative which will help to prolong the life of the infused oil.

This basil oil is great not only on salads but also with hard-boiled eggs, tomatoes, fish and cold chicken.

Makes 250 ml

3 good handfuls of basil leaves
250 ml light olive oil
2 tsp lemon juice

Wash and dry the leaves on kitchen paper. Finely chop the leaves (this can be done in a food processor), add the oil and the lemon juice and mix well. Pour into a container with a sealing lid, and pop into the fridge. Use within 5 days; shake well before use as the lemon juice will separate.

Alternatively, after 2 days strain the oil through an unbleached coffee filter paper, pour into a clean dry container with a sealing lid and keep in the fridge. Use within 3 days; shake well before use.

Warning Do not place fresh leaves in the bottle to make it look pretty, when the oil level drops and the leaves become exposed to the air they will turn mouldy and this will contaminate the oil and can cause salmonella. If you wish to use leaves to decorate the oil, make sure that they are properly dried before adding.

BAY

(also known as Sweet Laurel, Sweet Bay)
Laurus nobilis

This magnificent evergreen tree has always been part of my life, for my mother had a very large bay tree growing in the garden at both the houses where I spent my childhood and I also planted one in my first house, which grew so large it had to be moved. Even today I can picture my mother wearing an apron, as one did in the 1950s, picking handfuls of bay leaves which she used when making baked egg custards in her trusty, coal-fired Rayburn cooker.

Description

This is one of the few culinary herbs from the Mediterranean that is a slow-growing, long-living evergreen tree. In the right conditions it will grow to 8 m high and reach 3 m across. It has small, waxy, pale yellow flowers in spring, followed by oval green berries that turn black when ripe. These berries will only appear on the female tree, so if you wish to pick berries you will need a male tree planted nearby so that the flowers on the female tree will be pollinated and thus produce berries.

The oval, dark green leaves are shiny on the upper surface and matt on the underside; when held up to the light they are translucent, showing all the veins. About 80 years ago a number of False Bays were planted in the UK; it is also a laurel but does not have the flavour of the true, sweet culinary bay. The easiest way to see the difference between the two trees is to hold up a leaf to the light; if you cannot see through the leaf and it does not have any scent when you break it in half, it is the False Bay. If, on the other hand, you can see through the leaf, see the veins and the leaf smells wonderfully aromatic when broken, it is the true sweet bay.

So, bearing in mind its eventual height and spread, this herb needs to be positioned with care. Alternatively, it will flourish in a container where you can more easily control its growth and give it added protection in cold weather. In hot, not humid, climates, plant it in well-drained soil in partial shade. In cool climates, plant it in full sun in well-drained soil, and in cold climates, plant it in a container and protect it when temperatures fall below -10°C (14°F).

History in cooking

This herb has been used mainly as flavouring for many thousands of years. The Bedouin of North Africa traditionally used the leaves to flavour their coffee. Historically the leaves were not only used fresh, usually being added to a long cooking pot over the fire, but also dried then ground over fresh vegetables as we would grind salt and pepper.

Harvesting and uses

Leaves:
The evergreen leaves can be picked year round and have a wonderful warm, spicy scent and flavour with a hint of nutmeg and citrus. They add depth to all forms of food. To get the best from them, add fresh leaves at the beginning of cooking so that their flavour can slowly permeate the food.

Seeds:
Harvest seeds in the late autumn once they are fully ripe and slightly soft to the touch. In Mediterranean regions a cooking oil is extracted from the seed.

Properties

When used in cooking bay leaves promote the digestion and absorption of food; in particular they assist in the breakdown of heavy food, such as meat. They also stimulate the digestive tract, help to settle the stomach and are said to relieve flatulence!

Different varieties

Golden Bay
Laurus nobilis 'Aurea'
This is a golden-leaved variety of the standard bay tree, with a milder flavour.

Willow Leaf Bay
Laurus nobilis f. *angustifolia*
This bay has attractive, narrow, oval dark green leaves and is smaller in height, reaching 7 m. It can be used in the same way as the standard bay.

Indian Bay, Tej Patta, Malabathron
Cinnamomum tamala
The leaves of this evergreen bay are similar to those of its European cousin; they are dark green and oval with three main veins running the length of the leaf. Unlike the European variety, which can be picked from young, these leaves are not ready for harvesting until the trees are 10 years old. They can then be picked for the next 90 years and are renowned in Northern Indian cooking.

BAY- AND GARLIC-CRUSTED PORK

This is a very old recipe that my mum used to cook on Sundays. It was my job to chop the bay leaves and garlic and then pulverise them with the salt in a pestle and mortar. Pulverising the leaves releases their flavour into the salt, which is why this recipe tastes so good. Serve with roast vegetables or mustard mash and purple sprouting broccoli.

Serves 6

8 garlic cloves, peeled and sliced
8 bay leaves
coarse sea salt and freshly ground black pepper
4 medium onions, peeled (root ends left intact), each cut into 8 wedges
3 tbsp olive oil
1 pork spare rib (enough for 6 – ask your butcher to bone and roll as this makes it much easier to carve)

Pre-heat the oven to 170°C/325°F/gas mark 3.

Using a sharp knife, finely chop together the garlic and bay leaves. Tip them into a pestle and mortar with 2 teaspoons of coarse salt. Crush together until it forms a sort of paste.

In a large roasting tin, toss the onion wedges with 2 tablespoons of the olive oil and season with salt and black pepper. Push the onions to the edges of the tin and place the pork in the centre, fatty-side up. Rub the top with the remaining oil, then rub in the bay and garlic mixture, coating the skin evenly.

Roast until cooked, approximately 3 hours, then transfer the meat and onions to a serving platter. Let the meat rest, loosely covered with foil, for about 10 minutes before carving.

BOUQUET GARNI

A quote from one of my grandmother's cookbooks, *Food for Pleasure* (published in 1950 by Rupert Hart-Davis), reads: 'A bouquet garni is a bunch of herbs constantly required in cooking.' As far as she was concerned, this was the right way to use herbs.

A bouquet garni is a small bundle of fresh herbs that is used to flavour slowly cooked dishes. The herbs are tied together tightly with a long piece of string so that they can easily be removed from the casserole or stew at the end of the cooking time. Alternatively, you can enclose the herbs in a muslin bag, also attached to a long piece of string.

Different combinations of herbs will enhance different foods, and here are a few of the best bouquets garnis:

A standard bouquet garni for a meat or chicken casserole
1 bunch of parsley, including the stems
3 thyme sprigs
1 garlic clove, peeled
2–3 bay leaves

Other variations using the amounts of herbs to suit your palate and dish:

Bouquets garnis for meat
Oregano, thyme, bay and lovage *or*
Thyme, sage, parsley and bay

Bouquets garnis for poultry
Bay, lemon thyme, lemon balm and lemon grass (the grass ends) *or*
Rosemary, summer savory, hyssop and bay

Bouquet garni for game
Myrtle, bay, orange-scented thyme and parsley

Bouquet garni for fish
Welsh onions (the stems), French parsley, bay and tarragon

WHITE CHOCOLATE AND BAY MOUSSE

Nigel Slater rates in my top 10 of culinary experts; he uses herbs lightly, respecting their flavour and texture. We have, over the years, had many a discussion about culinary herbs – their merits and their garden prowess – and I have even been known to carry a crate of herbs up to London on the train especially for his garden. This is one of his recipes, which is sublime, to which I have added bay leaves, as these complement the cardamom pods and add another dimension to the infused milk.

As a chocoholic I must, like Nigel, recommend that you use good chocolate to make this recipe as it honestly will not work with less. Use Lindt vanilla or, even better, Valrhona vanilla, which is a Rolls-Royce of a chocolate.

Warning There can be an increased risk of salmonella poisoning when eating raw and lightly cooked eggs. Pregnant women, the elderly and young children should take particular care and such dishes are not recommended.

Serves 6–8

100 ml milk
3 bay leaves
8 plump cardamom pods
250 g white chocolate
200 ml double cream
3 egg whites
some top-notch cocoa powder, to dust

Place the milk and bay leaves in a small pan. Break the cardamom pods open and extract the seeds, crush them lightly and add to the milk and bay. Very gently warm the milk until it's just below boiling point. Remove from the heat.

Break the chocolate into small pieces and melt them in a bowl set over a pan of gently simmering, not boiling, water. Make sure that the bottom of the bowl does not touch the surface of the water, otherwise your chocolate will dry out and become lumpy. As soon as the chocolate starts to melt, turn off the heat and the residual heat will melt the rest.

In a bowl, whip the cream until it forms soft peaks, i.e. not too firm.

In another bowl, beat the egg whites until stiff and forming peaks.

When the chocolate is completely melted, remove the bowl from the pan. Pour the warm milk over the chocolate, passing it through a sieve to catch the bay leaves and cardamom seeds. Stir until the mixture becomes smooth. Scoop the mixture onto the beaten egg whites, and gently fold in using a large metal spoon, then fold this mixture into the whipped cream.

Spoon into small ramekins or espresso coffee cups and refrigerate for 3–4 hours until set. Dust with cocoa powder to serve.

RICE PUDDING WITH BAY LEAF

This simple heart-warming pudding is just brilliant on a cold winter's day, especially when served at a lunch with friends that goes on for hours. When infused with the bay leaf the pudding is spicy and warm – the herb totally complements this dish.

This is best made using full-cream milk, but if you are lucky enough to live in the country you could use green milk. As my son, when young, would say, it has not been 'past your eyes'. However, I should add a warning as green milk comes straight from the cow without being pasteurised. Pasteurisation is a process of heat treatment which kills harmful food poisoning bacteria, so if you do use un-pasteurised milk it could be harmful to vulnerable people such as children, people who are unwell, pregnant women and the elderly. If you use un-pasteurised milk or cream, be especially careful to keep them properly refrigerated as they have a very short shelf life.

As a child Mum served the rice pudding with a dollop of home-made jam. If she wasn't looking, my brother and I would make swirling patterns with the jam! Serve with jam, clotted cream or stewed plums, or simply on its own.

Serves 6

2 tbsp pudding rice
25 g butter, plus extra for greasing
2 tsp granulated sugar
600 ml full-cream milk
2 bay leaves
nutmeg

Pre-heat the oven to 200°C/400°F/gas mark 6.

Place the rice in a sieve and rinse it under cold running water. Grease an ovenproof dish with a little butter, add the rice, then the sugar and the milk. Stir well, and add the bay leaves, tucking them under the surface of the milk. Grate over the nutmeg and, finally, scatter small slices of butter over the surface of the pudding.

Place on a baking sheet and bake for 20–30 minutes, then reduce the temperature to 150°C/300°F/gas mark 2 for a further 1 hour or until the milk has been absorbed into the rice, the texture is soft and creamy and you have the wonderful golden skin.

Excess bay

As this is an evergreen tree that can be picked all year round, it is unlikely that you will have an abundance of leaves that you urgently need to preserve. However, if a friend gives you a branch and you wish to preserve the leaves for future use, I recommend drying a few. Alternatively, infuse them in salt, oil or vinegar. When using dried leaves in cooking, use half the amount of fresh ones mentioned in the recipe.

Drying bay leaves

Remove the leaves from their branches. Spread them out, with space between each leaf, onto some muslin that has been stretched over a simple wooden frame. Place the rack of leaves in a dark room that is warm, dry and well ventilated. Turn the leaves over every other day until fully dry. When the leaves are dry and crisp enough to crumble, they are ready for storage. Put the leaves into a dark glass jar with a screw top.

Bay salt

This salt is simple to make, delicious to use and it makes a great Christmas present.

Makes 250 g salt

250 g non-iodised salt
6 bay leaves

With a pestle and mortar, pound the salt with the leaves so it picks up the flavour of the bay. Bottle the salt with the crushed bay leaves and keep in a dark cupboard.

The flavoured salt can be used immediately and is best used within 3 months.

Bay oil

This is an unusual oil but is certainly worth making if you have a glut, as the flavour is beautiful and the oil can be used with many dishes, from mayonnaise to marinades.

For more information about preserving and the risks of using herbs in oils, see page 36.

3 good handfuls of bay leaves
250 ml mild olive oil
2 tsp lemon juice

Wash the leaves and dry on kitchen paper. Finely chop the leaves (this can be done in a food processor), add the oil and the lemon juice and mix well. Pour into a container with a sealing lid, and pop into the fridge. Use within 5 days; shake well before use as the lemon juice will separate.

Alternatively, after 2 days strain the oil through an unbleached coffee filter, pour into a clean dry container with a sealing lid and keep in the fridge. Use within 3 days; shake well before use.

BERGAMOT

(also known as Oswego Tea, Bee Balm, Blue Balm, High Balm, Low Balm, Mountain Balm, Mountain Mint or Wild Bergamot)
Monarda fistulosa

I have a soft spot for this herb which has, in summer, a magnificent flamboyant flower that looks like a hat that could be worn to a society wedding or the Chelsea Flower Show. It is a native of North America, where it was introduced to the settlers by the Oswego American Natives. So that there is no confusion, this herb bears no resemblance or similarity to the small fruit which is also called bergamot, *Citrus bergamia*, which is predominantly found in Italy. It is from that fruit that the bergamot essential oil is extracted.

Description

Bergamot is a hardy herb perennial that dies down in winter, reappearing in the spring. When in flower it will reach 1.2 m high and will spread, in light soils, to 45 cm. The bergamot flowers appear from summer until early autumn, and they are a lovely lilac with mauve bracts. The leaves are highly aromatic, toothed and slightly hairy.

Bergamot grows well in moist, nutrient-rich soil, preferably in a semi-shady spot, especially in deciduous woodland. They will tolerate full sun, though, if the soil retains moisture. Like many other perennials, bergamot should be dug up and divided every 3 years, discarding the dead centre.

History in cooking

It is said that in the 18th-century bergamot became known as 'Oswego Tea' when a Quaker botanist sampled a tea made from the leaves at Fort Oswego, New York, and gave it this name. It became such a popular tea during the Colonial period that in the mid-18th century the settlers started sending bergamot seeds back to England. While visiting my daughter in the USA I bought a number of old medicinal herb books which show that the early North American settlers had learnt of the medicinal properties of bergamot from the Native Americans. They used it to treat many ailments, including making a tea from the leaves to help respiratory difficulties.

Harvesting and uses

Leaves:

Pick the leaves from late spring until early autumn before the plant flowers, because they become bitter as they age. They have a warm, minty, spicy flavour. Use the leaves with cheese, pork and vegetables such as cauliflower. Their spicy flavour also enhances fish dishes.

Flowers:

These can be picked throughout the summer until early autumn. Remove the flowerets individually from the flower head and scatter over salads, both sweet and savoury.

Properties

Bergamot is a member of the mint family, and like mint it is very beneficial as a digestive. A tea made from the leaves is said to help insomnia, nausea and flatulence.

Different varieties

Lemon Bergamot
Monarda citriodora
This bergamot is an annual, and it has the most superb, intense, lemon-scented leaves that are great for use in puddings, savoury dishes and for making a delicious cup of tea. The flowers are a beautiful mauve surrounded by pale mauve bracts.

Bee Balm Bergamot, Red Bergamot
Monarda didyma
The leaves of this variety can be used with pork, fish and salad dishes. They also make a good cup of tea. It has a 'wow' factor – the red flower with dark red bracts. These look great when scattered over a green salad.

BERGAMOT AND COUSCOUS SALAD

A delicious fast salad. My mother spent hours steaming couscous to make it light and fluffy; sadly, she did not live to see the couscous that I can now buy in the supermarkets which just takes minutes to prepare and makes a wonderful simple meal. The flavour of the bergamot leaves and flowers makes this salad taste good and look good.

Serves 4–6

100 g couscous
200 ml boiling water
25 g unsalted butter
2 bunches of
spring onions, chopped
225 g tomatoes, skinned,
chopped and drained
1 tsp chopped bergamot leaves
2 tsp bergamot flowers (petals
removed from the green calyx)
4 tbsp olive oil
3 tbsp lemon juice
salt and freshly ground
black pepper

Put the couscous in a bowl and pour over the boiling water – read the packet for specific instructions, as some brands need more water, some less. Add the butter, stir, then cover and leave to stand for 5 minutes.

Fluff up the couscous with a fork and pour into a serving bowl. Allow to cool before adding the chopped spring onions, tomatoes and bergamot leaves and petals. Stir well, then add the oil and lemon juice and mix well. Season to taste with salt and black pepper.

BERGAMOT WITH SALMON STEAKS

This is a lovely late-spring dish, when the bergamot leaves are at their most succulent. The combination of flavours of the salmon and the bergamot leaf is subtle and complementary. Serve with new potatoes and a crisp green salad.

Serves 4

4 salmon steaks (or cod or halibut)
40 g unsalted butter
1 tbsp olive oil
1 tbsp chopped bergamot leaves,
plus whole ones to garnish
2 tsp plain flour
150 ml white wine

Rinse the salmon steaks and pat dry with kitchen paper. Melt the butter with the olive oil in a large frying pan. Add the salmon steaks and the chopped bergamot leaves. Cook the fish over a moderate heat for 3 minutes on each side until lightly browned. When the steaks are cooked, remove them from the pan and put them in a warmed serving dish.

Add the flour to the juices left in the pan, stir well for 1 minute then add the white wine, stirring to prevent any lumps developing. Bring to the boil and cook for 2 minutes.

Pour the sauce over the salmon steaks and add some extra leaves to garnish.

PORK TENDERLOIN WITH BERGAMOT SAUCE

Pork combines well with the minty, aromatic spicy flavour of the bergamot sauce to make this a special supper. Serve with mashed potato and fresh green broccoli.

Serves 4–6

2 pork tenderloins
(approx. 150 g each)
75 g butter
olive oil

For the bergamot sauce
2 shallots, very finely chopped
40 g plain flour
250 ml hot vegetable
or chicken stock
2 tbsp bergamot leaves,
finely chopped
salt and freshly ground
black pepper
1 tbsp crème fraîche

Pre-heat the oven to 200°C/400°F/gas mark 6.

Pat the tenderloins dry with kitchen paper and cut into 1.5 cm thick slices.

Melt half the butter with a splash of oil in a frying pan over a medium heat. Gently fry the pork slices, turning once halfway through cooking, for about 5–7 minutes until cooked. Arrange the slices in a warmed serving dish.

Prepare the sauce by sweating the shallots in the remaining butter until soft. Stir in the flour and cook for about 1 minute, stirring all the time. Whisk in the stock and simmer until it thickens, stirring occasionally to prevent it sticking. Add 11/2 tablespoons of the chopped bergamot leaves. Simmer for several minutes then season with salt and black pepper to taste.

Remove from the heat, stir in the crème fraîche and pour over the arranged pork slices. Garnish with the remaining chopped bergamot leaves.

BERGAMOT AND GOOSEBERRY JELLY

This jelly emphasises the warm, spicy, mint flavour of the bergamot when combined with the sharp flavour of the gooseberries. It is a good accompaniment for cold or hot pork, roast lamb and Cheddar.

Makes approx. 2 x 350 g jars

1 kg gooseberries,
topped and tailed
1 bunch of bergamot leaves
900 ml cold water
approx. 450 g sugar
2 tbsp lemon juice
2 tbsp white wine vinegar
4 tbsp chopped bergamot leaves

Wash and sort the gooseberries and add the good ones to a large pan with the bunch of bergamot leaves and the water. Bring to the boil and simmer until the fruit is soft and pulpy. Pour into a jelly bag and leave to drain overnight.

Next day, measure the juice and add 450 g of sugar for every 600 ml of liquid. Pour the juice and sugar into a heavy pan, bring back to the boil and boil steadily until setting point is reached, about 20–30 minutes (see page 21). Skim off the surface scum, stir in the lemon juice and vinegar and the chopped bergamot leaves.

Pour into warm sterilised jars (see page 12) and seal when cool. This will keep in unopened jars for 1 year. Once opened, store in a fridge and use within 1 month.

Excess bergamot

Bergamot flower ice cubes

Bergamot flowers are ideal for freezing in ice cubes. Pick the flowers when they are fully open. These cubes look lovely not only in drinks but also added to fruit salads or in an ice bucket on special occasions.

bergamot flowers
cooled boiled water

To keep the ice cube clear, use boiled water that has been left to cool. Fill the ice-cube tray with the water, then add a single flower to each section. If you find the flowers difficult to handle, use a pair of tweezers to place them in the water. Leave to set in the freezer for 12 hours.

Once frozen these ice cubes can be bagged, but they will stick so I do advise keeping them in the trays. Use within 3 months.

Bergamot sauce

This sauce goes well with cold or hot lamb and cold pork.

1 small bunch of bergamot leaves
caster sugar (enough to cover the leaves when chopped)
white wine vinegar

Remove the leaves from the stalks and chop them very finely. Add the sugar and keep chopping, this way the oils and flavours of the bergamot are amalgamated into the sugar.

Once you are happy that it is all mixed together, transfer the bergamot and sugar to a small bowl. Stir in the white wine vinegar – enough to just make it runny but not so much that you have lots of vinegar. Check the sweetness and add extra sugar if required.

This will keep in the fridge in a sealed jar with a non-metallic lid for 7 days.

Bergamot vinegar

bergamot leaves
white wine vinegar

Fill a wide-mouthed bottle with bergamot leaves and pour white wine vinegar over them to fill the bottle completely. Screw on the lid and stand in a dark place for 2–3 weeks.

Strain through unbleached coffee filter papers into sterilised bottles (see page 12). Label and store – it will keep in a dark cupboard for a couple of years.

BORAGE

(also known as Burrage, Common Bugloss,
Star Flower, Bee-bread)
Borago officinalis

I have positive and happy memories of this herb, from making necklaces by stringing flowers together in my teens, to using the flower heads in ice cubes to fill an ice bucket for a special occasion in my twenties, to the present day when harvesting my French beans. For besides having a beautiful flower, this is the one herb that helps with the pollination of vegetables, as all forms of bees love it, hence one of its common names: 'Bee-bread'. Personally I think that its culinary delights are overlooked. Interestingly, the leaves are covered in tiny hairs, which some people can find annoying as they can irritate the skin but do no harm. So it is important when using leaves for salads that you choose young succulent leaves, which you will find taste like cool cucumber and whose tiny hairs, which are annoying when mature, simply dissolve on the tongue.

Description

Borage is an attractive herb with pretty blue flowers that looks lovely in the garden or in the vegetable garden. Each plant lasts 1 year, and once it has flowered it will happily disperse its seeds around the garden. Luckily the seedlings are easily removed if you find you have a profusion of them, and they also taste delicious added to salads.

Please do not, like a few friends of mine, confuse this herb with alkanet, *Anchusa officinalis*, which looks similar and belongs to the same family. Alkanet is a perennial so it will appear in the same spot in the garden every year. The difference between the two is recognisable, once you know: the leaves of alkanet are long, lance-shaped and hairy; borage leaves are oval, medium-sized and hairy. The flowers on both are blue, but borage has black stamens that look rather like a bird's beak and the flower hangs down. Alkanet flowers look at you and are smaller than borage flowers with a white centre – more like their cousins, Forget-me-nots.

Sow borage seed from spring until midsummer direct into the garden soil or into a large container, as it has a long tap root that dislikes being disturbed once it gets growing. It prefers a well-drained light soil, however, saying that, it thrives in my very heavy clay soil when in a sunny position.

History in cooking

Records of the use of borage date back to the ancient Romans and Greeks; it has been used medicinally as a tea to reduce high temperatures and as a remedy for colds and flu. Interestingly, in Roman times they considered borage a pot herb/vegetable and added it to their vegetable stews.

Harvesting and uses

Leaves:

The young leaves of this herb are by far the best for using in the kitchen. As this is a bit of a thug of a herb, there are always new shoots and new leaves appearing from spring until the first hard frosts. Always pick the leaves before the flowers form. When eaten fresh the leaves have a cool cucumber flavour and are excellent in salads or with cream cheese, fish and vegetables. When cooked they have a light refreshing flavour which makes a lovely summer soup.

Flowers:

Pick the flowers from late spring right through the summer until the first frosts. Ideal for adding to fruit and savoury salads, rice dishes, puddings of all sorts and ice cubes.

Properties

The leaves and flowers are rich in potassium and calcium and therefore a good blood purifier and a tonic. Because it is a tonic plant for the adrenal glands, borage provides an invaluable support for a stressful lifestyle.

Different varieties

White-flowering Borage
Borago officinalis 'Alba'
This can be used in exactly the same way as the blue-flowering borage.

BORAGE SOUP

This is a versatile soup as it can be served both hot and cold, which makes it a perfect British summer dish – when the weather can also be very hot or cold.

Serves 4

50 g unsalted butter
50 g long grain rice
750 ml hot home-made (see page 13) or a good bought chicken stock or vegetable stock
225 g borage stems with young leaves and a few flowers, to garnish
salt and freshly ground black pepper
175 g crème fraîche or double cream

Melt the butter in a large pan, add the rice and cook on a low heat for a few minutes, stirring all the time. Add the stock, cover and simmer for 15 minutes.

Remove the flowers from the borage stalks and set aside for later. Remove the borage leaves from the stems, wash, and add to the stock and rice. Simmer for a further few minutes until the rice is cooked.

Remove from the heat, check the seasoning, and using a hand blender or a food processor, blend the soup. Serve hot with a swirl of crème fraîche or double cream, or pour it into a bowl and allow to cool before placing in the fridge.

When serving cold, stir the soup well before serving and spoon into individual bowls. Add a swirl of crème fraîche or double cream and garnish with a few bright-blue borage flowers.

BORAGE, PEAR AND RASPBERRY SALAD

A true summer salad bursting with colour. The young borage leaves with their cool cucumber flavour complement the pear and raspberries.

Serves 2

10 young borage leaves, finely sliced (don't worry, the hairs dissolve on the tongue)
1 handful of wild rocket leaves, coarsely chopped
4 tbsp raspberries
3 pears (Conference, Williams or Comice), peeled, cored and sliced
lemon juice (optional)
3 tbsp olive oil
1 tbsp balsamic vinegar
borage flowers

In a serving bowl, mix together the borage leaves and wild rocket. Add the raspberries, then the sliced pears. If you want to make this in advance, slice the pears and squeeze some lemon juice over to prevent them turning brown.

Make a vinaigrette with the olive oil and vinegar, pour over the salad and toss. Scatter the borage flowers over the top and serve.

BORAGE ICE CUBES

Add colour to your drinks and fruit salads with these pretty cubes. As with bergamot, pick the borage flowers when they are fully open.

borage flowers
cooled boiled water

To keep the ice cube clear, use boiled water that has been left to cool. Fill the ice-cube tray with the water, then add a single flower to each section. If you find the flowers difficult to handle with your fingers, use a pair of tweezers to place the flowers in the cube. Leave to set in the freezer for 12 hours.

They will keep in a freezer for up to 3 months before becoming cloudy.

BORAGE FLOWER ICE BOWL

Slightly fiddly to make but spectacular to look at, this is worth the effort for a special occasion or when you want to show off. Perfect for serving fruit such as strawberries, or slices of nectarines, peaches and melons.

stems of borage flowers and leaves
cooled boiled water

Remove the flowers from their stems.
Take two clear glass mixing bowls that fit inside one another. Half-fill the larger bowl with cool boiled water and sit the smaller bowl inside. Float the smaller bowl about 2 cm above the base of the larger bowl and hold it in position by weighing it down with gravel, a stone or a weight, then tape it centrally into place.

Arrange the flowers or leaves by tucking them into the water between the 2 bowls. When you are happy with their position, top up the bowl with more cooled boiled water. Place the bowls in the freezer for at least 24 hours. When you want to use the bowl, take it from the freezer, remove the tape and gravel and leave the ice bowl to melt slightly. This makes it easier to remove the glass bowls.

Excess borage

Borage flowers can be prolific and one of the best things you can do with this abundance is to crystallise them. They can then be used in a multitude of ways, including decorating puddings and cakes and placing on home-made chocolates.

Crystallised borage flowers

When I wrote my book *Cooking with Flowers* I discovered that there are a number of methods for crystallising flowers, the most common being to dip them in beaten egg white with sugar – with or without alcohol. However, the technique I prefer uses gum Arabic and rosewater, as this preserves the flowers for a few months when kept in an airtight container. This method does take time, so be patient.

Rosewater can be bought from the dispensary of any large pharmacy. Tell them that you wish to use the rosewater for cooking and they will make it up using tap water rather than purified water, which has had its salts removed. (The salts are necessary to control any bacteria.) Gum Arabic can also be bought from pharmacies or shops selling cake-making and icing accessories.

1 tbsp rosewater
1 tsp gum Arabic
borage flowers
icing sugar or caster sugar

When crystallising flowers it is essential to be well prepared, because the fresher they are when you are doing it, the better the end result. So prepare the gum Arabic solution first by pouring the rosewater into a small jar with a close-fitting lid and a wide-enough neck to be able to pop flowers in and retrieve them. Add the powdered gum Arabic. Replace the top and shake the bottle until the powder has dissolved, about 1–2 minutes. Do not be tempted to put the powder into the jar before the rosewater because it is then incredibly difficult to make the powder dissolve fully.

Pick the borage flowers in the late morning, choosing perfect specimens. Remove them from the stems, making sure you have no green parts. Dip each one in water to remove any insects or dust, then very gently dry them on some kitchen paper.

Pre-heat the oven to 110°C/225°F/gas mark ¼.

Immerse the flowers completely in the gum Arabic solution, by dropping them one at a time into the jar. Retrieve them from the jar using a fine artists' paintbrush and put them on a sheet of greaseproof paper that has been covered with sugar. Sprinkle more sugar over the top and use another fine paintbrush to remove any sugar that has made lumps in the heart of the flower.

Place the now well-sugared flower on a clean sheet of greaseproof paper on a wire rack and dry in the oven with the door ajar. This will take approximately 2–3 hours. When they are hard to the touch remove from the oven. Store them in layers between greaseproof paper in airtight jars or rigid containers. Stored this way they will keep for up to 6 months.

CARAWAY

(also known as Kümmel, Karon, Karuij, Alcaravea and Field Cumin)

Carum carvi

My grandmother and mother both used the seeds of this herb profusely in vegetable dishes and in cakes and biscuits. One childhood recipe that I remember well is baked potatoes covered in seeds and cheese.

Caraway is used in many countries from India to Europe, Australia and Northern America. In the UK it is one of our native herbs but has recently become endangered in the wild, due to changes in agricultural practice. Where it grows wild it is known as Field Cumin.

Description

Caraway is an attractive biennial which produces leaves in the first year, and in the second year attractive small clusters of tiny white flowers with a hint of pink throughout the early summer. The leaves are similar to its cousin the carrot – light green and feathery with a delicate parsley-like flavour. The root is comparable to parsnip, but it is much smaller and has a mild anise flavour.

Caraway is easily grown from seed sown direct into the garden or into a large deep pot placed in a sunny position. This is preferable to sowing in shallow seed trays as it has a long tap root which hates being transplanted and, being a biennial, it will bolt and run to seed if it feels that it is going to die.

Either sow in early autumn when the seed is fresh, which is also when you get the best germination, or in the spring after all threat of frost has passed. In the garden, sow direct into a well-prepared site in a well-drained soil in a sunny position. If you are growing caraway for a root crop, sow in rows then thin to 20 cm apart and keep free of weeds. Caraway perpetuates itself in the garden by self-sown seeds, which will, with a little control, maintain a rotation of crop.

History in cooking

This is a very ancient herb which has survived relatively unchanged for thousands of years. Records show that it was used in the Stone Age, and it has also been found in Egyptian tombs and at the ancient caravan stops along the Silk Road. In Elizabethan feasts it became a traditional way to finish the banquet, and it was mentioned by Shakespeare in Henry IV, when Falstaff is offered a Pippin apple and a dish of caraways. It has been, and still is, popular in Europe, and when Queen Victoria married Prince Albert, the UK renewed its interest in his favourite seed.

Harvesting and uses

Leaves:
Gather fresh young leaves in the late spring and early summer of the first season for use in salads. They are not worth drying or freezing.

Flowers:
Pick in the second summer to use in salads – both savoury and sweet.

Seeds:
Harvest in the second autumn. Use with vegetables, meats, and in cakes and breads. In Europe, caraway seed is inextricably linked with cooked cabbage, especially sauerkraut.

Roots:
Dig up roots in the second autumn for use as a food crop. They can be used as you would other root vegetables, such as parsnip, but caraway root has a much stronger flavour. Either steam, boil or roast.

Properties The seeds of this herb are rich in mineral salts and proteins and are extremely beneficial for the digestive system as they ease stomach cramps and nausea. When chewed at the end of a rich meal they relieve indigestion and help to clear the breath of garlic.

Different varieties None.

TUNISIAN SALAD WITH CARAWAY SEED AND MINT

A warm aromatic salad that is great to serve either as a starter with a little toasted pitta bread or as a main course. Caraway seed and mint is a classic Middle-Eastern combination; anise and mint are both good for the digestion.

Serves 2 as a main course,
4 as a starter

450 g aubergine
4 tbsp olive oil
2 garlic cloves
700 g green or red peppers,
halved and seeded
coarse sea salt and freshly
ground black pepper
25 g canned or marinated
fresh anchovies
1 tsp caraway seeds
3 large green chillies, seeded
and finely chopped
2 tbsp lemon juice
1 tbsp small capers
2 tbsp chopped mint (use a
spearmint, not a peppermint)

Pre-heat the oven to 200°C/400°F/gas mark 6.

Wash and dry the aubergine, rub 1 tablespoon of the oil over the skin and place it, whole, in a roasting tin. Cook in the oven for 20 minutes. Add the unpeeled garlic, peppers and 2 tablespoons of the oil to the aubergine in the roasting tin. Season with salt and cook for a further 30 minutes.

Roughly chop the anchovies. Remove the roasting tin from the oven, cool, then skin and roughly chop the peppers, garlic and aubergine. Return all the vegetables to the roasting tin, then add the caraway seeds, chopped chillies, lemon juice, capers and anchovies and the remaining oil. Season, then mix well and cook, uncovered, for 10–15 minutes until the liquid has evaporated. Place in a serving dish, sprinkle with chopped mint and serve at room temperature.

This salad can be kept for a few days in a fridge. Before serving, remove it from the fridge and leave at room temperature for a minimum of 40 minutes to allow the flavours to develop.

CARAWAY ROAST POTATOES

This early-autumn dish epitomises how using herbs can simply transform a dish. The aroma of the caraway seeds as they roast will enhance the potatoes and bring everyone to the table. Serve with rashers of crispy bacon and soured cream or crème fraîche.

Serves 4

16 small potatoes
(Desiree or Estima)
2 tbsp olive oil
1 tbsp caraway seeds
1 tbsp sea salt
Freshly ground black pepper

Pre-heat the oven to 200°C/400°F/gas mark 6.

Wash and dry the potatoes, then pierce the skin a couple of times to enable the steam to escape during cooking. Toss the potatoes in olive oil in a roasting tin, making sure they are well covered, then sprinkle over the caraway seeds, sea salt and black pepper.

Place the tin in the oven and roast for 35–45 minutes until cooked and golden brown.

RED CABBAGE, CARAWAY AND APPLE FLAMANDE

The scent of this cooking conjures up images of my mother in her kitchen with her sleeves rolled up, her inimitable apron fastened on and her tiny hands bedecked in rings. This is such a useful dish; it goes well with sausages and all meats, cold or hot, as well as cheese – especially a true farmhouse Cheddar.

Serves 4

1 medium red cabbage, outer leaves removed, cut into quarters and shredded
40 g unsalted butter, plus extra for greasing
4 eating apples (Cox's or something crisp), peeled, quartered and cored
1 tbsp caster sugar
2–3 tbsp red wine vinegar
salt, freshly ground black pepper and nutmeg
2 tsp caraway seeds
1 bay leaf

Pre-heat the oven to 150°C/300°F/gas mark 2.

Put the shredded cabbage into a buttered casserole in layers with the quartered apples, sprinkling the layers with the sugar, vinegar, salt, black pepper, nutmeg and caraway seeds. Add the bay leaf to the first layer.

Dot the top surface with butter. Cook, covered, for 3–3½ hours.

SPICED CARAWAY PEARS IN WINE

I make this in the autumn when the pears are in season. Many fruits are enhanced by caraway, and pears are no exception. This is a pudding for special friends.

Serves 6

2 tsp caraway seeds
750 ml red wine
1 cinnamon stick, 4–6 cm long
3 cloves
¼ tsp freshly grated nutmeg
zest and juice of 1 orange
2 tbsp redcurrant jelly
200 g brown sugar
6 firm pears
double cream, to serve

Pre-heat the oven to 150°C/300°F/gas mark 2.

Using a deep ovenproof or flameproof casserole dish with a lid, fry the caraway seeds on a medium heat until they start to release their aroma. Then add the wine, cinnamon, cloves, nutmeg, orange zest and juice, redcurrant jelly (this was always my mum's hidden ingredient), and the sugar. Slowly, stirring all the time, bring to simmering point and cook until all the sugar has dissolved.

Peel the pears, leaving the stalks intact, and add to the simmering liquid. Cover with a lid, and then put in the oven for 1½–2 hours, depending on the ripeness and size of the pears. Leave to cool. Once cold, place in the fridge for at least 24 hours to marinate.

To serve, remove the pears from the marinating liquid. Place on a heatproof serving dish with their stalks up. Place the casserole back on the hob, bring to the boil and reduce the liquid until it becomes syrupy.

Serve the pears with the hot liquid strained over and with a dollop of double cream.

CARAWAY SEED CAKE

Caraway seeds feature in many old recipes, especially in baking where the anise caraway flavour of the seeds can be tasted clearly. Here is a traditional recipe that I have brought up to date using modern ingredients.

This cake used to be served for tea; it makes a good weekend cake, ideal after a long walk – or even for taking on the walk.

Serves 8

150 g soft butter, plus extra for greasing
225 g plain flour
½ tsp baking powder
150 g caster sugar
3 large eggs
2 tbsp milk
1 tsp vanilla extract
3 tsp caraway seeds

Pre-heat the oven to 180°C/350°F/gas mark 4. Butter an 18cm-diameter round cake tin, or a 1 kg loaf tin, and line with greaseproof paper.

Sieve together the flour and baking powder into a large bowl. In another large bowl, cream together the butter and sugar until light and fluffy, then beat in the eggs, one at a time, adding 1 teaspoon of flour with each egg to prevent the mixture curdling. When the eggs are well incorporated, gently stir in the rest of the flour. Stir in the milk mixed with the vanilla extract and the caraway seeds, mixing lightly.

Spoon the mixture into the prepared tin and bake for 50 minutes, or until a skewer inserted into the centre of the cake comes out clean. Leave to cool in the tin for 10 minutes then turn out onto a wire rack to cool completely.

Serve in wedges or slices, spread with plenty of butter. This cake will keep in an airtight container for up to 3 days.

Excess caraway

The seeds of caraway are worth collecting as you can use them in the winter months to spice up many dishes.

Harvesting caraway seeds

It is important to recognise when the seeds are ripe for harvesting. If you are unsure, gently tap the plant: if the seeds fall, it is time.

Harvest the seeds on a dry, sunny day and always collect seeds after midday so that any morning dew will have dried away. It is worth taking a paper bag or a seed tray lined with newspaper to the plant, then you can collect as many seeds as possible and prevent them spreading around the garden. Also take a plant label to identify the seeds at once – in case you're harvesting other things.

Once you have collected enough seeds, clean them by removing them from the stems. Discard the stems and spread the seeds out thinly on some muslin or kitchen paper, place in a dry, airy room and leave for a few days until the seeds are totally dry. Check the seeds before storing, though, as there is no point in keeping damaged or eaten seeds. Store the seeds in a dark glass jar, cardboard box or paper envelope that is labelled. They will keep in this way for 1 year.

CATMINT

(also known as Catnep, Catnip)
Nepeta cataria

Catmint or Catnep is well known for being a cat's aphrodisiac and less well known for being a culinary delight. I first discovered catmint being used in a kitchen in Italy, where it was cooked with wild mushrooms – simply delicious. Since then I have added catmint to many dishes because the minty, spicy, peppery flavour of the leaf goes so well with vegetables, chicken and pasta.

Description

Catmint in flower is beautiful; it produces masses of clusters of pale pinkish-white tubular flowers in summer that, as they open, become a haven for bees and butterflies. This herb is a hardy perennial and will die back into the ground in winter, reappearing in the following spring. The oval, grey-green leaves are very pungent when crushed, like mint with a hint of musk.

Catmint can be raised either from seed in spring, cuttings in early summer or by dividing established plants in the autumn. Plant in a sunny position in a well-drained soil in full sun or light shade. This plant dislikes sitting in a heavy wet soil because in winter it can be known to 'rot off' if it becomes excessively wet.

History in cooking

Catmint tea has been well known in Europe since the Roman times as a refreshing tea that could be drunk to settle the stomach. In the Middle Ages the leaves were used to flavour meat, and the young shoots were used in salads.

Harvesting and uses

Leaves:

These have an aromatic mint, spice and pepper flavour and are quite strong, so go steady the first time you use this herb in the kitchen. Use freshly picked young shoots in early spring in salads, with vegetables and fungi, or rubbed on meat – this is particularly good with lamb. Mature leaves in summer and into autumn have a bitter mint flavour that can be used with fungi and in casseroles, stews, soups and sauces. The leaves freeze well and can also be preserved in butter, oil or vinegar. They make a good savoury jelly that goes well with meat dishes – again, especially lamb.

Flowers:

Pick from early summer until autumn. The whole of the flower is edible. When preparing the flowers for use in a recipe, remove any green bits otherwise the flavour of the flower will be impaired (the leaves have a more powerful flavour). The flowers combine well with pasta, rice and vegetables of all sorts, adding an extra bite. Always add at the end of cooking.

Properties

Catmints, especially the *Nepeta cataria*, contain citronellal; a lemon-scented volatile oil which has anti-viral properties. It also contains thymol, a substance also found in thyme, which is an antiseptic that helps kill any minor bugs that might be in the food prior to cooking. It also helps balance fatty foods, therefore making them easier to digest. There is a bitter flavour to the leaf which, as with all other bitter herbs, stimulates digestion and so is good for your liver and kidneys.

Different varieties

Lemon Catmint

Nepeta cataria 'Citriodora'

This variety has grey-green leaves that have a mint, thyme and lemon flavour with a slight bitter tang. Good with fish, chicken and for making salad dressings. It has creamy pink flowers.

Italian Catmint, Nepetella

Nepeta nepetella

Italian catmint has oblong, narrow, grey-green leaves with spikes of very pale mauve and a hint of blue flowers in summer. It is this variety that I eat with wild mushrooms. It has an amazing flavour which is aromatic and minty with a slight bitter note.

CATMINT AND POT-ROASTED CHICKEN

Catmint combined with poultry, and in particular chicken, makes a great flavoursome combination. I love recipes where I put all the ingredients together in a dish, with a firm-fitting lid, bung it in the oven and walk away, returning a few hours later to find the kitchen full of enticing aromas. This is one such dish. Accompany it with mashed potato or a lovely crisp green salad with a Lemon Catmint dressing, if you like. Make the dressing by combining 3 tablespoons of olive oil, 1 tablespoon of balsamic vinegar and 1 tablespoon of chopped lemon catmint leaves.

Serves 4–6

3 large sprigs (1 handful) of catmint or catnip, leaves removed from the stem
sea salt and freshly ground black pepper
1.2 kg chicken
1 rosemary sprig
4 red onions, quartered
2 large Bramley apples, cored and cut into large cubes
olive oil
600 ml dry cider

Pre-heat the oven to 190°C/375°F/gas mark 5.

Finely chop the catmint leaves with 1 teaspoon of sea salt. Rub the salt and catmint mix inside the chicken's cavity and all over the outside. Put the rosemary sprig in the middle of the chicken.

Place the onions and apples in a casserole dish and add 2 tablespoons of olive oil. Sprinkle with a little salt and black pepper and toss well so everything is covered with oil. Put the chicken on the top, rub the skin with a little oil, and pour over the cider. Cover the casserole and put in the centre of the oven. Cook for 1 hour and 35 minutes. At the end of the cooking time, either check the chicken with a cooking thermometer or check the legs and thighs; the meat should be just falling off the bone.

Remove the chicken from the dish. Strain the juice away from the onions and now-collapsed apple. Liquidise the onion and apple to a smooth purée and add some of the cooking juice to make a thin sauce. Carve the chicken into portions and serve with the sauce poured over.

MUSHROOM, CATMINT AND POTATO PIE

This is a useful dish as it can be a light lunch, a light supper or a side dish with cold meats. It really shows off how well catmint goes with mushrooms, as it complements and enhances their flavour without dominating. The mashed potato topping has eggs added to it – this was my mother's trick; without doubt it makes the best mash you have ever eaten. Serve with a crisp green salad or some fresh cooked spinach.

Serves 4

50 g unsalted butter, plus extra for greasing
350 g brown mushrooms (even better if they are fresh field mushrooms)
2 garlic cloves, peeled and sliced very finely
1 tbsp chopped catmint leaves
1 tbsp chopped flatleaf parsley
salt and freshly ground black pepper
200 g Gruyère, cut into small pieces

For the mashed potato
1.5 kg potatoes for mashing (such as Estima, King Edwards or Desiree)
50 g unsalted butter
100 ml hot milk
2 eggs, beaten
75 g Parmesan, freshly grated

Pre-heat the oven to 190°C/375°F/gas mark 5 and lightly butter an ovenproof dish.

First make the mash. Wash the potatoes, but do not peel. Place in a large pan of cold, salted water and bring to the boil. Cook until tender. Remove from the heat, drain, and peel the skins – which should just slip off. Mash with the butter and hot milk, stir in the beaten eggs and two-thirds of the grated Parmesan.

While the potatoes are cooking, wash the mushrooms and cut into thick slices if large or quarters if small. Fry them with the butter and garlic until golden and sweet. Stir in the catmint, cook for 1 minute, then add the parsley, salt and black pepper. Smooth half of the mashed potatoes over the bottom of the dish, scatter with the Gruyère, then add the cooked mushrooms and all their cooking juices. Top with the remaining mashed potato, smooth over and sprinkle with the remaining Parmesan.

Bake in the oven for 30 minutes until the crust is golden brown.

CATMINT-INFUSED VEGETARIAN GOULASH

The dry, aromatic minty flavour of the catmint enhances this vegetarian goulash. Serve with fresh pasta or egg noodles.

Serves 4

2 tbsp olive oil
2 medium onions, sliced
2 tsp wholemeal flour
1 tsp paprika
250 g skinned tomatoes or 400 g can of Italian tomatoes
1 tsp tomato purée
a pinch of soft brown sugar
275 ml hot water
1 tbsp catmint leaves, removed from the stem and finely chopped
225 g cauliflower florets
225 g new or small carrots, cut into chunks
225 g new or small potatoes, cut in half
½ red pepper, seeded and chopped
salt and freshly ground black pepper
150 ml soured cream or Greek yoghurt

Pre-heat the oven to 170°C/325°F/gas mark 3.

Heat the oil in a flameproof casserole, add the onions and fry gently until soft and clear, then stir in the flour and three-quarters of the paprika.

Roughly chop the tomatoes and add to the casserole. Mix the tomato purée and the sugar with the hot water and add to the casserole with three-quarters of the catmint leaves. Bring to the boil, stirring all the time. Add all the vegetables, and the seasoning. Cover and bake in the oven for 30–40 minutes.

Remove from the oven, stir in the soured cream or yoghurt, plus the remaining paprika. Serve decorated with the remaining catmint leaves.

TAGLIATELLE AND NEPETELLA SAUCE

Both nepetella and catmint have a dry mint flavour which goes so well with tomatoes and the sharpness of capers. The combination reminds me of hot summer days in the Mediterranean.

Serves 4

olive oil
1 garlic clove, finely chopped
2 tbsp nepetella or 1 tbsp catmint leaves, finely chopped
1 tbsp parsley, finely chopped
50 g fresh or preserved capers (rinse preserved ones and drain these well), coarsely chopped
250 g skinned tomatoes or 400 g can of Italian tomatoes, chopped
a pinch of soft brown sugar
400 g fresh or dried tagliatelle
salt and freshly ground black pepper
freshly grated Parmesan

Heat some oil in a large frying pan, add the garlic and soften. Add the nepetella or catmint, parsley and capers. Turn the heat down low. Add the tomatoes and the sugar. Cook gently for 5–10 minutes.

While the sauce is cooking, bring a large pan of water to the boil and add the tagliatelle. If the pasta is fresh, cook for a few minutes until al dente, if dried, cook according to the packet instructions.

Once the sauce is cooked, remove from the heat and season with salt and black pepper to taste.

When the tagliatelle is cooked, drain, add to the sauce and stir well. Serve at once with the Parmesan.

Excess catmint

Catmint butter

This can be used to fry mushrooms, for serving with lamb cutlets, or even used as a base to a fruit crumble. It is important to use unsalted butter in this recipe because it is mild in taste and the added herbs will provide the flavour.

Makes 125 g butter

handful of catmint leaves, removed from their stems
125 g unsalted butter

Gently chop the catmint leaves to release the oils, then mix the leaves with the butter. (The simplest and easiest way of blending the herb and butter together is to use a fork.)

When it has been thoroughly mixed, pack the herb butter into a roll of greaseproof paper and place in the fridge for up to 24 hours before use. The longer you leave it, the better the flavour.
This butter can be frozen; put it into a plastic container and label it. It will keep for up to 3 months.

CELERY LEAF

(also known as Wild Celery, Smallage, Ajmud, Persil)

Apium graveolens

Having been growing herbs professionally for over 25 years I
still find it magical when I discover something new about a herb
I thought I knew a lot about. Celery leaf is one such herb, for not
only is it the origin of commercially cultivated celery, but it can also
be found growing wild throughout Europe and North Africa. So I
was fascinated to find out that a descendent of this wild form is
considered an important minor spice in India, where the seed is
used in several tomato-based Indian curries.

Description

The main difference between the cultivated celery you buy in the
shops and the herb is that the mature stems of the wild form are
bitter and inedible, unlike those of the cultivated varieties.
This hardy herb lasts two years and will reach a height of 1 m when
in flower during the second year. Clusters of tiny green-white flowers
appear early in the second summer followed by ridged grey-brown
seeds. The bright, aromatic, mid-green leaves are similar to those of
its cousin, French parsley, with which, when young, it is often
confused.

If you are growing it just for leaf not for seed, sow it annually in
the late spring into a prepared site in the garden when all threat of
frost has passed. Celery leaf likes a good deep soil that does not dry
out in summer, and is a hungry plant so always feed the chosen site
with well-rotted manure in the previous autumn.

History in cooking

Historically, celery leaf has been used for thousands of years; there
are records that show that the seeds were found in Tutankhamen's
tomb (1327 BC). Also it is known that the ancient Greeks used it,
as did the ancient Egyptians. The salad stem, celery (*Apium
graveolens* var. *dulce*), was originally bred in the 17th century from
the wild form.

Harvesting and uses

Leaves:
The young shoots can be picked throughout the growing season and
are delicious in salads or added to mashed potato. They are also
great added to soups or sweated down with onions. In my opinion,
the mature tough leaves are inedible and bitter.

Flowers:
These have a light celery flavour, great in tomato salads. Pick them
in the second year in early summer.

Seeds:
Harvest these in the second season in late summer and early

autumn, when they are fully ripe and start falling from the seed head. These are very useful; grind them in a pestle and mortar or add them whole to stews, casseroles and soups. They are also lovely added to dough for flavoursome bread. In India celery seed is an important minor spice.

Stems:

The stems are best cut in the first season before they produce flowers in the second spring.

Roots:

As a cousin of the carrot, this herb produces good-sized tap roots. It was traditionally grown as a root crop. Harvest the roots in the second year of growth.

Properties

Because of the deep tap root, the leaves are very beneficial, being high in calcium, iron, carotene and vitamins B1, B2, C and K. The seeds are also beneficial. However, a slight but noteworthy word of caution: there are some people who are allergic to the seeds and it has been known to cause an anaphylactic reaction similar to that for a peanut allergy.

Different varieties

None.

CELERY LEAF AND MASHED PARSNIP PATTIES

My aunt, many years ago, introduced me to mashed parsnips. This dish is not only delicious in its own right, but when combined with celery leaf, with its unique flavour, it makes a lovely light supper or lunch.

Serves 2–4

750 g large parsnips, peeled and cut into large chunks (discard any woody cores)
1 small onion, finely chopped
1 garlic clove, crushed
125 g ricotta or cottage cheese
2 tbsp celery leaf, finely chopped
2 eggs, separated
salt and freshly ground black pepper and nutmeg
butter, for greasing
grated Cheddar, or any hard cheese

Pre-heat the oven to 200°C/400°F/gas mark 6.

Boil the parsnips in a large pan of slightly salted water until tender. Drain and mash with the onion, garlic and ricotta and add the finely chopped celery leaf. Beat in the egg yolks and season well with salt, black pepper and nutmeg.

Whisk the egg whites until stiff then fold into the parsnip mixture. Place about 6–8 spoonfuls of the mixture into a greased baking dish (depending on its size), sprinkle each one with grated cheese, and bake for 30–35 minutes until nicely browned. Serve immediately.

CELERIAC AND CELERY LEAF SALAD

Celeriac, celery stems and celery leaf together make a light and refreshing dish. Topping it off with pomegranate seeds not only makes it look a picture, but adds further texture and flavour and creates a mouthwatering salad. This is lovely served with cold meats or soft cheeses and some crusty home-made bread.

Serves 4–6

1 medium-sized celeriac, washed, peeled, and finely sliced
1 large handful of young celery leaf stems, leaves removed, stems washed and finely sliced (do not use the large stems which have flowers on, as these will be very bitter)
2 tbsp celery leaf, finely chopped
2 tbsp ripe pomegranate seeds
3 tbsp olive oil
1 tbsp lemon juice
salt and freshly ground black pepper

Mix together the sliced celeriac and the celery stems with the celery leaf and 1 tablespoon of the pomegranate seeds. Combine the olive oil and lemon juice to make a salad dressing, and season to taste. Dress the salad, and toss well, then add the final tablespoon of pomegranate seeds and serve.

CELERY SEED CHEESE STRAWS

These straws are always eaten with gusto. I remember making them with my mother, then in turn making them with my own children. Some people can be allergic to the seeds, so do check before serving this dish to others, as it has been known to cause an anaphylactic reaction similar to that for a peanut allergy. Serve either on their own, with salads, or for use with dips.

Makes approx. 24

100 g unsalted butter, plus extra for greasing
100 g plain flour, plus extra for dusting
150 g mature Cheddar, finely grated
1 tsp celery seed
freshly ground black pepper
1 egg yolk

Pre-heat the oven to 220°C/425°F/gas mark 7. Lightly grease a large baking sheet with butter and cover it with a piece of baking parchment.

Sift the flour into a large bowl, add the grated cheese, celery seed and black pepper and mix well. Cut the butter into small cubes, add them to the flour and rub them into the mixture using your fingertips. Once the mixture has become very fine crumbs, add the egg yolk, stirring it in using a palette knife or butter knife (rather than a spoon) to keep the mixture lighter.

Gather the now-forming pastry into a ball. Dust the work surface with flour and gently roll out the dough into a square approximately 5 mm thick. With a sharp knife, cut the square into strips and then each strip into roughly 7–8-cm lengths. Carefully lift them onto the baking sheet, leaving a small space in between each one.

Pop them into the oven for about 6 minutes. After this time, check them – they should be a pale golden colour. If they are not, leave them to cook a few minutes longer.

Remove the baking sheet from the oven and allow the straws to cool and to firm up before transferring the baking parchment with the straws on it to a wire rack to cool completely.

Excess celery seed

Celery seed salt

This is a useful way to store an abundance of seeds. Make sure that the seeds are totally dry before you start and that they are cleaned – no stems or damaged seeds. This salt can be used as a seasoning and is often used to enhance the flavour of the cocktail Bloody Mary.

2 tbsp celery seeds
5 tbsp sea salt

Combine the celery seeds with the sea salt in a food processor or pound small amounts at a time in a pestle and mortar.

Store in a jar with a tightly fitting lid in a dark cupboard for up to 6 months.

CHERVIL

(also known as Kerbel, Kervel, Cerfoglio)
Anthriscus cerefolium

This, in my opinion, is an underrated herb, as its delicate anise flavour can permeate food very subtly. It is also a robust herb to grow, surviving cold winters to give fresh leaves as soon as the weather picks up. My mother always had it in her garden, and even when she moved into a flat she had it in pots outside her kitchen door. It was one of her must-have herbs when making a 'Salsa Verde' (see page 233) which she served with new potatoes or poached white fish.

Description

Chervil is an attractive hardy herb that lasts 2 years; however, many who are growing it for leaf production will re-sow it each year. It will reach a height of 60 cm when in flower in the second year. The tiny white flowers, which have a hint of pink, grow in clusters from spring until early summer. The light green, fern-like leaves have a slight anise flavour. In the early autumn or spring, when the night temperatures drop, the leaves can develop a purple tinge which does not impair the flavour.

This is an easy herb to grow as it is raised from seed that germinates rapidly in the warmth of spring as the air and soil temperatures rise. The seed must be fresh as it loses it viability after 1 year. Young plants are ready for cutting about 6–8 weeks after sowing, thereafter continuously providing leaves as long as the flowering stems are removed. Plant in the garden in a light soil that retains moisture in the summer but is not waterlogged in winter. A semi-shaded position is best because chervil will bolt if the soil dries out or it gets too hot. For this reason some gardeners sow it between rows of other garden herbs or vegetables, or under plants that drop their leaves in autumn, to ensure the chervil has some shade during the summer months.

History in cooking

This herb has been used for thousands of years throughout Europe and North Africa, and it is said to be a native of Siberia. It was almost certainly brought to the UK by the Romans in their wagon train. It is considered to be one of the Lenten herbs (a herb traditionally eaten in quantities during the Christian period of Lent, especially on Maundy Thursday), and is thought to have blood cleansing and restorative properties.

John Gerard, the Elizabethan physician who was superintendent to Lord Burleigh's gardens, wrote in his book *Gerard's Herbal* of 1636: 'The leaves of sweet chervil are exceeding good, wholesome and pleasant among other salad herbs, giving the taste of Anise seed unto the rest.'

Harvesting and uses

Leaves:

Leaves can be picked 6–8 weeks after spring sowing. They are then available all year until the first hard frosts. They are not damaged by frosts, but they do become limp and unusable until the temperature picks up.

It is best to use the leaves fresh as they are not easy to dry and when frozen then thawed they are a bit mushy. However, this mush can happily be used in soups and sauces when you do not need the perkiness of fresh leaves. The leaves are good in salads, soups and sauces, and in vegetable, chicken, white fish and egg dishes. Always add freshly chopped chervil leaves towards the end of cooking to preserve their flavour.

Stems:

Packed with flavour, the stems can be used from spring onwards, and unlike the leaves they can be used all through cooking. They are particularly good for flavouring sauces, stocks and soups.

Properties

Eaten raw the leaves add additional vitamin C, carotene, iron and magnesium. They are also a good appetiser and carminative. A tea can be made from the leaves to stimulate digestion and alleviate circulation disorders, liver complaints and chronic catarrh.

Different varieties

None.

ASPARAGUS AND CHERVIL SOUP

This was one of my mother's standbys – she was immensely proud of her asparagus bed which had a ceremonious cut each year. The combination of asparagus and chervil is excellent as the light anise of the chervil acts as a digestive with the asparagus.

Serves 4–6

3 tbsp olive oil
2 leeks, washed well and finely sliced
2 baking potatoes (Estima or Marfona), peeled and finely chopped
1.5 litres home-made (see page 13) or good bought chicken stock
1 kg asparagus, washed and trimmed, tough ends removed
a generous handful of chervil
425 ml double cream
salt and freshly ground black pepper

Heat the oil in a large pan and fry the leeks on a moderate to low heat until very soft. Add the potatoes and stir so they absorb the oil. Add the stock, increase the heat slightly to return to the boil, then cook for 10 minutes.

Slice the asparagus stems and tips into 2-cm pieces and add to the potatoes. Boil for a further 7 minutes or until tender. Strip the chervil leaves from their stems and add the stems to the soup. Cook for a few minutes, remove the soup from the heat, then liquidise.

Finely chop most of the chervil leaves, reserving some whole ones to serve. Stir the chopped leaves into the soup with the cream.

Season to taste and thin with water, if wished. Garnish with chervil leaves and serve hot or cold.

CAMEMBERT IN ASPIC

According to my grandmother she had this wonderful dish when lunching with Lady Jekyll and she had never forgotten it – and nor has anyone who has eaten it since.

My grandmother's version was very heavy going and took hours to prepare, so here is my adaptation. The light anise flavour of the chervil goes so well with the stronger tastes of cheese and consommé, and balances out the flavours well. Delicious served with dry toast or oat biscuits for a light lunch.

Serves 4–6

415 g beef consommé
1 bunch of chervil, finely chopped (including the stems), reserving some to garnish
1 ripe Camembert or a round ripe Brie (approximately 250 g)

Very gently warm the consommé and the chervil, but do not boil. Remove the outer white skin of the Camembert or Brie. Choose a serving bowl just a bit bigger than the cheese and pour in some of the warmed consommé. Add the cheese, pour over the remaining consommé and place in the fridge, covered with cling film, until set (about 2–3 hours).

Garnish with some fresh chervil.

MARINATED TROUT WITH CHERVIL AND PEPPERCORN DRESSING

Chervil's light flavour enhances that of many fish, and when combined with dill the flavours complement each other. This dish makes a lovely summer meal, either for a light supper or lunch, or even as a first course served with brown bread or new potatoes, depending on your appetite.

Serves 4

500 g rainbow trout fillets
6–8 tbsp olive oil
juice of 1 lemon
1 bunch of dill leaves, finely chopped, reserve some whole ones to serve
1 tbsp coarse sea salt
freshly ground black pepper
chervil leaves, to serve

For the chervil and peppercorn dressing
4 tbsp crème fraîche
1 tbsp single cream
2 tbsp chervil leaves, finely chopped
1 tsp green peppercorns, soaked for 1 minute in boiling water then drained

Wash the trout fillets and pat them dry with kitchen paper. Place them in a shallow china dish, pour over the olive oil and 2 tablespoons of the lemon juice, scatter over the dill, then sprinkle with sea salt and a small amount of black pepper. Cover with cling film or foil and leave in a cool place, not the fridge, for at least 12 hours, turning the fillets occasionally.

When you wish to serve, whip together the crème fraîche and cream and fold in the chopped chervil and drained green peppercorns.

Remove the trout from the marinade, scraping off the salt and the black pepper (do not worry about the dill). Using a very sharp knife, slice the fillets into paper-thin slices and arrange on 4 plates with a spoonful of the whipped cream and chervil dressing. Sprinkle the fish with the remaining lemon juice, scatter over some fresh chervil and dill leaves and serve with any remaining cream dressing.

Excess chervil

Chervil sauce

This is a lovely, delicate fresh sauce which shows off the full potential of chervil. It is good with poached chicken, chicken salad, white fish and hard- or soft-boiled eggs.

Makes approx. 450 ml

12 chervil sprigs
150 ml single cream
25 g unsalted butter
1 tbsp plain white flour
300 ml hot chicken stock (home-made, if possible, see page 13)
salt and freshly ground black pepper

Remove the chervil leaves from the stalks and reserve 2 tablespoons of leaves for use later. Put the stalks and any remaining leaves into a small pan with the cream and slowly bring to just below boiling point, stirring all the time. Remove from the heat, cover, and allow to cool and infuse for at least 20 minutes.

Melt the butter in a medium pan, stir in the flour and cook for 1 minute. Add the hot chicken stock, stirring well until blended. Strain the infused cream into the pan and cook gently for a few minutes. Add salt and black pepper to taste. Chop the reserved chervil leaves, stir into the sauce and serve.

CHICORY

(also known as Blue Endive, Bunks, Strip for Strip, Blue Sailors,
Succory, Wild Chicory, Wild Succory)
Cichorium intybus

This herb holds so many memories for me. As a child I disliked it; Mum and grandmother often used to cook the chicons, and to a child's palate they were very bitter. When my children were young we took a canal trip through France on the Canal du Midi and there are two things I especially remember from this trip: the first was Hannah and Alistair going to buy the fresh bread every morning, proudly practising their French, and the second was seeing chicory in full flower growing wild along the canal banks in the bright sunshine.

Description

Chicory is stunning when in flower; the blue flowers in midsummer are a clear blue, so it is worth growing a few plants for the flowers alone. Chicory will reach a height of 1 m when in bloom, so plant it at the back of the border or against a fence so that it does not blow over. It is a hardy perennial which will die back into the ground in winter, reappearing the following spring. The leaves are mid-green, hairy underneath, and coarsely toothed.

It can be easily grown from seed either sown in the spring or late summer, using fresh seed, or by division of the roots in the following spring (make sure you get a growing bud with each piece of root). It prefers a sunny site in a light, preferably alkaline, soil. If you are planning to harvest the roots, prepare the site well prior to seed sowing by digging deeply and applying loads of well-rotted compost and/or manure.

History in cooking

The use of chicory can be traced back to the ancient Egyptians who, like the Arabians, used to blanch the leaves as a salad; a custom continued to this day. Careful English wives grew chicory among their herbs, as it was good for purging and for the bladder. Since the 17th century, dried, roasted and ground roots have been used as a coffee substitute. In fact, Dickens in his *Household Words* described the extensive cultivation of chicory in England for just this purpose.

Harvesting and uses

Leaves:

Gather leaves from early spring until early autumn and use them fresh, as they do not dry or freeze well. Young leaves can be added to summer salads to give a light, bitter flavour. Forced leaves can be used as a winter salad as they have a strong bitter flavour.

Flowers:

Collect flowers in early summer until early autumn and use them in salads.

Roots:

Dig up the roots from the second year onwards in late autumn and shorten to 20 cm. Remove all the side shoots and leaves and stack the roots in dry sand in the dark. Roasted chicory roots are still widely used as an excellent substitute or adulterant for coffee. Young roots can be harvested early in the second autumn, boiled like carrots and served with a white sauce, which makes a good contrast to the bitterness of the root.

The chicory roots can also be blanched, and the result is known as a chicon or endive. Traditionally the blanching was done in mid-autumn. A few roots were dug up from the garden, the tops cut off to just above the crown, then the roots were planted close together in a box of loamy soil. They were kept in total darkness, and after 4–6 weeks the roots had produced tight, blanched, new top growth. If you want to try this at home, bear in mind a couple of practical points: do not allow any light in during the forcing period or the chicons will become bitter, and always delay the picking of the forced chicon until you need it, because after just 1 hour of being in the light they will become limp.

Properties

We need to rediscover an appreciation of bitter foods like chicory as they benefit the endocrine and digestive system. There is an old saying 'Bitter to the tongue is sweet to the tum'. Fresh leaves contain vitamins A, B and C.

Different varieties

Magdeburg or Brunswick
These are the best for producing roots which can be used as a coffee substitute.

Pain de Sucre (Sugar Loaf)
This looks like lettuce and can be used in the same way. Does not require blanching.

Red Verona
This has crimson-red foliage and is good in salads.

Witloof (Brussels Chicory)
This is the one grown for the chicons.

Radicchio
A red, loose-leafed chicory, rather like lettuce and not suitable for blanching.

BRAISED CHICORY

This is just as my mother and grandmother cooked chicory. The full flavour of the chicory can be appreciated in this dish – clean and fresh with a hint of bitter. I usually serve this with boiled ham or chicken, but it is also very good with grilled tomatoes.

Serves 4

4 large heads of chicory
300 ml vegetable stock
grated zest and juice of 1 orange
salt and freshly ground black pepper
grated nutmeg
25 g hazelnuts, coarsely chopped (optional)

Cut the chicory in half lengthways and place in a large pan. Pour over the stock, orange zest and juice, seasonings and nuts (if using). Bring to the boil, cover, lower the heat and simmer for 5–10 minutes, until the chicory is tender but still crisp.

Drain the chicory, reserving the cooking liquid, place in a serving dish and keep warm. Reduce the cooking liquid over a high heat to about 150 ml and pour over the chicory. Serve immediately.

CHICORY AND CHEESE BAKE

The clean bitter flavour of the chicory combined with the light saltiness of the ham and the creamy soft cheese makes this a good supper and a delicious comfort food.

Serves 4

50 g butter, plus extra for greasing and cooking
450 g chicons, washed and dried
275 g lean cooked ham
1 tbsp oil
salt and freshly ground white pepper
2 tbsp plain flour
250 ml milk
150 ml dry white wine
100 g soft cheese
2 tbsp chicory leaves, washed, dried and finely chopped
2 egg yolks, beaten
2 tbsp breadcrumbs
1 tbsp chopped parsley

Pre-heat the oven to 200°C/400°F/gas mark 6 and grease an ovenproof dish with butter.

Cut the chicons and ham into strips about 1 cm wide. Heat the oil in a frying pan, add the chicons and ham, season with salt and white pepper and fry, keeping to one side. Melt the butter in a medium pan, add the flour and cook until golden. Stir in the milk a little at a time and simmer for 5 minutes, stirring continuously. Add the wine, slowly stirring all the time until amalgamated. Add the cheese in small pieces and stir until melted, then add the chicory leaves. Remove the sauce from the heat and stir in the beaten egg yolks.

Tip the ham and chicons mixture into the greased ovenproof dish. Cover with the cheese sauce, sprinkle with the breadcrumbs and parsley and dot with butter. Bake in the oven for 25 minutes until golden brown on top.

CHICORY AND STILTON SALAD

The bitterness of the chicory combined with the salty pungency of the Stilton really makes this salad.

Serves 3–6

6 chicons
1 handful of chicory, green leaves torn into pieces
200 g shelled walnuts
200 g Stilton (or use Roquefort)

For the dressing
6 tbsp olive oil
2 tbsp French tarragon vinegar (see page 316), or lemon juice
2 tsp Dijon mustard
½ tsp caster sugar (optional)

Pre-heat the oven to 150°C/300°F/gas mark 2.

Remove the leaves from each chicon, wash them carefully and pat dry with kitchen paper. Place the leaves in a shallow bowl with the green chicory leaves.

Cook the shelled walnuts in the oven on a baking sheet for 4–10 minutes until toasted. Remove from the oven and leave to cool.

Remove the rind from the Stilton, crumble into small pieces and add to the cooled walnuts. Mix well, then scatter over the chicon leaves. Combine the dressing ingredients until well amalgamated. Drizzle over the salad just before serving.

CHICORY AND ORANGE SALAD

Adding fruit to salad leaves (especially the clean, bitter flavour of chicory) adds more depth and flavour, particularly to this zesty salad. Serve with crusty bread and/or thin slices of smoked salmon.

Serves 2–4

350 g radicchio (red-leafed chicory)
100 g endive (curly chicory leaves)
100 ml crème fraîche
salt and freshly ground white pepper
generous pinch of sugar (optional)
15 g butter
1 tbsp flaked almonds
1 orange, peeled and divided into individual segments with pips removed and broken into mouthfuls

Separate the radicchio and endive leaves, wash thoroughly under cold running water and shake dry. Tear the radicchio leaves into large pieces and cut the endive into strips.

Season the crème fraîche with salt, white pepper and the sugar, if required. Melt the butter in a frying pan over a medium heat and cook the almonds until golden brown.

Mix the crème fraîche with the radicchio, endive and orange segments, then sprinkle with the toasted almonds.

Excess chicory

Chicory can over-produce, but there is only so much chicory salad or chicons that one can eat. My solution to over-production and to keep my plants producing lush young growth is to cut the plants hard back, put the excess on my compost, and wait for the next lush flush.

CHIVES

This was one of the first herbs I grew; it is very versatile. The leaves, having a mild onion flavour, combine well with so many dishes that it is nearly indispensable. At my childhood home my mother grew chives all along the edge of the path. It always looked stunning in mid-spring when it was in full flower. I remember thinking, at that age, that the flowers looked like soldiers wearing their bearskins on guard duty outside Buckingham Palace.

Description

Chives is a pretty hardy perennial that dies back into the ground each winter, reappearing early in the spring. It has attractive round purple flowers in summer that are composed of individual little purpley-mauve, star-shaped flowers which taste of sweet onion. The green, cylindrical hollow leaves have a mild onion scent and flavour.

This herb can be easily raised from seed sown in spring under protection at a temperature of 20°C. Alternatively, sow the seeds in late spring into prepared open ground. Established clumps should be divided every 3 years in the spring to encourage them to put on new growth. Plant in a rich moist soil in a sunny position. Keep well watered throughout the growing season. In the autumn, give the area a mulch of well-rotted manure. Both chives and garlic chives flourish in containers; plant them into a soil-based potting compost.

History in cooking

This is one of the most ancient of herbs, with records of its existence and use dating back to 3,000 BC. It is the only member of the onion group to be found growing wild in Asia, Europe, Australia and North America. Historically it was used as an antidote to poison and to staunch blood flow.

Harvesting and uses

Leaves:

Cut fresh leaves with scissors from early spring to mid-autumn, and either use fresh or preserve by freezing as leaves or in a herb butter (see page 93). They are delicious freshly picked, snipped and included as a garnish or flavour in omelettes, scrambled eggs and salads or added to soured cream as a filling for jacket potatoes. They are good sprinkled on soup and on the top of a thick bacon omelette or grilled meat, too. The leaves should be added towards the end of cooking, because if they are cooked for too long they lose their delicious onion flavour and become bitter.

Flowers:

You can pick the flowers from mid-spring until midsummer, but they are best used in early summer. They have a sweet onion flavour, which is great scattered over salads, with rice, and many other dishes. Divide the flower heads into individual bulbils and add at the end of cooking, otherwise the sweet onion flavour will disappear.

Properties

When the leaves or flowers are sprinkled onto food they stimulate the appetite by arousing the digestive juices in the mouth, therefore helping to promote digestion. They are also a beneficial antioxidant and the leaves are mildly antiseptic.

The two herbs mentioned below are hardy herbaceous perennials which die back in winter. They can both be preserved in exactly the same way as chives, and the flowers of both can also be eaten as you would chives.

Different varieties

Garlic Chives, Chinese Chives
Allium tuberosum
Garlic chives has clusters of white star-shaped flowers in summer and flat, solid, thin, lance-shaped, mid-green leaves which have a mild, sweet garlic flavour.

Welsh Onion, Japanese Leek
Allium fistulosum
Large, creamy white, global flowers appear early in the second summer among long, green, hollow cylindrical leaves. Dig up the bulbs any time from early summer until early autumn.

GARLIC CHIVES BUBBLE AND SQUEAK

My mother never wasted food. There was always a set routine to the meals so that if anything was left over it either became soup, was added to casseroles or used in one of my favourites: bubble and squeak. This was usually served on Saturdays – before the Sunday roast which marked the beginning of Mum's culinary week. Adding garlic chives to bubble and squeak adds a subtle flavour, and in late summer the flowers make the dish look most attractive. Perfect served with a home-made tomato sauce (see page 12) or cold meats.

Serves 2–4

450 g cooked mashed potato
225 g cooked cabbage or kale, cut into fine slices
115 g Cheddar, grated
1 egg, beaten
2 tbsp finely chopped garlic chive leaves
freshly grated nutmeg
salt and freshly ground black pepper
plain flour, to coat
sunflower or light olive oil
2 complete flower heads (when in season), to garnish

Mix together the potato, cabbage or kale, cheese, egg, garlic chives, nutmeg and add salt and black pepper to taste. Divide and shape into 8 patties.

Chill, if possible, for 1 hour in the fridge, as this helps the mixture to become firm and stops it falling apart when you fry it. Once the patties are cold, toss each in flour.

Heat some oil in a large frying pan until it is quite hot. Gently lower the patties into the pan and fry for about 3 minutes on each side. Remove carefully, as they can disintegrate at this point, and place on a plate lined with kitchen paper to drain off excess oil.

Serve hot and crisp, scattered with flowers, if available.

WELSH ONIONS, FETA CHEESE AND CUCUMBER SALAD

Welsh onions have larger leaves than chives and so are ideal for cooking very quickly. They add a light onion flavour to this salad, which combines well with the feta cheese to make a simple, appetising summer dish. This salad makes a great filling for pitta bread, for taking on picnics or for eating at a barbecue.

Serves 4

2 bunches of Welsh onions
extra virgin olive oil, for drizzling
250 g feta
1 small cucumber
1 small cos lettuce or 2 little gem, washed and roughly shredded
5 sprigs of good spearmint (Moroccan or Tashkent), chopped

For the dressing

juice of 1 lemon (plus a little zest)
3 tbsp extra virgin olive oil
1 tsp Dijon mustard
salt and freshly ground black pepper

Trim the Welsh onions of any wilted greens. Heat a frying pan (do not use any oil) or use a griddle, if you have one. Place the onions in the pan and fry on each side for about 45 seconds. Remove from the pan, place on a plate and drizzle with olive oil.

Make the dressing by whisking all the ingredients together in a small bowl. Season well and set aside.

Remove the feta cheese from the packet and break it up into small pieces.

Peel and halve the cucumber lengthways. Run a teaspoon along the seed cavity to remove the seeds and discard. Finely slice the cucumber, then toss together with the lettuce, Welsh onions, chopped mint and dressing.

Scatter the broken feta cheese over the salad and serve.

SEA BASS WITH CHINESE GARLIC CHIVES

This is a quick stir-fry dish which is simple to make and is transformed by using garlic chives. Serve with plain boiled rice and some steamed broccoli.

Serves 2

2 sea bass (about 450 g in total)
1 tbsp plain flour
salt and freshly ground black pepper
3 tbsp sunflower oil
175 g garlic chive leaves, snipped into small pieces using scissors
1 tbsp dry sherry or rice wine
1 tsp caster sugar
1 head of garlic chive flowers, if in season, divided into individual flowers

Remove the scales from the sea bass by scraping them with the back of a knife, working from the tail towards the head. Then fillet the fish (if you cannot do this yourself, ask the fishmonger to do it for you).

Cut the fillets into large chunks and dust them lightly with the flour, salt and black pepper. Heat 2 tablespoons of the oil in a wok or a large non-stick frying pan. When the oil is hot, toss in the fish chunks and quickly turn the pieces to seal them. Remove from the pan and set aside. Add the garlic chives to the wok, stir fry for 10 seconds, add the fish, sherry or rice wine, bring to the boil and add the sugar. Serve decorated with garlic chive flowers, if in season.

CHIVE FISH CAKES

My children were particularly fond of fish cakes, which we made and served with a home-made tomato sauce (see page 12). The chives give it a light onion flavour which is ideal for children. This is a useful recipe as it turns a small amount of fish into a meal for 4 people, and it is an ideal supper for friends who drop by unexpectedly.

Serves 4

500 g floury potatoes, peeled and cut into large chunks
500 g fish (salmon, haddock, cod, hake or any large-flaked white fish)
milk (enough to almost cover the fish)
1 bay leaf
2 tbsp chive leaves, cut into small pieces with scissors
salt and freshly ground black pepper
50 g plain flour
50 g butter
sunflower or light olive oil, for frying
120 ml white wine
300 ml single cream

Pre-heat the oven to 170°C/325°F/gas mark 3.

Place the potatoes in a large pan of cold water set over a high heat, bring to the boil and cook for 20 minutes, until they are tender.

Wash the fish, place in an ovenproof dish, almost cover with milk and add a bay leaf. Place in the oven and cook for 10–15 minutes until the fish is opaque and will easily come away from the bone or skin when you pull it (bearing in mind that different types of fish take varying times to cook).

Drain the potatoes, putting them back into the empty pan over a moderate heat for a few minutes if they seem wet, then mash them with a potato masher.

Lift the fish from the milk, reserving the liquid, then pull the flakes away from the bones and skin. Tip the fish into the mashed potato; add 1 tablespoon of the chive leaves and season with salt and black pepper. Mix briefly and gently, so as not to crush the flakes of fish.

Shape the mixture into patties, about the size of a small ball, gently flatten, then coat each one lightly in flour. Don't panic if your patties all look different, it all depends on the size of the fish flakes. Melt a little butter and oil in a frying pan and fry the fish cakes until they are lightly golden – this should take no more than a couple of minutes on each side. Remove from the pan and keep warm in an oven set to its lowest temperature.

Wipe the frying pan out with kitchen paper, add the wine, bring to the boil and simmer until there are only a few tablespoons left. Reduce the heat, pour in the cream and a glassful of the fish milk and bring back to the boil, turning it down to simmer so that it thickens but does not separate. Season with salt and black pepper. Add the remaining spoonful of chopped chives, then pour the sauce over the fish cakes and serve.

SMOKED MACKEREL AND CHIVE PANCAKES

I often make this recipe, especially when the chives are in flower. Smoked mackerel has a flavour which combines particularly well with the Gruyère and the light onion flavour of the chives, however you can change the fish to salmon if you wish.

Serves 4

30 g butter
2 shallots, finely chopped
4 tbsp white wine
1 bay leaf
200 g smoked mackerel, skin and bones removed and broken into chunks
30 g plain flour
150 ml semi-skimmed milk
salt and freshly ground black pepper
1 tbsp chopped chives
50 g Gruyère cheese, finely grated
30 g fresh breadcrumbs
Chive leaves for garnish, and flower heads when in season, divided into individual flowers

For the pancakes
100 g plain flour
2 eggs
300 ml milk
2 tbsp snipped chives
1 tsp extra virgin olive oil

Pre-heat the oven to 200°C/400°F/gas mark 6.

Start by making the pancakes. Sift the flour and a good pinch of salt into a bowl, add the eggs and half of the milk, and mix well with an electric hand mixer for 2 minutes or until the batter is smooth with bubbles rising to the surface. Alternatively you can use a whisk, which will take a bit longer. Stir in the remaining milk and the chives.

Heat an 18–20 cm non-stick frying pan. Add a little oil, then pour in enough batter to coat the bottom of the pan. Cook over a moderate heat until golden brown on the base, then flip the pancake over and briefly cook the other side. Remove from the pan to a plate. Repeat with the rest of the batter, adding a little more oil every so often, to make 8 pancakes in all. Stack the pancakes on the plate, interleaving them with greaseproof paper.

Melt one-third of the butter in a large, deep pan and cook the shallots for 2 minutes. Add the wine and bay leaf, cover tightly and cook over a fairly high heat for 3 minutes, shaking the pan a few times. Strain the cooking juices through a fine sieve and pour back into the large pan. Bring to a simmer, then add the smoked mackerel chunks and poach for 2 minutes. Remove the mackerel pieces with a slotted spoon. Reserve the cooking liquid.

Melt the remaining butter in a small pan, stir in the flour and cook for 1 minute. Whisk in the reserved cooking liquid and the milk. Bring almost to the boil, then simmer for 3–4 minutes, stirring, until thickened and smooth. Add the chives and season with salt and black pepper to taste. Add the mackerel and stir gently.

Lay out all the pancakes and divide the mackerel mixture among them. Fold the pancakes into triangles. Arrange the filled pancakes in an ovenproof dish, then pour the remaining sauce over the top and sprinkle with the Gruyère and breadcrumbs. Bake for 20 minutes or until the sauce is bubbling and the top is golden brown. Garnish with cut chive leaves and chive flowers, when in season.

Excess chives

Chives is one herb that I do like to preserve for use in the winter. Here are two methods which are quick and easy to do.

Chive butter

A useful reserve, especially when you are busy, as this can be made in advance and used not only in scrambled eggs, omelettes and cooked vegetables, but also with grilled lamb or fish and it is brilliant on jacket potatoes.

Makes 100g butter

4 tbsp chives or garlic chives, cut into small pieces using scissors
100 g unsalted butter, softened
1 tsp lemon juice
salt and freshly ground black pepper

Cream together the chives and softened butter until well mixed. Beat in the lemon juice. Add salt and black pepper to taste.

Cover and cool the butter in the fridge until ready to use. It will keep for several days in the fridge, or alternatively it can be frozen in a labelled container and used within 3 months.

Chive ice cubes

Chives, being an herbaceous perennial, dies back in winter. This is disappointing if, like me, you suddenly decide on a winter's day that you fancy a simple chives omelette with a crisp salad and some rosemary chips, and then you remember the chives are over. So here is a useful way of preserving a bit of summer for use in winter.

chive or garlic chive leaves

Cut your chives in the late morning, wash and remove any brown or beige leaves, then gently dry them on some kitchen paper.

Using scissors, snip the chive leaves into the individual sections of an ice-cube tray. Once full, transfer to the freezer. Do not add water. Freeze for 48 hours.

Before you remove the tray from the freezer, get some freezer bags ready, because once you take the tray out of the freezer the leaves thaw very quickly. Pop the individual chive ice cubes into a few freezer bags and immediately return to the freezer. You then have portion sizes that are ideal for that winter omelette.

CORIANDER

(also known as Chinese Parsley, yuen sai, pak chee, Fragrant green, dhania (seed)
dhania pattar, dhania sabz (leaves))
Coriandrum sativum

I find it amazing to think that neither my mother nor my grandmother ever used this herb in any of their recipes. I remember vividly when coriander came to fame in the UK. At that time my herb farm was wholesale and Delia Smith was inspiring people to cook via her television programme. She used coriander in one dish. and that was it; we could not grow enough of it. Supermarkets did not sell herbs back then so the garden centres suddenly became desperate to get their hands on it.

This is one herb you either like or dislike – there seems to be no middle of the road. Having hand-potted many thousands of plants, I must admit to disliking the scent (which said to resemble a crushed bed bug) but I do like the flavour, which is ironic.

Description

Coriander is a tender herb and lasts for only 1 year, so it needs to be grown from seed each year. It has pretty clusters of small white flowers in summer. The leaves come in two forms: the first and lower mid-green leaves are broad and have a strong scent; the second to appear are the upper leaves which are finely cut and have a more pungent scent. The whole plant is edible, and this includes the root because coriander belongs to the same family as the carrot, and so the roots are most delicious. When you harvest it, pull up the whole plant so you get the roots and the leaf in one go. The seeds are also edible and, on ripening, develop a delightful orange-like scent; they are used widely as a spice and a condiment.

To grow coriander in the garden, choose a light, well-drained soil that has been nourished with well-rotted manure or compost in the previous autumn, in a partially sunny position. As this herb hates being transplanted, choose your site carefully and sow it where you want to crop it. Sow the large seeds thinly, either direct into the garden or into a large pot (not a small one, otherwise you will get hardly any leaf before it flowers).

History in cooking

Coriander has been cultivated for over 3,000 years. There are records from the 21st Egyptian Dynasty (1085–945 BC), and seeds were found in tombs of this period. It is mentioned in the Old Testament: 'when the children of Israel were returning to their homeland from slavery in Egypt, they ate manna in the wilderness and the manna was as coriander seeds'. It is still one of the traditional bitter herbs to be eaten at the Passover when the Jewish people remember their great journey. Coriander was brought to Northern Europe by the Romans who, combining it with cumin and vinegar, rubbed it into meat as a preservative.

Harvesting and uses

Leaves:
Pick the leaves from late spring until late summer when about 10 cm in height and bright green in colour, and before the plant flowers. Alternatively, pull up the whole plant when the leaves reach 10 cm high. The leaf should be added to dishes just before serving, as it tends to go slimy when cooked and it loses flavour. It goes well with spicy dishes and vegetables, especially carrots, and meat, chicken and fish.

Flowers:
Pick when the whole cluster is in flower, from late spring until late summer, and use in salads or with rice. The flowers have a flavour which is a mixture of the seeds and the leaf – warm, aromatic and slightly scented.

Seeds:
Watch the seeds carefully, as they ripen suddenly in late summer and early autumn and will fall without warning. You can cut the flower stems just as the smell of the seeds starts to change and become pleasant. Cover the seed heads with a paper bag, tie the top of the bag around the stems and hang upside down in a dry, warm airy place. Leave for about 10 days. The seeds should come away from the husk quite easily and can then be stored in an airtight container. Coriander seeds keeps their flavour well.

Roots:
These are best harvested before the plant runs to flower – from late spring until early autumn. The flavour is a combination of the leaf and seed with definite earthy undertones. Add to soups, stews, casseroles and curries.

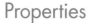

Properties
The main medicinal use for coriander is to treat both the loss of appetite and dyspeptic complaints. It is good for the digestive system, reducing flatulence and stimulating the appetite by aiding the secretion of gastric juices. The roots are high in potassium and iron.

Different varieties
None.

CORIANDER, CARROT AND ORANGE SOUP

This is a great summer and autumn soup, and as it freezes well, it is a lovely way to preserve coriander – which is notably difficult to do. Serve with fresh crusty bread.

Serves 4–6

a large bunch of coriander, with roots (if possible)
1 tbsp olive oil
4 large carrots, roughly chopped
1 onion, roughly chopped
900 ml vegetable or chicken stock
juice of 1 orange

Cut off the roots from the coriander, wash well and then slice. Roughly chop the greens.

Heat the oil in a large pan over a medium heat. Sauté the carrots and onion for a few minutes until the onion has softened a little. Pour in the stock and add the coriander roots. Bring to the boil and cook until the carrots are tender, about 10–15 minutes. Remove from the heat and allow to cool slightly.

Add the orange juice and the roughly chopped coriander leaves. Purée the soup until smooth. Reheat before serving, but do not boil.

CORIANDER AND HERB COUSCOUS

There are many herbs in this recipe, and here coriander is included in both seed and leaf form. The seed has that lovely orange tone and the leaves a more earthy one, and when combined with the other herbs these individual flavours still shine through. This couscous goes well with grilled fish or chicken, or is delicious simply on its own.

Serves 4

250 ml vegetable stock
200 ml orange juice
1 tsp paprika
½ tsp ground cinnamon
1 tsp ground cumin seed
1 tsp ground coriander seed
4 tbsp olive oil
salt and freshly ground black pepper
400 g couscous
juice of 1 lemon
150 g fresh dates or 75 g dried dates, stoned and chopped
1 large orange, peeled and roughly chopped
6 tbsp garlic chive leaves, snipped into small sections
20 g coriander leaves, finely chopped
20 g flatleaf parsley, finely chopped

Place the stock and orange juice in a large pan with all the spices and 1 tablespoon of the olive oil, season, and bring to the boil. Pour the boiling liquid over the couscous, cover with cling film and set aside. After 5–10 minutes, fluff up the couscous with a fork. Stir in the remaining 3 tablespoons of oil and the lemon juice, dates, chopped orange pieces, garlic chives, coriander and parsley. Mix well and season to taste. Serve.

VICKI'S MEXICAN ENCHILADAS

Over the past two decades I have employed many people to help me on the herb farm and nearly all have been foodies – not only enjoying cooking but also growing what they ate on their own allotments. Vicki is a vegetarian and enjoys cooking. This is one of her favourite recipes. The coriander in the salsa combines well with and complements the tomatoes.

Serves 4 for lunch as a starter, or
2 as a main course

For the salsa
1 medium green chilli,
seeded and finely chopped
400g can whole tomatoes, drained
1 red onion, finely chopped
3 heaped tbsp coriander leaves,
roughly chopped,
plus extra to garnish
juice of 1 lime
salt and freshly ground
black pepper

For the enchiladas
110 g Wensleydale cheese, grated
150 g mozzarella, grated
4 large flour tortillas
200 ml crème fraîche
oil for greasing

Pre-heat the oven to 180°C/350°F/gas mark 4.

First make the salsa. Into a large bowl put the chilli, tomatoes, half the onion, all the coriander leaves and the lime juice. Season well with salt and black pepper and mix thoroughly. Set aside.

Mix the two cheeses together in a bowl. Put the frying pan over a high flame to pre-heat and when hot, dry-fry each tortilla for 6 seconds on each side. Place 1 tortilla on a flat surface and spread 1 tablespoon of salsa over it, but not quite to the edges. Sprinkle over 1 heaped tablespoon of the mixed cheeses, followed by 1 tablespoon of the crème fraîche. Roll up each tortilla and place in a lightly oiled, ovenproof baking dish with the sealed-side down. Repeat with the others, then spread the remaining crème fraîche on top of the tortillas in the dish and sprinkle the rest of the salsa over the top, followed by the remaining cheese and red onion.

Place the dish on a high shelf in the oven for 20–25 minutes. Garnish with extra coriander and serve immediately (if you don't, they can become soggy).

CHICKEN AND CORIANDER CURRY

This is a really great curry which has all the flavours and textures a curry should have. It is made all the better by using the coriander roots, too, which bring additional texture. Serve with basmati rice.

Serves 4–6

3 tbsp oil
1 bay leaf
1 large bunch of coriander, finely chopped, including 4 or 6 roots, washed and chopped (reserve some leaves to serve)
1 onion, thinly sliced
salt
3 tbsp water
1 tbsp turmeric powder
½ tsp chilli powder, or to taste
½ tsp paprika
2 tbsp ground ginger
2 tbsp crushed garlic
4 or 6 boneless and skinless chicken breast fillets, cut into chunks (or use chicken thighs)
1 tomato, thinly sliced
¼ tsp sugar
3 cardamom pods, lightly crushed
3 cloves
1 cinnamon stick, about 4–6 cm long
1 tbsp ghee or unsalted butter
1 tbsp ground coriander seed salt, to taste

Heat the oil in a deep casserole or a large, deep frying pan with a lid over a high heat. Add the bay leaf, coriander roots and three-quarters of the onion to the pan. Season with a little salt and fry until golden brown. Add a spoonful of water and stir so that the onions break down. Add the turmeric, chilli, paprika, ginger and garlic and stir well. Reduce the heat to medium–high.

When the liquid starts to dry, add a spoonful of water and stir again. Add the chicken and tomato. Season with salt and sugar and stir. Add the cardamom, cloves, cinnamon, ghee or butter and another spoonful of water. Reduce the heat to low, cover and simmer for 30–35 minutes. Remove the lid, and if there is water left in the pan, raise the heat to medium. Add the ground coriander seed salt and cook until all the water has evaporated to the consistency you require.

In another frying pan, add a little oil and the remaining onion, sprinkle a little salt and fry for a few minutes, or until golden brown and crispy. Remove from oil and set aside on kitchen paper. Spoon the curry onto serving plates and sprinkle with fresh finely chopped coriander leaves and the fried onions.

CORIANDER, MINT AND PITTA SALAD

This is an easy lunch which tastes so refreshing on a hot summer's day. The earthy flavour of the coriander leaves combined with clean spearmint makes this salad come alive.

Serves 2–4

4 large tomatoes
½ cucumber, cut into 1-cm dice
1 red onion, finely sliced
400 g can chickpeas, drained and rinsed
2 large pitta breads

For the dressing
4 tbsp olive oil
juice of 1 lemon
2 tbsp chopped coriander
2 tbsp chopped spearmint (either Moroccan or Tashkent)
salt and freshly ground black pepper

Boil a kettle, put the tomatoes in a large bowl and pour over the boiling water. Leave them to stand for a few minutes. With a slotted spoon, remove the tomatoes one at a time and peel. Once all are peeled, slice thinly.

To make the dressing, put the oil and lemon juice into a large bowl, whisk until amalgamated, and add the coriander and mint. Check the seasoning and add salt and black pepper to taste.

Put the cucumber, tomatoes, onion and chickpeas in a bowl. Pour over the dressing and then toss together until well mixed. Immediately before serving, using a knife, split the pitta breads in half, then pop into the toaster for 1 minute until crisp and lightly browned. Tear into bite-sized pieces and add to the salad. Mix well and serve.

Excess coriander

Fresh coriander chutney

If you have a blender or food processor this recipe is simplicity itself and will complement any curry. Alternatively, it is great as a dip with poppadoms.

1 bunch of coriander
1 garlic clove
1 finely chopped green chilli
1 tbsp ground almonds (optional)
1 tbsp finely chopped spearmint leaves (either Moroccan or Tashkent)
salt and caster sugar, to taste
2 tbsp lemon juice
olive oil (optional)

Blend together all the ingredients in a food processor until smooth. Add a few drops of olive oil if the mixture is too dry. The flavours are best when served fresh, but at a push it will keep, covered, in a fridge for a few days.

CURRY LEAF

(also known as Curry Tree, Indian Bay, Nim Leaves, Kahdi Patta, Karapincha)
Murraya koenigii

For the past few years I have treasured a curry leaf seedling, nursed it through the winters and eaten just a few leaves each year. I am extremely proud of this plant and would love to be able to produce it here in our cold climate. So you can imagine my excitement when I saw this herb growing in a garden for the first time. I had just arrived in Sydney and was about to give an address in the Herb Garden of the Royal Botanic Gardens. Still suffering from jet lag, I wandered into the garden to be confronted by a prolific curry leaf tree. It looked stunning, and I realised that my little plant at home was, even after a number of years, a mere baby and I would need more patience before I could pick it regularly.

Description

The curry leaf is considered a tropical and sub-tropical evergreen shrub or small tree. It produces clusters of small, creamy white, sweetly scented, star-shaped flowers from late summer, which are followed by small, black fruit. The fruit is edible but its seed are poisonous if digested. The oval, soft, glossy, aromatic leaves are divided into 11–21 individual leaflets which have a marvellous aroma when crushed and an even better flavour when eaten, reminiscent of a mild korma. It can only be grown in a garden in the tropics or sub-tropics, where it prefers a fertile light soil in partial shade. When growing it outside the tropics, it will need protection when the night temperatures fall below 13°C.

It can be grown from fresh ripe seed in the autumn, but it is easier to propagate from semi-ripe stem cuttings in late spring and early summer.

History in cooking

The use of curry leaves as a flavouring for vegetables is described in early Tamil literature dating back to the 1st century AD. These leaves are absolutely necessary to create the authentic flavour of Southern Indian and Sri Lankan cuisine.

Harvesting and uses

Leaves:

The best time to harvest leaves is either side of flowering in warm tropical climates, spring to midsummer in cold climates. The leaves when fresh have a very short shelf life; they may be stored in the freezer for up to a week. They are usually dried, so if you have a tree and wish to dry them, follow the instructions for Stevia (see page 309) or Lemon Verbena (see page 180). In some recipes the leaves are either oven-dried or toasted immediately before use, or quickly fried in butter or oil – this scented oil is then poured over dishes to add richness and flavour. Equally, the leaves can be dropped into hot oil before adding the main ingredient. Since Southern Indian cuisine is predominantly vegetarian, curry leaves seldom appear in non-vegetarian food; the main applications are thin lentil or vegetable curries and stuffings for samosas. Because of their soft texture they are not always removed before serving.

Properties

Fresh leaves eaten raw are reputedly a good cure for dysentery, and they are also used as an infusion for a drink that is said to stop vomiting. The traditional medicinal use of the curry leaf to treat diabetes has recently attracted a great deal of interest. Medicinal research has found special compounds which could provide the basis for an effective new medicine to treat diabetes in the near future.

Different varieties

None.

CURRY LEAF-INFUSED POACHED TROUT

I cannot describe how brilliantly the flavour of the curry leaf infuses the fish without it being overpowering; it makes this a simple, perfect summer meal. Serve with new potatoes and a green salad.

Serves 4

4 trout, cleaned and gutted
salt
6 whole black peppercorns
12 curry leaves,
plus 4 extra to garnish
1 small onion, cut into thin rings
1 lemon, cut into thin slices, reserve
4 slices to garnish
110 ml white wine
75 g butter

Place the trout in a large frying pan or a heavy-based roasting tin. Sprinkle with a little salt and the peppercorns. Place 3 curry leaves inside each trout. Lay the onion rings on top of each trout and arrange the lemon slices over them. Pour in the wine and enough water to just cover the fish. Bring it to the boil on top of the hob, reduce the heat and let it simmer, uncovered, for 6 minutes.

When the trout are cooked, lift them out gently and place them on individual plates. Put a little pat of butter onto each and top with a curry leaf and a slice of lemon.

CURRY LEAF RICE

This fragrant rice enhanced with curry leaf is lovely as an accompaniment to many dishes, for example spinach, mushrooms or grilled fish.

Serves 4

550 g basmati rice
3 tbsp virgin olive oil
20 curry leaves, finely chopped
(or use dried leaves and crumble
them into the oil)
1 onion, finely sliced
2 garlic cloves, finely chopped
salt and freshly ground black
pepper
½ tsp garam masala
2 tsp plain breadcrumbs
3 curry leaves, left whole for
garnish

Wash the rice in a colander with water that has been boiled and allowed to cool slightly, then cook it in boiling water. Once cooked, strain and run under cold water so that it does not stick. Leave it to one side.

Heat the olive oil in a large frying pan. When hot, add the finely chopped curry leaves, onion and garlic and a sprinkling of salt to stop the onions catching. Turn the heat down and fry over a low heat until you can smell the curry leaves and the onions are tender, about 5 minutes. Watch that the leaves don't burn. Add the garam masala and cook for 1 minute. Add the breadcrumbs and stir for 1 minute. Add the cooked rice and, with a spatula, turn over until thoroughly coated and reheated, being careful not to mash the rice. Season with salt and black pepper to taste.

Garnish with the whole curry leaves and serve.

CURRY LEAF KEDGEREE

Kedgeree was a family staple which we often used to have on Fridays. I remember when I was growing up that the smoked haddock was always bright yellow and the dye used to come off and colour the milk. Mum always added boiled eggs and peas to her smoked haddock, and just before serving she stirred in double cream, masses of freshly ground black pepper and a handful of chopped French parsley. I have adapted her recipe so that it includes the curry leaf.

Serves 4

500 g undyed smoked haddock
275 ml milk
3 tbsp vegetable or sunflower oil
3 onions, sliced and chopped
12–14 fresh or dried curry leaves
4 cardamom pods, split
1 cinnamon stick (about 4–6 cm long), broken into pieces
400 ml water
280 g basmati rice
½ tsp turmeric
pinch of salt
50 g butter
2 eggs
handful of coriander leaves, finely chopped
1 lime or lemon, cut into 4 wedges

Put the fish in a deep frying pan (with a lid), pour over the milk and cover and simmer for 4 minutes. Take off the heat and leave to stand, covered, for 10 minutes to allow the fish to gently finish cooking.

Meanwhile, heat the oil in a deep frying or sauté pan (with a lid). Add one-third of the sliced onions, all the curry leaves, cardamom and the cinnamon stick and fry until the onion is soft and golden, about 7–8 minutes, stirring often.

Lift the fish from the milk with a slotted spoon, discard the skin and any bones, cover to keep warm and set aside. Add the milk to the water and add extra water if necessary so that you have a total of 600 ml.

Rinse the rice in a colander, drain, then stir it into the onion and spices over a medium heat. Keep stirring for 1 minute so the rice is coated, then pour in the milk and water mix and stir in the turmeric. Bring to a boil, then simmer for 10 minutes, covered, lowering the heat if it starts to stick on the bottom.

In a separate frying pan, fry the remaining onion with a pinch of salt (which helps to stop it burning), on a medium heat, stirring occasionally, until deep golden, about 20–25 minutes. When done, spread on kitchen paper and leave to become crisp.
When the rice is tender, remove from the heat, drop the butter on top so it melts in, then lay the whole pieces of fish on the rice. Cover and leave the flavours to mingle.

Meanwhile, put the eggs in a pan, cover with cold water and bring to the boil, then boil for 6 minutes (for lightly boiled). Remove from the heat and plunge into cold water, cracking the shells against the side of the pan. Peel off the shells and quarter the eggs.

To serve, break the fish into big pieces with a fork, throw in the coriander and stir gently to mix without breaking up the fish, adding the eggs at the end. Season, scatter the crisp onions on top and serve with lime or lemon wedges.

Excess curry leaf

Curry leaf chutney

If you are lucky enough to have a curry tree or are able to source a good supply of leaves, this is an excellent chutney that will keep for a few weeks in the fridge. Serve as an accompaniment to curries or with poppadums.

250 g curry leaves, washed and dried
20 green chillies, seeded and finely chopped
2 tsp vegetable oil
1 tsp Bengal gram (obtainable from Indian supermarkets),
or use chickpeas and crush them before frying
½ tsp white mustard seeds
juice of 1 lemon
salt

Grind the curry leaves and green chillies in a pestle and mortar or in a food processor until they make a smooth paste.

Heat the oil in a pan, add the Bengal gram or chickpeas and mustard seeds and sauté until they crackle. Remove from the heat, add to the paste and mix well. Add the lemon juice and check for seasoning. Cool and transfer to an airtight jar and place in the fridge.

DILL

(Also known as Dillweed, Dillseed, Aneto, Aneth and Sowa)
Anethum graveolens

I think this is one of the 'must-haves' of a good family kitchen, as it is so immensely useful. The aroma and taste of dill transports me back to my childhood. My mother used dill like most households used parsley, so for me it was the norm. I grew up with the leaves being added to mashed potato or sprinkled over courgettes, the flowers being added to pickles and the seeds being pounded and added to soups and sauces. Today it can be found in many prepared fish dishes from gravlax (salmon marinated with dill leaf) to pickled gherkins.

Description

This attractive, feathery, green annual herb, with its clusters of small yellow flowers followed by flat aromatic seeds, is a delightful addition to the garden. It is easy to muddle visually with fennel; if you are at all unsure, simply eat a tiny bit of the finely divided leaf, then you can immediately tell the difference. Fennel has an anise flavour and dill, well, it is difficult to describe, it's dill – no anise but a light aromatic flavour that combines well with so many foods.

To grow it successfully in the garden it is best to sow it in a row either in a prepared site in the garden or in a deep pot or window box in a sunny position. Dill, being an annual, will bolt to flower if transplanted or if the compost is allowed to dry out (when grown in a container). This is great if you need flowers or seed quickly, but you would miss out on the delicate flavour of the leaves.

History in cooking

Dill has a long history; it has been in cultivation for thousands of years and is mentioned in the Ebers papyrus around 1500 BC. Historically dill was used with pickled and preserved food.

Harvesting and uses

Leaves:
For the best flavour, pick before the plant starts to flower – from spring to late summer. The leaves can be used with courgettes, cucumbers, potato dishes, carrot dishes and all forms of fish.

Flowers:
Pick as soon as the flowers start to form, from late spring to late summer. They have a sweeter flavour than the leaves, but not as strong a flavour as the seeds. They are lovely added to salads.

Seeds:
These can be harvested in the green from summer to early autumn to use immediately or for use in pickling. Alternatively, harvest the seeds when they turn brown and start to drop for use throughout the year. They can be used in many dishes and for pickling.

| Properties | Throughout the world dill seed is well known for its medicinal qualities. The seeds contain volatile oils, the main one being carvone which has antispasmodic, diuretic and carminative properties. The whole plant is used not only for its flavour but also for its digestive properties, for both the seed and leaf when used in cooking are said to improve the appetite and digestion. |

Different varieties

There are many forms of dill seed available from various seed merchants; some have been bred for leaf crop, and some especially for seed.

Varieties worth looking out for are:

Indian

Anethum sowa
This Indian variety has a more rounded, spicy flavour.

Bouquet

Anethum graveolens
A popular American variety.

Dukat

Anethum graveolens
A popular leaf variety.

Mammoth

Anethum graveolens
Excellent for pickling.

Vierling

Anethum graveolens
This variety has dark, bluish-green leaves which are great for salads and other vegetable dishes.

COURGETTE, DILL AND PARSLEY PANCAKES

Courgettes and dill was one of my mother's signature combinations. This recipe shows off how delicious the partnership is but I've parsley to this mixture whichs adds another level of flavour and a lovely green colour. These pancakes can be eaten hot or served cold with a green salad.

Makes 6–8 pancakes

6–7 tbsp light olive oil or sunflower oil
1 large onion, grated
2 courgettes, grated
2 tsp dill seed
75 g feta
2 tbsp dill leaf
2 tsp chopped flatleaf parsley
2 tbsp plain flour
2 eggs
salt and freshly ground black pepper

Heat 1 tablespoon of the oil and fry the grated onion gently until soft and translucent. Gently squeeze the grated courgettes in your hand to remove any surplus moisture. Add the dill seed and the courgettes to the onion and cook quickly for 2–3 minutes. Set aside to cool.

Whisk the cheese, dill leaf, parsley, flour and eggs together in a mixing bowl, season with salt and black pepper, then add the contents of the frying pan and mix well.

Wipe out the frying pan and add enough oil to shallow fry. When hot, drop in tablespoons of the courgette mixture, allowing room for them to spread. Cook until golden brown on one side before turning over.

When cooked on both sides, remove from the pan, drain on kitchen paper and serve.

SALMON, DILL AND POTATO SOUP

Soups are a nourishing and economical way to feed a family for lunch. This recipe ticks all the boxes and is brilliant on a gloomy summer's day when you want the sun to come out. The dill seed and leaf goes so well with the salmon and bring out all its wonderful flavours. Serve with a green salad, and/or good bread.

This is best made with fresh salmon. If possible, ask the fishmonger to give you the salmon bones and tail to make the stock with. When buying in a supermarket, try to buy a piece with the skin, which you can then use to flavour the stock.

Serves 6–8

1 kg salmon, piece or fillet
900 g potatoes, peeled and cut into large chunks
30 g unsalted butter
a generous handful of dill leaves, stalks removed and chopped (reserve the stalks for the stock)
200 ml single cream
salt and freshly ground black pepper

For the stock
8 whole black peppercorns
2 tsp dill seed, ground in a pestle and mortar
zest of 1 lemon
1 large carrot, peeled and chopped into chunks
a generous handful of celery leaves (the herb) plus stalks, washed and roughly chopped (or use 2 celery sticks, cut into chunks, plus the leaves)
3 bay leaves
a handful of flatleaf parsley leaves, plus stalks, washed and roughly chopped
1 large onion, peeled and roughly chopped

Prepare the salmon by removing all the bones and the skin. Cut the fish into large chunks.

Next make the stock. Put 3 litres of water into a large pan with the salmon skin, bones, peppercorns, crushed dill seeds, lemon zest, carrot, celery leaves, bay leaves, parsley stalks, dill stalks and chopped onion. Bring to the boil, remove any scum that appears, then lower the heat and simmer for 30 minutes. Strain through a fine sieve into a clean pan. You need 1.5 litres of stock; if you do not have enough, don't worry, just add some water.

Heat the stock over a high heat and add the potatoes. Simmer for roughly 15 minutes until the potatoes are just soft. Add the salmon chunks and lower the heat to just simmer for approximately 10 minutes until the salmon is cooked. Remove from the heat, stir in the butter, chopped dill leaves and the cream, to taste. Return to the heat, reheat gently, do not boil, and check the seasoning, adding salt and black pepper to taste.

DILL MUSTARD

This mustard is particularly good with smoked salmon, trout or mackerel. It is also great added to mashed potato, salad dressings and sauces, or combined with either crème fraîche or cream cheese as dips for vegetables or pretzels. A word of warning when adding mustards to hot food: remember that the pungency of mustard is destroyed by heat, so only add it to finished sauces or stews.

Makes 3 x 125 ml jars

80 g black mustard seeds
30 g white mustard seeds
600 ml water
115 g English mustard powder
200 ml cider vinegar
1½ tsp salt
50 g light brown sugar
1 tsp ground dill seeds
(use a pestle and mortar)
1½ tsp turmeric
50 g chopped dill leaves

Place both the mustard seeds in a china or glass bowl, add in 600 ml of water and soak for 24 hours prior to use.

The next day, add the mustard powder, vinegar, salt, sugar, ground dill seeds and turmeric. When thoroughly mixed, place the bowl over a pan containing water, ensuring the water does not touch the bottom of the bowl. On a very low heat, gently cook the mustard seed for 4 hours, stirring occasionally. Check regularly that the water has not evaporated and never boil the mixture as the mustard will lose its flavour and become bitter. Once cooked, allow to cool and add the chopped dill leaves.

Cover the herb mustard and keep it in the fridge. This will keep for up to 4 weeks. It will keep longer in the fridge if you put the mustard into a glass jar with a sealing lid. Once opened, use within 4 weeks.

Alternatively, you can cheat and simply mix 50 g of chopped dill with 50 g of good ready-made coarse grain mustard and 50 g of ready-made smooth Dijon mustard. If it is too thick, add a small amount of white wine vinegar to obtain the correct consistency.

Excess dill   Dill freezes beautifully, so if you have a glut and want to have some leaves in winter, simply pick a bunch, wash it, pat it dry with kitchen paper and put it into a plastic bag and then into the freezer. When required, remove the bag from the freezer and crush it immediately; that way you will have crushed, chopped dill with no effort. If, however, you do delay, it will thaw, and go mushy.

Dill vinegar

This vinegar is lovely for making salad dressings, or fish marinades.

Makes 500 ml

dill leaves to fill a 500 ml bottle
2 tbsp crushed dill seed
500 ml white wine vinegar

Fill a clean, empty bottle with fresh dill leaves and the crushed seeds. Top up with white wine vinegar and seal. (Use a plastic or plastic-lined top as vinegar destroys metal.)

Leave on a sunny windowsill for a month, shaking from time to time, and then strain off the liquid through on unbleached coffee filter paper into another sterilised bottle. Put a sprig of dill in the bottle for identification purposes and decoration.

For those who cannot wait for 4 weeks for the vinegar to infuse with the herbs, here follows a quick method which is good for emergencies. Put the herbs and vinegar into a covered glass or china bowl over, but not touching, a pan of cold water. Bring the water to the boil, then immediately remove the bowl from the pan. Leave it to cool for about 2 hours before using the vinegar.

This vinegar will keep, bottled in the same way as above, for a number of years, whichever method you use.

ELDER

(also known as Elderflower, Elderberry, Common Elder,
Black Elder)
Sambucus nigra

Near where I live, in late spring you can see people with large black plastic bin liners walking around the country lanes collecting elder flowers; this could be for their own use but is more commonly for the local company that makes elderflower cordial. There are also farms close by that have acres of elder trees which not only look beautiful in flower in late spring, but also magnificent in autumn with the branches weighed down with bunches of the tiny blue–black fruit. This is one of the most useful herbs I grow in my garden; it looks good, smells good and does you good – what more can you ask of a plant?

Description

Elder is a sprawling, multi-stemmed shrub or small tree that drops its leaves in winter. It has attractive, flat clusters of lightly scented, creamy white, star-shaped flowers in late spring that are followed by masses of small, round blue–black fruits. The leaves are mid-green, large with sawn-edged leaflets. These leaves are toxic and should not be eaten.

When growing in the garden this plant prefers a fertile moist soil in sun or dappled shade. Choose your site carefully because in the right conditions elder can grow very rapidly, reaching 1.2 m in one season.

History in cooking

Stone-Age sites in Europe reveal that elder has been valued by mankind for its flowers and fruit for thousands of years. They were used by medieval monks in the kitchen and for herbal medicine, and also by the Native American Indians, who also used the fruit as food and for medicinal compounds.

Harvesting and uses

Flowers:
Pick them in the late spring just before they are fully open. They are lovely in the kitchen, not only for making the famous elderflower cordial but also for mousses, sorbets, jellies and with stewed fruit.

Berries:
Pick the fruits in early autumn when they are dark purple–blue. It is advisable to cook them rather than eat them raw, as when raw they work as a good laxative and diuretic!

Properties

The berries are high in vitamins A, B and C, and in the minerals calcium, potassium and iron. They are also high in anthocyanin, so are considered an antioxidant.

Different varieties

Warning Please be cautious when picking this herb in the wild and make sure you know which variety it is, for some are very poisonous. For example, the seeds inside the Red Elder (*Sambucus racemosa*) berries are poisonous even when cooked, and the berries of dwarf elder (*Sambucus ebulus*) can cause severe diarrhoea.

American Elder, Black Elder, Common Elder, Rob Elder, Sweet Elder
Sambucus candadensis

This native American shrub has numerous small white flowers in flat cymes (see page 347) throughout the summer and dark purple berries in early autumn. The leaves are long, sharply toothed and bright green. All parts of the fresh plant can cause poisoning (children have been poisoned by chewing or sucking on the bark), however, once cooked the berries are safe and are commonly used in pies and jams.

GOOSEBERRY ELDERFLOWER FOOL

Gooseberries are a firm family favourite and when we moved to the herb farm we inherited 6 cider-apple trees, some elder trees, gooseberry bushes, rhubarb and an amazing plum tree. This is a recipe I created using the harvest from the plants we found here.

Serves 6

450 g gooseberries, topped and tailed
4 tbsp sugar
10 heads of elderflower, shaken to remove insects then run under a cold tap
150 ml milk
2 egg yolks
1 tsp arrowroot
30 g sugar
150 ml double cream
fresh elderflowers, to decorate

Put the gooseberries in a medium pan with the sugar. Bring to the boil, stirring gently, and cook until the sugar is melted. Add the elderflowers, tied up in a muslin bag or jelly bag, and simmer until the gooseberries are soft and pulpy. Leave to cool completely.

Remove the elderflowers, squeeze as much juice out as possible then put them in the compost bin (if you have one). Keep the muslin bag for washing later. Place the cooked gooseberries in a serving dish.

Make the custard by heating the milk in a medium pan to the point of boiling. Beat the egg yolks, arrowroot and sugar together in a jug and pour the hot milk into the jug. Mix well then return to the pan. Heat gently until the custard thickens, but do not boil. Strain through a sieve into a clean bowl and leave to cool.

Whip the cream to the same consistency of the gooseberries. Gently stir the cream into the gooseberries and then fold in the custard. Try to give it a marbled effect in the serving bowl. Place a few elder flowers on top to decorate.

ELDERBERRY SOUP

This is a wonderful spicy-sweet autumn soup that heralds the start of winter. Interestingly it is served cold, which, in my opinion, enhances the unique dry and lightly fruity flavours of the berries.

Serves 6–8

875 g elderberries, washed and removed from the stems
1.5 litres water
1 cinnamon stick, about 2.5 cm long
4 cloves
1 large lemon, sliced, plus juice to taste
½ litre unsweetened grape juice
150 g sugar, plus extra to taste
1 tsp arrowroot (or use cornflour)
2 tbsp cold water
Soured cream, to serve
Grated nutmeg, to serve

In a large pan, combine the berries, water, cinnamon, cloves and lemon slices and cook slowly for about 40 minutes until soft. Force the pulp through a sieve, pressing as much through as possible. Add enough unsweetened grape juice to make 1.75 litres of liquid, and return to a large clean pan. Add the sugar and, stirring regularly to dissolve the sugar, cook over a gentle heat for 10 minutes.

Dissolve the arrowroot in the 2 tablespoons of water then add to the elderberry and grape juice mix. Keep stirring until it thickens, adjust to taste with extra sugar and lemon juice.

Pour into a large bowl, cover, and refrigerate for at least 4 hours before serving in individual bowls with a dollop of soured cream and a light sprinkle of grated nutmeg.

ELDERBERRY AND DAMSON CRUMBLE

This is a real autumn fruit crumble which I forage for each year, as we have elder growing around the farm and a large damson tree nearby. The dry fruity flavour of the elder with the intense flavour of the damson is extremely good. Delicious served with crème fraîche or clotted cream.

It is a good idea when cooking acidic fruit not to use an aluminium pan. I suggest you use a stainless-steel or non-stick pan as this will prevent a chemical reaction between the pan and the fruit.

Serves 4–6

6 bunches of elderberries
500 g damsons, washed and stoned (you can substitute plums if you wish)
100 g caster sugar
100 g plain flour
50 g unsalted butter
50 g soft brown sugar
50 g porridge oats

Pre-heat the oven to 170°C/320°F/gas mark 3.

Wash the elderberries well and then, using a fork, remove the berries from the stalks. Place them in a medium-sized pan.

Add the damsons to the pan with the elderberries, add the sugar, then cook over a low heat for 20 minutes or until the fruit is soft. Check the surface for the appearance of any missed damson stones and also check for sweetness, as both these berries can be very acidic.

Place the flour, butter and brown sugar in a bowl and rub together with your fingers until well mixed (if you have a food processor this can be done in an instant). Add the oats. (If you are using a processor, do not over-process.)

Place the fruit in an ovenproof dish and sprinkle over the crumble mixture. Using the back of a fork, press the crumble down; this will make it become crispy. Bake the crumble in the oven for 15–20 minutes until the topping is golden brown. Leave to stand for 5–10 minutes before serving.

Excess elder

Elderflower cordial

This cordial is best made with fresh flowers that have been picked on a sunny day when they are still creamy in colour and before they fade to white. At this time they have the highest amount of pollen, which contains the yeast that gives extra flavour to the cordial. The cordial can be diluted with still or carbonated water, depending on your preference, and is best served chilled.

Makes approx. 4.5 litres

4.5 litres water
450 g sugar
juice and thinly peeled rind of 2 lemons
3 tbsp white wine vinegar
12 elderflower heads (shake the flowers well to remove insects prior to washing)

Bring the water to the boil in a large pan then pour it straight into a sterilised container (see page 12). Add the sugar, stirring until dissolved.

When cool, add the lemon rind and juice and the vinegar and elderflower heads. Cover with several layers of muslin and leave for 24 hours.

Filter through muslin into strong, sterilised (see page 12) glass bottles with corks or screw lids. The cordial is ready after 2 weeks. This delicious nectar will keep for weeks if it is given a chance, which is very rare in this household.

Elder wine

This is a recipe from my mother's *Mrs. Beeton's Household Management*. This was a revised 1949 edition with new pictures as the original illustrations, from the original edition printed in 1861, were lost in the Blitz in 1940. The berries make a delicious wine, rich and fruity.

If you are going to make this, I advise getting a 5-litre fermentation jar with a rubber bung that has a hole in it, into which you can fit a glass or plastic fermentation lock. The first reason for the bung and fermentation lock is that it will stop the fruit flies attacking your wine for, if they do, your wine will be sour. The second reason is that yeast produces more alcohol if fermented without air, so the lock allows the wine to ferment without letting in air but allowing the gases to escape.

Makes approx. 10 x 750 ml bottles

13½ litres water
3 kg elderberries, washed

To each 4.5 litres liquid, add:
1.35 kg sugar
450 g raisins
20 g ground ginger
6 cloves
½ tsp dried yeast
150 ml brandy

Bring the water to the boil and leave to stand for 1 minute so that it is no longer bubbling. Strip the washed berries from the stalks and pour the water over the berries making sure they are covered. Let them stand for 24 hours, then bruise well and push through a sieve.

Measure the juice obtained and pour it into a preserving pan or large pan with the sugar, raisins, ginger and cloves. Boil gently for 1 hour, and skim when necessary.

Let the liquid stand until just warm, then stir in the yeast and pour everything into a clean, dry cask or fermentation jar. Cover the bung hole with a folded cloth, let the cask remain undisturbed for 14 days, then stir in the brandy and bung tightly.

Once you notice the bubbling stop (after about 6 months) your wine is ready for siphoning. For this you will need a length of plastic tubing, as this will help leave the sediment behind in the jar. Decant into sterilised bottles (see page 12), tightly cork them and store in a cool, dry place. The wine will keep for 3–4 years.

FENNEL

(also known as *Finocchio Selvatico*,
Wild Fennel, Sweet Fennel)
Foeniculum vulgare

Bronze Fennel,
Foeniculum vulgare
'Purpureum'

I have fond memories of a summer holiday spent on Majorca where I either sat on the beach watching my children sail, or went biking around the island, which I discovered is covered in wild fennel. One evening we got into conversation with the proprietor of the bistro where we were eating and I mentioned the fennel. In response he gave us a glass of 'Hierbas', which is a local liqueur made from fennel seeds and wild marjoram from the island. The predominant flavour was the anise of the fennel; it is a very strong digestive.

Description

Fennel is an attractive hardy herb which dies back in the winter, reappearing the following spring. In summer the small yellow flowers grow in flat clusters and are followed by anise-flavoured, small brown seeds. The leaves are feathery, mid-green and also have an anise flavour when eaten.

In the garden, different conditions produce very different results. A hot dry spot produces the sort of plant one sees by the Mediterranean roadside – a clump 1.2–1.5 m high with thin, highly aromatic leaves that make the whole plant look sparse. In a decent garden soil fennel looks more like a huge dome of green candyfloss.

It can be easily raised from seed sown in early summer into an open sunny position in fertile well-drained soil.

History in cooking

Fennel is as ancient as the Egyptian papyrus documents in which it is mentioned. The Greeks thought very highly of fennel and used it for slimming and for treating more than 20 different illnesses, and the Romans ate its leaf, roots and seeds in salads and baked it in bread and cakes. In Anglo-Saxon times fennel was used on fasting days, presumably because, as the Greeks had already discovered, it stilled the pangs of hunger.

Harvesting and uses

Leaves:

The best flavour is in the new shoots as they appear from late spring until early autumn. These are lovely chopped over salads and cooked vegetables, added to soups and as a stuffing for fish.

Flowers:

Pick these in summer just as they come into bloom. Add them to pickles and salads.

Stems:

The young stems, produced from summer until early autumn, have a great flavour and can be used in salads or in pickles. Mature stems are excellent for adding to the barbeque coals.

Seeds:

Gather the seeds in the green in late summer, or when brown in early autumn to early winter if you wish to dry them. Cut them off still attached to the stems, and hang them upside down in a light airy room. Once the seeds have dried, strip them from the branches and put them in an airtight glass jar. They can be used in sauces, fish and meat dishes, and in bread.

Properties

Fennel is a renowned digestive that is used to flavour many types of liquor. It also helps to ease dyspepsia and flatulence. The seeds chewed at the end of the meal not only clear the breath but also help to soothe indigestion, especially after a spicy meal.

Different varieties

Bronze Fennel

Foeniculum vulgare 'Purpureum'

This is a hardy herbaceous perennial with flat umbels of flowers in summer and lovely soft, striking, bronze feathery leaves. These have a milder anise flavour than the green variety but can still be used in cooking.

Florence Fennel, Finnocchio

Foeniculum vulgare var. *dulce*

This variety is grown as an annual because you dig up the sweet anise-flavoured white bulb in the early autumn. This herb is highly favoured as a vegetable in Italy. If you want it to produce good bulbs you should not let it flower. The leaf is feathery and green, very similar to the green variety. It should be sown in shallow trenches during the early summer in a rich, well-composted soil for the bulbous roots to reach maturity by the autumn. When the swelling is about the size of a golf ball, draw some soil around it. After 2–3 weeks the bulbs will have blanched and grown in size. The best size for harvesting is roughly the size of a tennis ball.

FENNEL AND COURGETTE SALAD

Anise-flavoured fennel and crunchy courgettes are abundant in the garden at the same time, and when combined with oranges this salad sings. Serve with salmon or cold pork, or simply with fresh crusty bread.

Serves 2–4

1 courgette, grated then drained
1 bulb Florence fennel, finely sliced
zest and segments of 1 orange
1 tbsp flaked almonds
100 g wild rocket leaves, roughly chopped
250 g feta, drained and roughly broken into small pieces
1 tbsp fennel leaves, finely chopped

For the dressing
2 tsp clear honey
3 tsp olive oil
3 tsp orange juice
salt and freshly ground black pepper

Combine the grated courgette, with as much liquid squeezed out of it as possible, with the sliced fennel, the orange segments and zest in a large bowl and mix well.

Toast the almond flakes in a frying pan, with no oil, for about 3–4 minutes or until golden. Set aside to cool.

Make the salad dressing by combining the ingredients and mixing well. Pour the dressing over the fennel and courgette, cover the bowl and put in the fridge for at least 1 hour.

Put the wild rocket leaves in a large salad bowl, then place the fennel and courgette mixture in the centre. Scatter over the feta cheese, the toasted almonds and the finely chopped fennel leaves.

SEA BASS WITH FENNEL AND OLIVES

We ate this in Majorca, where it is made with the wild fennel that grows all over the island and is served on wooden platters. This simple dish, with the anise flavour of the fennel leaves combined with the fresh sea bass is, in my opinion, sheer heaven.

Serves 2

Olive oil
2 sea bass fillets, each approximately 100 g
2 tbsp fennel leaves, finely sliced
sea salt and freshly ground black pepper
1 tsp fennel seeds, crushed
2 bulbs Florence fennel, halved and finely sliced
2 garlic cloves, peeled and finely sliced
4 large handfuls of green chard, finely sliced

For the sauce
1 garlic clove, finely sliced
6 anchovy fillets
4 tbsp olive oil
2 large handfuls of small black olives, stones removed
75 ml double cream
2 tbsp flatleaf parsley, roughly chopped

Pre-heat the grill to a medium heat, line a baking sheet with greaseproof paper and rub it with olive oil.

Using a sharp knife, score the skin side of the fish fillets (about halfway through the fish) and stuff with the fennel leaves. Place the fish, skin-side up, on the baking tray and cover with a few good glugs of olive oil and salt, black pepper and crushed fennel seeds. Grill for 5–7 minutes until the skin is crisp and the fish is cooked through.

Gently fry the Florence fennel slices and garlic with a pinch of salt in 2 tablespoons of olive oil until softened and lightly coloured. Add the chard and cook until the stalks are soft.

To make the sauce, gently fry the garlic and anchovies in the olive oil until soft. Chop half the olives, keeping the other half whole, and add these to the garlic and anchovies. Fry for another minute. Remove from the heat and add the cream and parsley. Check the seasoning, adding pepper if required.

Serve the fish and vegetables with the warm sauce poured over the top. Decorate with the remaining whole olives.

FENNEL AND CHICKEN STEW

The succulent Florence fennel bulbs give a light anise flavour to this stew, which gently enhances the chicken, making a delicious combination. Serve it with new potatoes and French beans.

Serves 4

3 tbsp olive oil
1.5–1.75 kg chicken, jointed into 8 pieces
salt and freshly ground black pepper
12–16 shallots, peeled and left whole
125 g pancetta
2 garlic cloves, finely chopped
1 tsp fennel seeds, lightly crushed
1 tbsp Pernod (optional, but good for special occasions)
250 ml dry white wine
350 ml hot chicken stock
2 bay leaves
2 tbsp thyme leaves (removed from stems)
2 bulbs Florence fennel, sliced into thick slices
2 tbsp butter combined with 2 tbsp plain flour to make a smooth paste
4 tbsp crème fraîche
2 tbsp fennel leaves, finely chopped

Heat the oil in a large flameproof casserole. Season the chicken pieces with salt and black pepper and fry, in batches, over a medium–high heat until browned on all sides. As each batch is cooked, remove using a slotted spoon and set aside.

Add the shallots and gently fry until lightly browned, then remove and keep with the chicken pieces. Pour the oil out of the casserole, add the pancetta and fry until golden, stirring regularly. Add the garlic and fennel seeds and fry for 1 minute, but do not brown. Add the Pernod and wine and stir well.

Once it is bubbling, add the stock, bay leaves and thyme leaves. Return the chicken and shallots to the casserole, cover and simmer gently for 10 minutes, stir in the fennel slices, cover, and gently simmer for a further 30–35 minutes until the chicken is tender.

Lift the vegetables and chicken out of the casserole and place in a warmed ovenproof dish. Slowly add the butter and flour paste to the cooking juices, whisking all the time, until you have a smooth thick sauce. Once mixed, cook gently for a further few minutes, add the crème fraîche, check the seasoning, then pour over the chicken, fennel and onions. Sprinkle with fennel leaves to serve.

FENNEL SEED RUB

I love the fact that when you pound the fennel seeds in the salt the lovely anise flavour is released into it, making this a very useful accompaniment for fish or meat.

Makes enough to rub into 4 kg of meat or fish

4 tbsp fennel seeds
1 tbsp sea salt

Pound together the fennel seeds and salt in a pestle and mortar, then rub all over your chosen meat or fish. Alternatively, put the rub into a dry container with a tight-fitting lid and store in a dark cupboard for up to 3 months.

FENNEL SEED-ENCRUSTED SLOW-ROASTED PORK BELLY

To say this is a family favourite would be an understatement. I usually serve the crackling from the pork as I make the gravy and, before I have sat down, it's gone. Fennel is renowned for breaking down fatty food, which is why it is so good with the crackling – it does not just taste delicious, it helps you digest this wonderful treat.

I am lucky enough to live near a country town that has an independent butcher. Steve purchases his pork locally; they are reared outside and are free range. It is the best pork I have ever eaten. With this cut of meat I ask him to score the skin so that it makes fantastic crackling. If you need to do this yourself, use a new clean Stanley knife or a very sharp knife and slice the skin lengthways at 1-cm intervals.

Serves 6–8

2 kg pork belly
olive oil
2 tbsp fennel seed rub
(see page 126))
2 onions, peeled and cut in half
2 carrots, scrubbed and cut in half
2 bulbs Florence fennel, cut in half
2 tbsp thyme leaves (common, French, compact or broad-leafed)
1 whole garlic bulb, unpeeled and divided into individual cloves
1 tbsp plain flour
a little water or vegetable stock

Pre-heat the oven to 170°C/325°F/gas mark 3.

Rub the pork all over with olive oil, then coat it in the seed rub, making sure you push it into the cuts in the skin.

Place the vegetables, thyme leaves and garlic cloves in a roasting tin and place the pork, skin-side up, on top of the vegetables. Make sure the vegetables stay under the pork otherwise they will burn. Add a little water to the bottom of the roasting tin and pop into the oven for 2½–3 hours. Keep checking the water to make sure it does not dry out; add a little more if necessary, but keep the water away from the meat. There is no need to baste the crackling; if you do it will not become crisp.

Once the pork is cooked, removed it from the oven and put it on a serving plate or a chopping board. Remove the vegetables and pop them into a warm serving dish.

To make the gravy spoon the fat off the cooking juices, add the flour and stir well, scooping up all the juices and the bits that have stuck to the bottom of the tin. Place on the hob over a low heat and, stirring all the time, add some water or vegetable stock to the roasting tin. Keep adding the stock until you have the consistency you like. Simmer for a few minutes then pour into a jug (you will not need to added extra salt and pepper because the wonderful seed marinade will automatically flavour this gravy).

If for some reason your crackling does not crackle, using a sharp knife, simply remove the skin from the cooked pork, place it on a rack and then put it under a grill set to the highest temperature. Keep an eye on it as it will only take minutes to rise and bubble. Once the first side is done, turn it over and do the same on the underside. Once that is cooked, turn it over again so it is skin-side up, allow to cool, then break it up into serving pieces. Pop it into a bowl.

Slice the meat; serve with the roasted vegetables and the gravy.

BAKED FENNEL

Both my grandmother and mother used to bake fennel. This is their recipe but with modern measurements. The flavour of fennel with cream is delicious, but that is only half of it, for fennel is also a digestive, helping one digest the richness of cream. Serve with grilled tomatoes and a crisp green salad.

Serves 2

2 bulbs Florence fennel
1 tbsp unsalted butter
1 tsp fennel seeds, ground
175 ml single cream
175 ml crème fraîche
2 tbsp freshly grated Parmesan

Pre-heat the oven to 170°C/325°F/gas mark 3.

Cut off the base of the fennel bulbs, removing any remains of the roots, then cut a cone shape into the base to remove the core. (This is only necessary if you have tough home-grown bulbs that you should have pulled earlier.) Cut the fennel from top to bottom, not sideways, into 5-mm-thick slices.

Melt the butter in a large frying pan set over a medium heat, add the fennel bulb and the ground fennel seeds, cook gently for about 3 minutes then stir in the cream and the crème fraîche until mixed. Transfer into a small baking dish and sprinkle with the Parmesan.

Bake in the oven for 20 minutes until the top is golden brown and the fennel is tender. If you are unsure, check by piercing it with a fork.

Excess fennel

Fennel and cucumber pickle

This is a brilliant way to use up an abundance of fennel stems in early autumn when you are preparing to cut back your fennel plants. This coincides well with the availability of cucumbers, which, if you grow your own, you can have in equal abundance. The great thing about combining fennel with cucumber is that some people find cucumber difficult to digest and fennel helps this; it also counteracts the acidity of the vinegar.

I have deliberately not put quantities here, as it all depends on how many cucumbers you have.

cucumbers
salt
fennel stalks and seeds
white wine vinegar
dill seeds
coriander seeds
black peppercorns

Wash, dry, then sterilise some wide-opening jam jars or kiln jars in an oven, set at minimum temperature, for at least 1 hour. If you are using metal lids, cut some greaseproof paper to line the lid as vinegar will, in time, corrode the metal.

Choose young fresh, rather than small, cucumbers. These will be very crisp and, equally important, have few seeds. Wash the cucumbers, do not peel, then slice into 5-mm thick pieces. Mix 600 ml of water per 50 g of salt, place the sliced cucumber in the salt water, making sure it is immersed, and leave for a minimum of 2 hours.

Cut down the fennel stalks, and wash and chop them into 3-cm pieces. The fennel stalks smell amazing when freshly cut.

Remove the jars from the oven and allow to cool until you can pick them up easily. Drain and rinse the cucumber well under a cold running tap.

Place 600ml of vinegar plus 2 teaspoons of salt in a pan (not an aluminium one), bring to the boil, remove from the heat and to allow to cool. In each jar place a layer of fennel stalks, then some sliced cucumber, and a sprinkling of the dill and coriander seeds and peppercorns. Then repeat as necessary with some stalks, some sliced cucumber, and some seeds, leaving a small gap at the top. Pour over the cooled vinegar to fully immerse the cucumbers, but not to the absolute brim. Cover.

This pickle will be ready in a month and will keep for 3 months.

GARLIC

(also known as Heal all, Aglio, Gift of the Gods)
Allium sativum

Wild Garlic, *Allium ursinum*

I cook with garlic as a matter of course, as do my children, for both my mother and grandmother used it well in cooking. It was never overpowering, it was simply part of the meal. And that is what garlic should be: a complement not a statement.

Description

Garlic is a hardy perennial that is grown each year as an annual. Each bulb is made up of several cloves enclosed in white papery skin. The cloves vary in colour from white to pink. The round heads of white flowers appear in summer only in warm climates. The mid-green, flat solid leaves smell and taste of mild garlic when broken or eaten.

Plant garlic cloves in early to mid-winter into a well-drained and sunny site that has been fed with well-rotted manure or compost at the end of the previous summer. Traditionally, for the best crop, garlic cloves are planted on the shortest day of the year and harvested on the longest.

History in cooking

Garlic is one of the oldest and most valued of all cultivated plants. It was certainly known to both the ancient Chinese and the ancient Egyptians, who considered it a health giver. Both the slaves constructing the pyramids of Cheops and the Roman soldiers were given garlic cloves daily to sustain their strength.

Harvesting and uses

Leaves:

Pick the leaves in spring until early summer. They can be added to salads, stir-fries, or used on baked potatoes.

Flowers:

Flowers are borne in summer in warm climates only. Pick the individual flowers just as they open. They have a light garlic flavour and so are good added to salads and scattered over potatoes.

Bulbs:

Lift the bulbs from late summer and divide into individual cloves. To know if you should peel the clove or not for cooking, I have always worked on this rule of thumb: peel it if you are going to slice, pound, chop or fry it. Do not peel it if you are either going to roast it (as this will help to stop it burning), or when you add it to boiling water. After you have roasted or boiled garlic cloves, remove them from the pan, then squish them to remove the soft pulp. The garlic will no longer be strong in flavour, but creamy and sweet. Add to sauces, soups, or simply mix with cooked vegetables or roasted meat.

Properties Garlic is high in many minerals including magnesium, zinc, sodium and potassium, and in vitamins A, B and C. It aids digestion, is an antioxidant, antispasmodic, carminative and diuretic. The flavour of garlic does not only enhance many meats, but will also aid the digestion of the meat.

Different varieties Wild Garlic, Ramson's Wild Garlic, Wood Garlic Devil's Posy, Onion Flower, Stinkplant, and Bear's Garlic
Allium ursinum
This is a hardy perennial with clusters of snow white, star-shaped flowers in spring and early summer, which grow on long stalks above broad, bright green leaves. It is often found growing wild in damp shady sites, especially on the banks of streams. It is recognisable by its strong oniony smell. If you wish to grow it in your garden, choose your site carefully because it is invasive. Plant in semi-shade in a moist fertile soil. The leaf has its best flavour and texture before flowering. Use sparingly in salads, or wilt and cook like a vegetable. The flowers are edible and are good added to salads.

GARLIC AND GREEN BEAN SALAD

This was one of my mother's favourite salads; the combination of the garlic with the French beans is lovely.

Serves 2–4

500 g dwarf French beans
25 g unsalted butter
2 garlic cloves, crushed
2 tbsp garlic leaves
(when in season)

Top and tail the beans, then cook in a pan of boiling water (do not salt as this will make the beans tough) for 6 minutes until firm and crunchy. Drain using a colander.

Using the same pan, melt the butter, add the crushed garlic and stir well to just cook but not brown. Add the beans and toss. Tip into a serving bowl.

Select some fresh young leaves of the new crop of garlic, finely slice and scatter over the beans. Serve.

BRUSSELS SPROUT MEZZE

The inspiration for this has come from many sources: my grandmother's book, Russian Food for Pleasure, my mother's jottings, and my travels. I love sprouts and combining them with garlic is brilliant; they both have strong flavours, but when combined they seem to balance each other.

Serves 2–4

2 tbsp olive oil
4 garlic cloves, peeled and sliced
1 small onion, peeled and chopped
30 g sun-dried tomatoes,
cut into fine strips
400 g chopped tomatoes
(home-grown or canned)
450 g Brussels sprouts, outer leaves
removed and stems trimmed
salt, sugar and freshly ground
black pepper, to taste
1 tbsp pesto (preferably home-made
but bought if the basil is over)
Freshly grated Parmesan,
to serve

Heat the oil in a pan with a close-fitting lid over a moderate heat. Slowly fry the garlic, onion and sun-dried tomatoes. When softened, add the chopped tomatoes. Cook for 5 minutes then add the sprouts. Season with salt, a pinch of sugar and a good grinding of black pepper. Cover and cook slowly for 20 minutes until the sprouts are tender. Stir in the pesto. Scatter over the grated Parmesan to serve.

ROASTED GARLIC AND BEETROOT

When roasted, garlic tastes totally different to when eaten raw; it is creamy and sweet – ideal with sweet vegetables like beetroot. This dish can either be served as an accompaniment to roast pork or chicken, or you can serve it with wild rice.

Serves 4

400 g fresh beetroot, peeled and cut into wedges
4 tbsp olive oil
2 tbsp balsamic vinegar
1 garlic bulb, cloves separated but unpeeled
1 tbsp thyme leaves, removed from the stems

Pre-heat the oven to 170°C/325°F/gas mark 3.

Put the prepared beetroot into a roasting tin, add the oil and vinegar and toss well. Add the separated garlic cloves and the thyme leaves. Give another good shake to cover everything in oil and vinegar then roast for 40 minutes until the beetroot are tender.

Serve just as it is or squish the garlic cloves, releasing the cooked garlic, and toss the beetroot in the pulp before serving.

Excess garlic Wild garlic pesto

In spring one can certainly have a glut of wild garlic. Here is an interesting pesto recipe which can be used to stir through vegetable dishes, stews, soups and sauces, or mixed with cream and served with cold chicken.

1 generous handful of young wild garlic leaves, washed, dried and finely chopped
½ tsp sea salt
2 tbsp pine nut kernels or ground almonds
2 tbsp freshly grated Parmesan
olive oil
freshly ground black pepper

Add the chopped garlic leaves and sea salt to a pestle and mortar and grind until you have a paste. Add the pine nut kernels or ground almonds and mix well, then add the grated Parmesan. Once you have a thick smooth paste, very slowly add the olive oil until you get the consistency you require.

Spoon into a jar with a screw top and keep in the fridge for up to 7 days.

GOOD KING HENRY

(also known as All good, Good King Harry,
Good Neighbour, Wild Spinach,
Lincolnshire Asparagus)
Chenopodium bonus-henricus

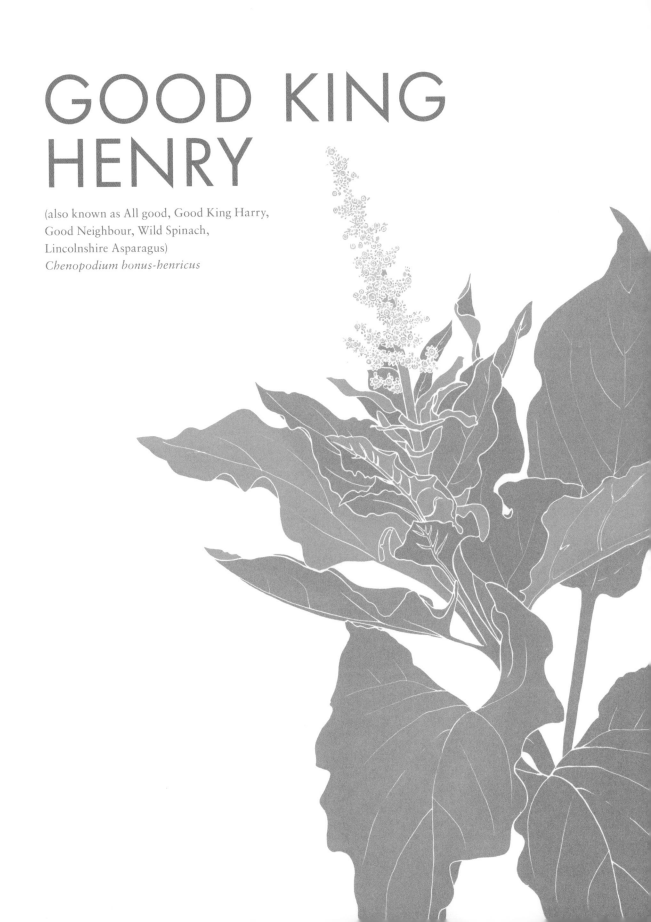

Over 30 years ago I was working on a herb farm in the west country which went under the name 'Tumbler's Bottom', and there I met Good King Henry and his cousin amaranth, both of which come from the Fat Hen family. It is this herb and its family that attracted me to the herb world. I was intrigued by their names and wanted to find out the origins. The research led me into finding out about all the herbs I grew, and the more I researched, the more I was fascinated. The outcome was my first herb collection which, in turn, led to me starting the herb farm and writing my first book in 1994.

Description

Good King Henry is a hardy perennial herb that dies back in winter, reappearing the following spring. It has tiny greenish-yellow flowers in early summer. The leaves are green and arrow or goosefoot shaped, depending on how you look at it.

In spring it can either be grown from seed or by division of established plants. Plant in a sunny position in a well-draining soil that has been fed with well-rotted compost or manure in the previous autumn. It will, however, tolerate any soil conditions, with the exception of waterlogged. If the soil is weak, though, the plant will be under fed and the leaves will be tough. Good King Henry can be grown in large containers using a soil-based potting compost. Feed weekly during the growing season to prevent the leaves becoming tough.

History in cooking

Good King Henry has been popular for hundreds of years until the last century. Traditionally the leaves were boiled and pounded with butter, the young flowering tips were eaten with salad, and the seeds were both added to gruel and dried and ground into flour for bread making. In Lincolnshire, Good King Henry was cultivated and became known as Lincolnshire spinach. It was immensely popular until the sixteenth century, when the spinach we know today arrived in this country from Asia and quickly replaced it and all other forms of the Fat Hen family. There was a slight blip in its favour after the Second World War when, due to the acute food shortage, it was cultivated and the wild varieties foraged.

Harvesting and uses

Leaves:

In early spring you will notice the appearance of new young shoots; these are now much prized by top restaurants as they can be eaten in the same way as asparagus. In mid-spring the young leaves, which are still tender, can be eaten raw in salads. From late spring onwards the leaves become tougher and need to be cooked; they are ideal for adding to stuffings, soups, purées and pies. Because of the plant's long tap root, they are more nutritious than spinach or cabbage.

Flowers:

Pick the flowering spikes as they begin to open in summer. These can then be steamed and served either hot tossed in butter, or cold with a vinaigrette. They are, because of their high seed content, very grainy and so not to everyone's taste!

Seeds:

As the seed pods start to turn light brown, from late summer until early autumn, collect the seeds by picking whole branches, laying them on trays of newspaper in a warm dry place out of the sun. Within a few days you will notice that the seeds are being released. Lift the flowering branch carefully and all the seeds will drop onto the tray. Leave these seeds on the tray for a further week, then sift them away from the chaff, (the stems and bits) and store them in an airtight container in a dark cupboard. They can be added to soups, or ground and used with flour to make pitta-type breads.

Properties

The leaves of Good King Henry and Fat Hen (see below) are rich in iron, calcium and vitamins B1 and C. It is recommended that they are included in the diet of anyone suffering from anaemia because of their high iron content.

Different varieties

Tree Spinach, Giant Goosefoot

Chenopodium giganteum

This is a hardy annual with tiny greenish flowers in summer and arrow- or goosefoot-shaped leaves with serrated edges. The new leaves have the most wonderful magenta colour which fades to green as it ages. The young leaves can be eaten raw in salads or cooked as spinach, when the colour will revert to green.

Fat Hen, Lambs Quarters, White Goosefoot, Common Pigweed, All Good, Muckweed

Chenopodium album

Fat Hen is a hardy annual with small, greenish white flowers in summer and green, lance- or goosefoot-shaped leaves. This herb can be found growing wild all over Europe, and its fatty seeds have been identified at Neolithic villages in Switzerland. The seeds can be ground into flour and used to make gruel.

GOOD KING HENRY CROQUETTES

This is a lovely simple supper dish or appetiser. One can use tree spinach or ordinary spinach leaves instead of Good King Henry leaves, if you wish, which taste like a strong version of spinach. Serve with a classic tomato sauce and jacket potatoes.

Serves 2

900 g young Good King Henry leaves
2 tbsp plain flour, plus extra for dusting
½ tsp freshly grated nutmeg
1 egg, beaten
Salt and freshly ground black pepper
Oil, for frying

Cook the Good King Henry leaves in a small amount of boiling water until it has reduced to a soft mound, about 5–7 minutes. Drain through a colander and, with the back of a wooden spoon, squeeze out as much liquid as possible. Set aside until cool.

Mix the cooked Good King Henry leaves with the flour, nutmeg and the beaten egg, and add the salt and black pepper. Put in the fridge to firm up, about 40 minutes, or longer if required.

Remove from the fridge, form the firm mixture into cakes or croquettes, roll in a small amount of flour, then fry briefly on either side in a pan with a little oil until uniformly golden.

GOOD KING HENRY OMELETTE

The flavour of the leaves of Good King Henry are enhanced when combined with eggs. This is a highly nutritious meal that is ideal for lunch or supper served with a crisp green wild rocket salad.

Serves 2

75 g unsalted butter
1 garlic clove, very finely chopped
225 g Good King Henry leaves, washed and chopped
Salt and freshly ground black pepper
6 eggs, beaten well with a whisk for at least 1 minute

In a non-stick frying pan, melt 1 tablespoon of the butter and cook the garlic and the Good King Henry until the leaves are fully wilted, adding a little more butter if required. Season, then pour in the beaten eggs and cook until they start to solidify.

TREE SPINACH MASH

This recipe has been inspired by my mother. She was often making interesting mashes because when I was growing up we had to make food stretch a long way, and she was incredibly inventive with the same ingredients. She created many variations on a theme, both to extend different root vegetables and to combine root vegetables with other soft-leaved varieties. This is one of her mashes that I have adapted for tree spinach, which has a dry spinach flavour. It is especially good during the summer, when one has the start of the maincrop potatoes and a mass of tree spinach leaves to hand. This is delicious with a roasted chicken.

450 g tree spinach leaves, cooked then puréed using a hand blender or food processor
900 g potatoes (Wilja or King Edward), cooked and mashed by hand for a rough texture with a knob of butter and 1 beaten egg
Salt and freshly ground black pepper
Grated nutmeg

Combine the puréed spinach with the mashed potato by hand rather than using a mixer – as this makes it too smooth and glue-like. Add the salt, black pepper and nutmeg to taste.

Excess Good King Henry

If you do have a glut of this herb I suggest you cook it like spinach, squeeze out any excess water, and pop it into a container. Once cold, seal, then freeze. This can then be used for mash, croquettes, sauces or soups.

HORSERADISH

(also known as Cranson de Bretagne, Rafano, Mountain Radish)

Armoracia rusticana, syn. *Cochlearia armoracia*

As a child I used to walk down the high street in Chew Magna every Sunday to get the newspapers for my parents. One Sunday I saw Mr Bell, our neighbour, sitting outside his cottage crying. This really worried me, for I had not seen a grown man cry before. He saw me, saw my concern and called me over. Smiling through his tears he said he was grating horseradish for the Sunday roast. As soon as I drew near, I also started crying from the pungency of root. So every autumn as I prepare the roots for preserving, I remember Mr Bell.

Description

Horseradish is a very hardy herbaceous perennial that dies back in winter, reappearing in the spring. It can be found growing wild throughout the UK. It has large mid-green leaves and white flowers in summer. One should consider carefully growing this herb in the garden as it is so invasive. It spreads when you dig up the plant, for it is impossible to remove all the root because it is very very long and any bit left in the soil will automatically produce a new plant. So once you begin to harvest you will start the plant spreading.

It is a most tolerant plant, liking all but the driest of soils. It prefers a sunny site but again will tolerate dappled shade. If large quantities are required, horseradish should be given a patch of its own where the roots can be lifted and the soil replenished each autumn. If you have a small garden, consider growing this herb in a dustbin, this makes it easy to control and very easy to harvest in the autumn.

History in cooking

Horseradish has been in cultivation and the wild for over 3,000 years. It is said to be one of the five bitter herbs (along with coriander, horehound, lettuce and nettle) which the Jews ate during the Feast of Passover.

In the Middle Ages horseradish was used as a painkiller as well as a condiment.

In the sixteenth century, John Gerard, an English herbalist, notes in his book, Gerard's Herbal, that horseradish (which he calls *Raphanus rusticanus*) grows wild in several parts of England. He says:

'The Horse Radish stamped with a little vinegar put thereto, is commonly used among the Germans for sauce to eate fish with and such like meates as we do mustarde.'

Interestingly, this herb was not cultivated in the USA until the mid 1850s, when the settlers started horseradish farms in the Midwest.

Harvesting and uses

Leaves:

These can be picked and eaten in early spring, particularly in salads. However, the flavour is not to everyone's palate – and that includes mine – as it is rather dry and mustard-like.

Roots:

Lift roots in autumn. The flavour of grated horseradish root is like an extremely strong radish; it can be used in coleslaw or dips, or with pickled beetroot, cream cheese, mayonnaise and avocado fillings. Make horseradish sauce to accompany roast beef and smoked oily fish.

Properties

The reason horseradish is used in sauces, vinegars and as an accompaniment to other dishes, is because the volatile flavouring oil which is released when it is grated evaporates rapidly, so it becomes nothing when cooked. But raw, that's a different story. The volatile oil contains vitamins A, B and C and is rich in sulphur, phosphorus potassium, iron and magnesium. Horseradish, due to its powerful flavour, stimulates the digestion.

Different varieties

Variegated Horseradish

Armoracia rusticana 'Variegata'
This variety is a hardy herbaceous plant with white flowers in summer and large, green/cream variegated, oblong-shaped leaves. The edible root can be used in the same way as the green-leaved horseradish.

Japanese Horseradish, Wasabi

Wasabia japonica syn *Cochlearia wasabi*
This is a sub-tropical plant that has edible leaves, flowers and rhizomes. The fleshy rhizomes are finely grated and prepared into a green paste which is famous in Japan. Like horseradish, the flavour rapidly deteriorates once the root is cut or grated.

ICED TOMATOES AND HORSERADISH SAUCE

This is a recipe from my grandmother's notebook. She was given it by a friend of hers called Nancy Shaw, and it appears in her book, *Food for the Greedy*, published in 1936.

'Very good to serve as a salad on a hot summer day with tomatoes skinned and put in the ice chest till very cold, and at the last moment some good creamy horseradish sauce poured over them. The sauce to be just slightly iced. With a joint of cold lamb this is excellent. The best horseradish sauce to use is made by grating some horseradish into mayonnaise to which has been added some cream.' Here is my adaptation.

Serves 6

450 g cherry tomatoes
150 ml double cream
2–3 tbsp grated horseradish
150 ml mayonnaise
Chervil or parsley leaves, to decorate

Place the cherry tomatoes in a bowl, pour over boiling water, leave for a few minutes then peel. Place the tomatoes in a serving dish, cover, and put in the fridge until they need to be served.

Lightly whip the cream. Put the horseradish in a bowl, stir in the mayonnaise and fold into the cream. Cover and place in the fridge.

When ready to serve, spoon the horseradish sauce over the tomatoes and decorate with the chervil or parsley leaves.

HORSERADISH EGG MOUSSE

My father would eat horseradish with everything if given half a chance. I have known him have horseradish cream with baked apples. He was extremely greedy when this mousse was served by my mother, you had to hope that the dish was not given to him first as it went round the table.

The combination of the eggs with the hotness of the horseradish and the coolness of the cucumber is delightful.

Serves 4

8 hard-boiled eggs, shelled
200 ml chicken stock
15 g gelatine
Sea salt and freshly ground black pepper
Pinch of cayenne
1 tbsp grated horseradish
150 ml double cream, lightly whipped
3 tbsp chopped chervil or dill
½ cucumber, peeled and coarsely grated, to garnish

Chop the eggs fairly finely and put in a large bowl.

Heat the stock and melt the gelatine in it, then strain it over the eggs and mix gently. Season with salt and black pepper and add the cayenne and horseradish. Fold in the cream and chopped herbs, then turn into a food processor and blend briefly, stopping before it becomes smooth.

Tip the mixture into a 900 ml soufflé dish and chill in the fridge for 3–4 hours, or overnight.

Serve chilled, with the grated cucumber scattered over the top.

STIR-FRIED BEEF IN HORSERADISH YORKSHIRE PUDDINGS

Infusing the batter with the horseradish counteracts the effect of cooking, so the flavour is brilliant.

Serves 4

75 g plain flour
2 medium eggs
125 ml whole milk
2 tbsp grated horseradish (if using preserved horseradish, drain the vinegar before use. If using bought, get the relish/sauce not the cream variety)
5 tbsp vegetable oil
25g butter
350 g beef steak, cut into thin strips
1 large onion, halved and thinly sliced
100 ml red wine
200 ml beef stock

Preheat the oven to 220°C/425°F/gas mark 7.

Place the flour, eggs and milk in a bowl. Season and mix with an electric whisk for at least 3–5 minutes, or until smooth and frothy on the surface. Mix in the horseradish. Pour the batter into a jug and leave to stand at room temperature for 1–2 hours.

Either put 4 tablespoons of oil into a large roasting tin, or if you have a 4-hole Yorkshire pudding tray, put 1 tablespoon of oil in each section. Place in the oven for about 10 minutes or until the oil just begins to smoke. Pour the batter into the tin. Cook for 15 minutes or until risen and golden.

While the pudding is cooking, melt half the butter with 1 tablespoon of oil in a large frying pan over a high heat. Stir-fry the beef for 5 minutes or until brown. Using a slotted spoon, transfer to a plate and set aside in a warm place.

Return the frying pan to the heat and add the onion. Cook for 5 minutes or until golden. Pour in the wine and bring to the boil for 1 minute or until almost all the liquid has evaporated. Add the stock and boil for a further 5 minutes, or until reduced slightly. Stir in the remaining butter to create a glossy gravy. Mix in the meat and season to taste.

HORSERADISH CREAM

This is a deluxe version of horseradish sauce that goes so well with meat, smoked fish and cheese. It is especially good served with cold beef, smoked mackerel or an avocado and apple salad.

Makes 125 ml

15-cm piece of fresh horseradish (or use 1 tbsp of preserved horseradish in vinegar, drained, and omit the lemon juice)
1 tbsp unsalted butter
2 tbsp fresh breadcrumbs
1 apple
2 tsp yoghurt
1 tsp lemon juice
pinch of salt
pinch of sugar
1 tsp chopped fresh chervil, French tarragon and dill
3–4 tbsp double cream

Wash, peel and grate the fresh horseradish.

Melt the butter in a frying pan and add the breadcrumbs. Fry until golden brown, remove from the heat and add the grated horseradish. Grate the apple into the mixture. Add the yoghurt, lemon juice, salt, sugar and chopped herbs. Set aside to cool, then chill in the fridge.

Just before serving, gently fold the cream into the mixture.

Excess horseradish

Horseradish vinegar

This is the best way to preserve horseradish for use throughout the year. Always strain the grated root before using.

Freshly grated horseradish root
White distilled malt vinegar

Per jar:
½ tsp salt
¼ tsp sugar

One very good tip for how to prevent your eyes streaming when grating horseradish is to wash and peel the root, then pop it in the freezer in a plastic bag. Leave for one hour; then remove and grate it.

Fill a small or medium jam jar to about two-thirds full with horseradish, depending on how much you have grated. Add the salt and the sugar, cover with the malt vinegar and shake well. If using a metal lid, put a piece of greaseproof paper on the underside to stop it corroding.

The vinegar can be stored for at least 1 year, if not longer.

HYSSOP

(also known as Herbe sacrée, Issopo)
Hyssopus officinalis

I love this Mediterranean herb, for in summer it abounds with bees and butterflies as they adore the blue flowers. It is one of my must-haves when I am designing a herb garden, especially if the herb and vegetable gardens are intertwined. The fact that hyssop attracts bees to the garden means that pollination of the vegetables increases and this, in turn, increases their yield. In the kitchen it has been a great stand-by herb; it adds another dimension to food and, I believe, is under used, so its full potential has yet to be discovered.

Description

Hyssop is a hardy herb with semi-evergreen leaves, which means that some leaves can be picked throughout the winter. It is short-lived, lasting about 4–5 years, with attractive spikes of small, dark blue tubular flowers throughout the summer. The small, lance-shaped green leaves are aromatic in scent and slightly bitter, not sour, in flavour when eaten straight from the plant. Like its cousins, rosemary and thyme, it prefers a well-drained soil and a sunny position in the garden.

It can either be grown from seed sown in the early summer or it is easily grown from cuttings taken from the new growth in late spring or early summer. This herb happily adapts to being container grown; plant in pots using a soil-based compost.

History in cooking

Historically, hyssop is said to have been mentioned in the Bible, however there is some dispute about whether it is this plant or an Origanum. It certainly was used by Hippocrates (460–377 BC) who recommended it for chest complaints – for which it is still used today.

Harvesting and uses

Leaves:
Pick young leaves from early spring until early winter to use fresh or, in summer, from non-flowering stems for drying. The leaves are quite strong in flavour, so do not be too lavish with them. Use them in salads, with meat stews, soups and stuffings. In the USA hyssop is added to apple pie.

Flowers:
Pick flowers in summer just as they open to use fresh or dry – the scent becomes more intense when dried. The flowers are delicious tossed in green salads.

Properties

It is said that this herb helps aid digestion, especially when eaten with rich, oily foods. It is also a beneficial antioxidant. Medicinally it is used to treat congestions and coughs.

Different varieties

Pink hyssop
Hyssopus officinalis 'Roseus'
Dense spikes of small, pale, sugar pink flowers from summer until early autumn. Small, narrow, lance-shaped, aromatic green leaves.

Rock hyssop
Hyssopus officinalis subsp. *aristatus*
Dense spikes of small, dark blue flowers from summer until early autumn. Small, narrow, lance-shaped, aromatic green leaves.

White hyssop
Hyssopus officinalis f. *albus*
Dense spikes of small white flowers from summer until early autumn. Small, narrow, lance-shaped, aromatic green leaves.

ROASTED PARSNIPS, HYSSOP AND DATES

The combination of the sweetness of the roast parsnips and dates with the bitter aromatic leaves of the hyssop transforms this roasted vegetable dish. Serve with mashed potatoes and roast meat or boiled ham.

Serves 2–4

500 g small parsnips, peeled, halved lengthwise and cut into 6-cm chunks (If using mature wintered stock, remove the centre core, especially if it has become woody)
350 g small onions, cut into quarters
4 garlic cloves, peeled and sliced
4 sprigs of hyssop leaves, removed from their stems
olive oil
125 g feta cheese, cubed
a handful of black olives, stoned
a handful of dates, stoned

Pre-heat the oven to 200°C/400°F/gas mark 6.

Put the prepared parsnips, onions and garlic into a heavy roasting pan with the leaves from 3 of the hyssop sprigs. Drizzle with olive oil and roast for about 45–50 minutes until golden. During the roasting, shake the pan several times to evenly brown the vegetables and to stop them sticking.

Scatter over the feta, olives, dates and remaining hyssop leaves. Return to the oven for 5–10 minutes.

HYSSOP-BAKED PEPPERS

This is a succulent rustic lunch or light supper. The aromatic bitter flavour of the hyssop combined with the sweetness of the peppers and ripe tomatoes is delightful. Make sure you serve this with some crusty fresh bread so you can mop up the juices.

Serves 2–4

4 red peppers
3 garlic cloves
salt
2 sprigs of hyssop leaves, removed from the stems and finely chopped
olive oil
16 ripe cherry tomatoes
8 anchovy fillets

Pre-heat the oven to 200°C/400°F/gas mark 6.

Halve the peppers lengthways, remove and discard the white core and seeds then lay the peppers, cut-side up, in a greased baking dish. They should fit snugly.

Peel the garlic, slice it finely and put a few slices in each halved pepper, together with a little salt, a pinch of hyssop leaves and 1 tablespoon of oil. (If you are using anchovies in olive oil, use this oil as it adds extra flavour.) Halve the tomatoes – there's no need to peel these small tomatoes – and tuck them into the peppers. Bake in the oven until the peppers have almost collapsed and are full of juice. Either drain the anchovies, if in oil, on kitchen paper or, if in brine, rinse and dry them. Roughly chop the anchovy fillets and stir a teaspoonful into each of the peppers. Return to the oven for 10 minutes, then serve.

SPANISH HYSSOP TORTILLAS

Tortillas or baked omelettes are easy and versatile; they can be eaten hot or cold, for lunch or for supper, smart or casual. My favourite way is to serve them warm with a rocket salad and a cold glass of white wine.

The use of hyssop in this recipe adds a clean, bitter minty flavour to the dish.

Serves 3–6

1 medium onion
275 g small Desiree potatoes
3 tbsp olive oil
Salt and freshly ground black pepper
2 tsp hyssop leaves, finely chopped
5 eggs

First peel and cut the onion in half, then thinly slice each half and separate the layers into half-moon shapes. If you have a food processor, slice the potatoes thinly, if not, use a potato peeler. Doing this by hand will take time, so to stop them turning brown, fill a large bowl with cold water and thinly slice the potatoes into the water. When they are sliced, drain them and rub them dry in a clean tea towel.

Heat 2 tablespoons of the olive oil in a heavy-based frying pan that is approximately 20cm in diameter and has a lid. When the oil is hot, add the potatoes and onions and toss them around in the oil to get well coated. Turn the heat right down to its lowest setting, add a good sprinkling of salt and black pepper, plus the finely chopped hyssop leaves. Put a lid on the frying pan and let the onions and potatoes cook gently for 20 minutes, or until tender. Turn them over halfway through and shake the pan from time to time, as they are not supposed to brown very much but just gently cook.

Break the eggs into a large bowl, whisk them lightly with a fork (do not over beat), and add some salt and black pepper. When the onions and potatoes are cooked, quickly transfer them to the eggs in the bowl.

Put the frying pan back on the heat and add the rest of the oil. Mix the potato and eggs thoroughly before pouring the whole lot into the frying pan and turning the heat down to its lowest setting immediately. Cook, uncovered, very slowly for 20–25 minutes. When there is virtually no liquid egg left on the surface of the omelette, turn it over to cook the other side. (The easiest way to do this is to place either the lid or a plate over the pan, invert the omelette onto it then gently ease the omelette back into the pan using a palate knife.)

Put the frying pan back on the heat, cook for a further few minutes. It should be cooked through but still moist in the centre.

HYSSOP FISH CAKES

Living where I do, I cannot simply pop to the shops, so I have a modern form of an old-fashioned larder where I keep cans of food. These prove immensely useful on days when either we are snowed in or I simply have not made time to shop. My larder includes canned tomatoes, honey, anchovies and tuna, to name but a few, and this is a great supper made from its offerings. Serve with a home-made tomato sauce (see page 12), green beans, or a fresh green salad.

Serves 4

approx. 150 ml olive oil
1 onion, finely chopped
1 x 250 g can tuna, drained
250 g left-over mashed potato
(or if making specially,
allow to cool before using)
1 tsp finely chopped hyssop leaves,
removed from the stem
2 eggs, beaten

Heat a little of the olive oil in a frying pan, add the onion and gently fry it until soft. Add to a mixing bowl and allow to cool.

Once cold, add the tuna and mix well. Add the mashed potato and the chopped hyssop and mix again, then add half of the beaten eggs. Form the mixture into 8 flat cakes. Dip each cake into the remaining egg.

Add some extra oil to the frying pan and return it to the heat. Add the fish cakes and gently fry them for 5 minutes on each side.

Excess Hyssop

Hyssop butter

This butter can be used with vegetables, soups, stews, casseroles and for grilled meat or fish.

Makes 125 g butter

A handful of hyssop leaves
125 g unsalted butter

Remove the hyssop leaves from their stems. Chop roughly, then add the butter and keep chopping the butter and hyssop leaves together to release the oils in the leaves into the butter.

Once you have reached the size of leaf you require, use a fork to gather up the butter. When it has been thoroughly mixed, pack it into a roll of greaseproof paper and place in the fridge for up to 24 hours before use. The longer you leave it, the better the flavour.

This butter can also be frozen for 2–3 months. Place it in a plastic bag or plastic container and don't forget to label it so you know which herb it is.

LAVENDER

(also known as Lavande, Lavanda)
Lavandula

Lavender is the quintessential herb; it smells good, looks good and does you good. It is the traditional English garden herb. Neither my mother nor my grandmother would have used it in cooking. It is a herb that I use sparingly. It is particularly useful in winter when I want another flavour rather than rosemary. It is also extremely good infused in sugar for making cakes, biscuits and puddings.

Description

This very popular herb can be either a hardy evergreen shrub with highly aromatic grey leaves or a tender evergreen shrub with more of a eucalyptus rather than lavender-scented leaf. It all depends on the variety. The standard lavender-scented plants have medium to long spikes of blue–mauve flowers all summer long, whereas the French forms have more of a eucalyptus scent to the leaves with a small, dark purple flower head which is topped with two coloured bracts that are often called ears. The varieties with the best culinary flavours are mentioned below, and these are all hardy.

Lavenders can be raised from seed but this does take time, and even more important it is far more reliable to raise the plant from cuttings taken from non-flowering stems in late spring. All the species need an open sunny position and a fertile well-drained soil. They will adapt to semi-shade as long as the soil is well drained, otherwise they may die in winter. If you have very cold winter temperatures, I recommend that you grow lavender in a container which can be given protection.

History in cooking

Historically the Romans first introduced French lavender to Britain when they invaded. They brought the flower heads over dried and ground them to use as a condiment. The use of lavender as a condiment was much more common in medieval times because fresh meat was rare and difficult to keep. Condiments were used to hide the disagreeable flavours and tastes of semi-cooked or half-rotten flesh.

Harvesting and uses

Leaves:
Harvest before flowering, all year round. Being evergreen, though, the best flavour is in early summer. The leaves can be used fresh or can be dried. The leaves can be added sparingly to roast meat and in stuffings.

Flowers:
Cut the flowers in summer, just as they open, to use fresh and also for drying. Dry on open trays or by hanging in small bunches. The flowers can be used sparingly in cooking. They are good for flavouring sugar, which in turn is good for baking biscuits and cakes.

Properties

I can find no other identified culinary properties regarding lavender except for its use as a flavouring. Medicinally, the oil is anti-microbial and has sedative properties; it is used to treat insomnia, panic, shock and nervous palpations. It is one of the best herbs for keeping flies out of the kitchen.

Different varieties

Common Lavender, English Lavender
Lavandula angustifolia (syn. L. spica, L. officinalis)
This hardy, perennial evergreen shrub has mauve–purple flowers on long spikes in summer and long, narrow, pale greenish–grey aromatic leaves. It is one of the most popular and well known of this group of lavenders. The flowers and leaves are good with meat and to infuse sugars.

Hidcote Lavender
Lavandula angustifolia 'Hidcote'
This is a hardy, perennial evergreen shrub with richly scented, short, rounded spikes of deep purple–blue flowers in summer and short, narrow, aromatic grey leaves. The flowers and leaves are good with meat and to infuse sugars.

Old English Lavender
Lavandula x intermedia Old English Group
This hardy, perennial evergreen shrub has aromatic, long, pointed spikes of clear pale blue–purple flowers in summer and long, narrow, aromatic silver–grey green leaves. The flowers and leaves are also good with meat and to infuse sugars.

French Lavender
Lavandula stoechas
This is a frost-hardy, perennial evergreen shrub. It has attractive, small, deep purple flowers clustered around small flowering stalks topped with a short mauve–purple bracts (ears) from early summer until early autumn. The short, green–grey narrow leaves are camphor-scented. The flower heads can be dried and used as a condiment, and are also good in baking – but use with discretion.

Lavender Viridis
Lavandula viridis
Another frost-hardy, perennial evergreen shrub. This unusual lavender has green bracts with a cream centre tuft. The leaves are green, narrow and highly aromatic with a eucalyptus scent and flavour. Good with strong flavoured meats.

GRILLED LEFT-OVER TURKEY WITH LAVENDER BUTTER AND A PIQUANT SAUCE

This recipe is a true 'hand-me-down'. It is a great way to use up left-over Christmas or Thanksgiving turkey. This is where, I guess, it originated, as my grandmother's maiden name before marrying was Hirsch, and I believe she was born in Hungary but lived her adult life in the USA. My mother adapted Ruth's recipe and I have adapted hers, so here is a third-generation recipe. The lavender adds an aromatic piquancy to the whole meal.

My grandmother wrote: 'Take a cold roast turkey, cut it into neat joints and cover with the herb butter. Grill over a slow fire and serve with a piquant sauce.' So, to be more explicit I have written out her recipes and put in the amounts. Serve with winter green vegetables.

Serves 4

300 g rice
8 slices cooked turkey

For the lavender butter:
20 leaves in summer or 35 leaves in winter from any of the following: Old English Group or 'Hidcote'
125 g unsalted butter

For the piquant sauce:
40 g unsalted butter
1 onion, finely chopped
1 garlic clove, finely sliced
Salt and freshly ground black pepper
40 g plain flour
300 ml turkey stock (made from the bones or a good bought poultry stock)
150 ml red wine
2 bay leaves
4 cloves
2 tsp lavender jelly (see page 158) or redcurrant jelly
A generous dash of Worcestershire sauce

Make the butter the day before you need it to allow the flavours to infuse. Remove the leaves from the stems and gently chop to release the oils. Then mix the chopped leaves with the butter. Cover and place in the fridge for at least 24 hours before use. The longer you leave it, the better the flavour.

On the day that you are serving this dish, make the piquant sauce. In a small pan, melt the butter and gently fry the onion and garlic with a good pinch of salt until soft. Add the plain flour, stir until it absorbs all the juices and cook for 2 minutes, stirring regularly. In a separate pan, add the stock with the wine, bring it to the boil and simmer for a few minutes to burn off the alcohol.

Turn the heat right down and slowly add about one-quarter of the infused stock to the cooked flour, stirring well to eliminate flour lumps. Once you have a smooth (excluding the onion lumps) paste, slowly add the remaining three-quarters of the stock.

Add the bay leaves and cloves to the pan and stir regularly until the sauce is cooked, about 5 minutes. Do not boil. Remove the cloves and bay leaves. Add the jelly and stir well. Add a dash of Worcestershire sauce (this was my mother's secret ingredient) and check the seasoning. If necessary, add more lavender jelly so that you get a hint of lavender, but it must not be overpowering nor too sweet. Keep the sauce on a low heat while you cook the rice and the turkey.

Cook the rice according to the packet instructions. Pre-heat a grill to low, smear all the slices of turkey with the lavender butter and place under the grill, turning from time to time so that all the turkey becomes slightly crispy.

To serve, place the grilled turkey on the rice, pour over some sauce and put the remainder into a jug so everyone can help themselves.

LAVENDER AND SWEET WINE JELLY

Fruit jellies are something that were a particular favourite at children's parties when I was a child. If you went to a fancy birthday party you often had a chocolate blancmange rabbit surrounded by bright green jelly. It always looked amazing and tasted not as good as it looked! This, on the other hand, is a scrummy pudding; the combination of the aromatic lavender with the sweetness of the dessert wine is a winner.

Serves 4–6

55 g fresh lavender flowers
275 ml water
275 ml white dessert wine
40 g lavender sugar
(see page 159)
1 x 11 g sachet powdered gelatine
juice of 1 orange

Put the lavender flowers, water and wine in an enamel or stainless-steel pan, not aluminium or on untreated metal. Heat very, very gently until it reaches just below boiling. Remove from the heat, cover, and let the water, wine and flowers infuse for 10 minutes.

Strain the liquid, using a nylon sieve, into a glass or china bowl and stir in the sugar until dissolved. Check the flavour and add more sugar if required.

Sprinkle the gelatine onto the orange juice and allow to soften, then warm gently until dissolved. Stir into the wine mixture and pour the jelly into 4 individual pretty glasses or bowls. Chill the jelly in a fridge until set.

Remove from the fridge when you serve the main course so that the jelly is not cold when served. Serve just as it is.

LAVENDER MERINGUE ICE CREAM

I learnt this recipe from my mother who used to have it on standby in the freezer for special meals or for unexpected dinners. She became renowned for it, especially during the first Pilton, 'Glastonbury Festival', which was held in our village, and when our home became the neutral ground between the show organisers and the village.

I have adapted her recipe by infusing the sugar with lavender, which when cooked as meringues is lovely, as it removes the harshness of the lavender to give one a warm aromatic flavour. Topped with fresh fruit it is summer on a plate.

Serves 6–8

For the meringues
3 eggs
175 g lavender flower-infused caster sugar (see page 159)

For the ice cream
300 ml double cream
dash of milk
1 tbsp kirsch

seasonal summer fresh fruit (such as redcurrants, raspberries or strawberries), for the topping

Pre-heat the oven to 140°C/275°F/gas mark 1 and line 2 baking sheets with non-stick baking parchment.

Make the meringues. A top tip for making meringues is to make sure that all the utensils are spotlessly clean; if there is the slightest trace of grease, your egg whites will not form those strong, firm peaks necessary for great meringues.

Separate the eggs, putting the whites into a mixing bowl. (The remaining egg yolks can be added to mashed potato, omelettes or for making custard.) Using an electric hand whisk on a slow speed, whisk the egg whites until they start to bubble, then slowly increase the speed to maximum. Keep whisking until the egg whites form stiff white peaks. With the mixer on the fastest speed, slowly add the sugar. When all is amalgamated, turn off your machine. If you over process at this point the egg whites may collapse.

With two spoons, scoop the mixture out onto the baking sheets to make individual meringues. Alternatively, put half the mixture into the middle of each sheet then, using the handle of a metal spoon, in swirling movements slowly draw the mixture out into a round about 2 cm deep. I usually make half and half so I have the options of different puddings.

Place the baking sheets in the oven for 45 minutes–1 hour. If you like gooey centres, remove the meringues from the oven immediately at the end of the cooking time but if you like crisp centres, turn the heat off, open the door of the oven and leave the meringues to cool inside. For the meringue ice cream I prefer crisp, because when you combine it with the cream it will become a bit gooey anyway.

Whisk the cream with a dash of milk until it is very thick, then add the kirsch. Break the meringues into chunks then fold into the cream. Immediately pop the mixture into a large serving bowl, cover with cling film and put in the freezer to set (about 2–3 hours, until firm). Remove the ice cream from the freezer just before you serve. Top with the fresh fruit. Delicious.

LAVENDER OAT BISCUITS

These lavender biscuits are lovely on their own, with a cup of tea, or served with clotted cream and fresh summer fruit, especially raspberries. The combination of the clean fruity flavour of the raspberries with the aromatic flavour of the lavender cooked into a sweet oat biscuit, to me signals summer.

Makes approx. 12 biscuits

75 g unsalted butter,
plus extra for greasing
75 g self-raising flour
75 g porridge oats
75 g sugar
1 tbsp golden syrup
1 tbsp milk
1 tsp lavender leaves, removed from the stem and finely chopped
1 tsp lavender flowers, removed from the flowering spike and left whole

Pre-heat the oven to 180°C/350°F/gas mark 4. Grease a baking sheet with butter, then line it with baking parchment.

Sift the flour into a bowl, add the oats and sugar and mix well. In a small pan over a low heat, melt the butter with the syrup and milk, and stir until well amalgamated. Add the flour, oats, sugar and lavender leaves and mix well. Remove from the heat and stir in the lavender flowers.

Place a tablespoonful of mixture onto the prepared baking sheet and shape into rounds, leaving a space between each. Pop into the oven and bake for 10–15 minutes until golden brown. Remove from the oven, leave on the baking sheet for 5 minutes, then lift the baking parchment onto a wire rack and leave the biscuits to cool completely.

Excess lavender

Lavender jelly

This is a great way to preserve the flavour of lavender. This jelly can be used in cakes and it is also lovely with roast lamb.

The following quantities should fill 4 x 450 g jam jars

1.75 kg cooking apples
1.75 litres water
1 kg sugar
8 tbsp lavender flowers (stems removed, but leave the flower heads unplucked as they can be put complete into a piece of muslin for cooking)
4 tbsp lemon juice

Wash and chop the apples and put them in a large pan with a lid. Add the water, bring to the boil, then simmer until the apples are soft and pulpy – this takes from 20–30 minutes, depending on the variety of apple. Pour carefully into a muslin (or jellybag, cheesecloth bag) and leave for a day or overnight to drain into a large bowl.

Once drained, measure the juice and add 450 g of sugar to every 600 ml of juice. Put the juice and sugar into a large pan and bring to the boil, adding the lavender flowers tied in a piece of muslin (or cheesecloth). Leave 1 tablespoon of flowers, removed from the flower heads, aside to go in the jelly as decoration, if you wish. However, remember that some people do not like bits in jelly. Boil for about 20 minutes until setting point is reached.

At this point, remove the flowers in the muslin and spoon off the surface scum. Stir in the lemon juice and reserved tablespoon of flowers, if you wish, and pour into warmed sterilised (see page 12) glass jars. Seal when cool, date and label.

Lavender sugar

With this sugar you can make lavender biscuits, cakes and puddings, including meringues.

Makes 350 g sugar

8–16 tbsp chopped lavender flowers
350 g granulated or caster sugar

Pick the flowers after midday, making sure they are absolutely dry before starting the sugar. If you are unsure, remove the flower heads from their stems and spread them out on a baking sheet lined with baking parchment. Place them in a very low oven (110°C/225°F/gas mark ¼) leaving the door open. Put the timer on as the flowers should be dry in 10 minutes, and you do not want to bake them.

Once dry, chop up the flowers and mix with the sugar. Put the sugar and flowers into a jar or tub with a lid. After a day, shake the container to make sure that the flowers are not making the sugar sticky and lumpy. After a week, give the container another shake and check the flavour of the sugar. If you feel it is not strong enough, seal the container again and leave for a further week. When you are happy with the strength of flavour, sift the sugar and flowers through a medium sieve. If you find that the sugar is lumpy, put it in a food processor and whiz it up until fine. Pour into an airtight container and store; it will keep for 6–12 months, depending on the humidity of your kitchen.

LEMON BALM

(also known as Balm, Bee Balm, Sweet Balm, Melissa)
Melissa officinalis

As a gardener you cuss this herb because, like its cousin mint, it is invasive; however, as a cook I find it is incredibly useful and underused. Neither my mother nor grandmother used lemon balm for cooking, although I found out that my grandmother kept bees and planted it around the bee hives. This is a traditional thing to do, as not only are the flowers high in nectar but also it was said that rubbing a new hive with the leaves encouraged the bees to settle while the scent of the herb stopped bees swarming.

Description

Lemon balm is a hardy herb that dies back in winter and reappears in the spring. It has clusters of insignificant pale creamy flowers in summer, and intensely lemon-scented, mid-green, oval, toothed textured leaves.

It can be grown from seed or division and is a tolerant plant that will grow in all soils provided it is not waterlogged. Ideally the best situation is a well-drained soil in a sunny position. A word of warning: it will be invasive in light fertile soils, but if you want to keep it under control it happily adapts to being grown in a container in a soil-based potting compost.

History in cooking

This herb is steeped in history; records show that over 2,000 years ago the ancient Greeks and Romans prescribed lemon balm not only for indigestion and over indulgence, but also to chase away melancholy. It was also popular in Elizabethan times for use in salads, as a tea and to flavour wine.

Harvesting and uses

Leaves:

The best-flavoured leaves are those picked before it flowers or from non-flowering stems, and are harvestable from early spring until autumn. When added to stewing fruit the leaves cut down the amount of sugar needed and also remove the tartness. Fresh leaves can also be added to cream cheese, vinegars, wine cups, teas, and chopped with vegetables.

Flowers:

Pick the flowers throughout summer but remove all the green parts before use, as they do not have a flavour. Add the flowers to salads – both fruit and leaf, and use in jellies and butters.

Properties

Lemon balm is high in vitamins A, B and C, and it is a natural carminative, antispasmodic and a great digestive. A tea made from the leaves is not only a digestive, it is also calming and relaxing and helps to sharpen the memory!

Different varieties

Golden Lemon Balm
Melissa officinalis 'All Gold'
This is similar to the standard lemon balm with the exception of the leaves, which are golden yellow. These leaves are prone to scorch, so plant in partial shade. To maintain good leaf colour, cut back in summer. This variety can only be propagated by cuttings or division.

Variegated Lemon Balm
Melissa officinalis 'Aurea'
This is also similar to the standard lemon balm, but has variegated gold and green leaves.

Both varieties can be used in cooking, however the leaf flavour is milder than that of the straight green variety.

LEMON BALM SALSA

This is good with grilled fish, grilled meat or any barbecue dish. The lemon balm leaves have a wonderful lemon flavour when crushed, so when combined with the ingredients below you can imagine how delightful this salsa is.

Serves 4

3 tbsp lemon balm leaves, finely chopped
1 hot chilli pepper, seeded and finely chopped
1 garlic clove, crushed
1 medium red onion, coarsely chopped
140 g jar sun-dried tomatoes, drained and chopped
juice of ½ lemon
6 tbsp light olive oil
1 tbsp white wine vinegar

Mix together all the ingredients, adding the oil a little at a time until you have a lovely thick salsa. Spoon into a serving bowl, cover, and put into the fridge for at least 30 minutes so that all the flavours blend together.

ALMOND AND LEMON BALM STUFFED APPLES

Baked apples was one of my dad's favourite dishes. He was not a cook, but if he found out that Mum was cooking this he always made brandy butter or horseradish cream, either of which goes amazingly well with all forms of baked apple. The lemon balm added to the centre of the apples lends a warm lemon flavour, rather than the sharper citrus flavour that a lemon would give.

Serve with clotted cream, home-made custard or, especially for my father, brandy butter.

Serves 4

4 large cooking apples (preferably Bramleys)
40 g unsalted butter, plus 25 g extra for dotting
2 tbsp sugar
50 g ground almonds
2 tbsp finely chopped lemon balm
zest of 1 lemon
1 tsp ground cinnamon
25 g flaked almonds, toasted
4 tbsp golden syrup

Pre-heat the oven to 180°C/350°F/gas mark 4.

Wash and generously core the apples. Carefully, using a sharp knife, put a shallow slit in the skin, not deep into the flesh, running all the way around the apple's diameter. Place the apples in a roasting tin.

Cream the butter with the sugar, beat in the ground almonds and stir in the lemon balm, lemon zest, cinnamon and flaked almonds. Using a small spoon, put a quarter of this mixture into each cored apple, then drizzle 1 tablespoon of golden syrup over each apple, dot with butter and bake in the oven for about 15 minutes, until the apples are soft but not mushy.

LEMON BALM, LIME AND LEMON SORBET

I make no apology for including so many sorbets in this book, for it is one of the best ways to taste the flavour of a herb and they are brilliant digestives. Historically the Romans ate sorbets between courses during their enormous banquets to cleanse their palates.

Serves 4–6

200 g caster or granulated sugar
275 ml water
1 large bunch of lemon balm, leaves removed from their stems and finely chopped
zest and juice of 5 limes
zest and juice of 5 lemons

Place the sugar and water in a small pan over a medium heat and stir with a wooden spoon until the sugar has melted. Bring to the boil then simmer for 5 minutes. Remove from the heat and allow to cool.

Once the syrup has cooled, mix in the lemon balm leaves and the zest and juice of the limes and lemons. Pour into a freezerproof container and place in the freezer.

Remove from the freezer after 30 minutes, break up the ice using a fork and return to the freezer. Repeat this 30 minutes later and then again 3 more times. If you are not serving this within 24 hours, cover the sorbet after the final mixing and use within a month.

Excess lemon balm

Lemon balm vinaigrette

This is a useful vinaigrette; it is delicious on salads, including seafood and chicken salads, and can also be used to marinate fish or chicken before cooking. Alternatively, it can simply be served in a little bowl for your guests to spoon over their cooked fish or chicken.

1 tbsp shallots, very finely chopped
2 tbsp lemon balm leaves, finely chopped
½ tsp lemon zest
6 tbsp fresh lemon juice
4 tbsp white wine vinegar
1 tbsp Dijon mustard
1 tbsp soft brown sugar
8 tbsp light olive oil

In a bowl, mix together the shallots, lemon balm leaves, lemon zest, lemon juice, vinegar, mustard and sugar, then very slowly add the oil. Decant into a bottle with a tight-fitting lid.

This vinaigrette will keep in the fridge for a week. Shake well before using.

LEMON GRASS

(Also known as Fever Grass, Bhustrina, Takrai)
Cymbopogon citratus

It is amazing to think that when I first started my herb farm over 20 years ago lemon grass was only just appearing in Chinese food stores, and now it is available for 52 weeks of the year in many of the chain supermarkets. Over the years I have become a huge fan of this herb, especially since seeing it actually growing and flourishing in South Africa. There I could appreciate how classically elegant, in true grass fashion, this plant is, rather than the small plants I raise and the small stumps of stem I first used to buy all those years ago.

Description

Lemon grass is a tropical clump-forming grass with clusters of tiny grass flowers that only appear in the tropics, and lemon-scented, linear, grey-green leaves with robust cream and beige cane-like stems.

You can raise lemon grass from seed or from division, but if you live outside the tropics you will need to do this in a warm environment. You can only successfully grow lemon grass outside where the night temperature does not fall below 8°C. So in the northern hemisphere this herb can be planted out in summer only. Plant in any soil, including a heavy soil, as long as the summers are hot and wet and the winters are warm and dry.

This herb makes an excellent container plant; use a loam-based compost and do not allow it to dry out in summer. In winter, bring the plant into a frost-free environment, 5°C minimum.

When the light levels and night temperatures drop the plant will go 'dormant', the grass gradually turns brown and the outside leaves shrivel. Reduce the watering to minimal over winter and cut back the grass to 10 cm above the stems. In early spring, as the days lengthen and the temperatures rise, you will notice the grass starting to grow; at this time cut off all dead growth and repot if necessary.

History in cooking

Lemon grass has been used for thousands of years in Thailand, China, Malaysia, Vietnam, Indonesia and the West Indies, where it is not just considered an important culinary herb, but is also highly valued for its many medicinal properties. This herb has only come to the fore in European and Australian cooking during the past 20 years.

Harvesting and uses

Leaves:

Pick these throughout the summer in cold climates and all year in tropical climates. Young leaves have a much fuller flavour than older ones, which tend to have a slightly bitter undertone. The fresh leaves and stalks have been traditionally used in Thai, Vietnamese and Caribbean cuisine. The lemon flavour complements curries, seafood, garlic and chillies. Tie a handful of leaves into a knot and add to water to flavour rice or steaming vegetables. Remove before serving.

Stems:

Cut the stems from mature plants throughout the summer months in cold climates and all year round in tropical climates. To prepare the swollen stems, cut at the base just where the stem joins the soil, and trim off the top leaves to save for later use. Peel off the outer green sheaths around the thick stem; this will reveal a white core. Slice finely or pound the white stem to release the oils and flavours before adding them to your chosen dish.

Properties

The leaves and stems are rich in iron, chromium, magnesium, zinc, selenium, potassium and phosphorus; they also contain vitamins A, B and C. The digestive properties are carminative and diuretic. A tea made from fresh leaves is refreshing as well as being a stomach and gut relaxant. It is also a good antidepressant.

Different varieties

East Indian Lemon Grass, Cochin Grass, Malabar Grass
Cymbopogon flexuosus

This is similar to lemon grass except it grows taller and the base stems have a red rather than beige colour. It has a good lemon flavour and can be used in the kitchen in exactly the same way as lemon grass.

Palmarosa, Rosha Indian Geranium
Cymbopogon martinii var. *motia*

This is a smaller tropical grass than the two lemon grasses, and the linear grey-green leaves have the most heavenly rose scent. Use the leaves to flavour cakes, puddings and syrups. Infusing the leaves in milk and then adding the milk to various puddings is a wonderful way of using this herb.

SPICY LEMON GRASS AND BUTTERNUT SQUASH SOUP

This is a great combination: aromatic lemon grass and spicy hot chilli with comforting butternut squash. A soup with gusto.

Serves 4–6

2 tbsp light olive oil
1-cm piece of fresh root ginger, peeled and grated
½ tsp finely sliced red chilli
1 tsp lemon grass stems, peeled and finely sliced
1 large onion, finely sliced
500 g butternut squash, peeled, sliced in half, seeded, then sliced into chunks
2 garlic cloves, finely chopped
1 tbsp light soy sauce
400 ml coconut milk or semi-skimmed milk
400 ml water
salt and freshly ground black pepper

Heat the oil in a large pan and fry the ginger, chilli, lemon grass, onion and butternut squash, stirring constantly until just beginning to colour. Add the garlic and cook for a few more minutes. Add the soy sauce, coconut milk or milk and water. Bring to the boil, then reduce to a simmer and cook for about 25 minutes until the squash is tender.

Either using a hand blender or a food processor, liquidise until smooth. Taste, add salt and black pepper as required. Re-heat, but do not boil, and serve.

SALMON AND LEMON GRASS PARCEL

Cooking fish in foil keeps in the moisture and all the nutrients. Combining it with lemon grass leaves is lovely, as all the aroma and lemony spicy taste of the leaves permeates the fish. Serve with boiled rice and green beans or a fresh green salad.

Serves 4

2 tsp butter
1 onion, very thinly sliced
3 garlic cloves, very finely chopped
2 tomatoes, skinned and finely chopped
a pinch of salt
2 lemon grass stems, peeled then pounded and finely sliced
1 tsp ground cumin
lemon grass leaves (to line the parcel)
300 g skinless salmon fillets, cut into large chunks
2 limes, sliced
1 tbsp coriander leaves, chopped
1 tbsp flaked almonds, chopped

Pre-heat the oven to 160°C/325°F/gas mark 3.

Melt the butter in a pan, then add the onion and gently fry on a very low heat until the onion is softened. Add the garlic and cook for a further minute.

Boil a kettle of water, place the tomatoes in a bowl and pour over the boiled water. Leave for a couple of minutes, drain, and carefully (don't burn your fingers) peel the tomatoes. Add the chopped tomatoes, salt, the lemon grass stems and the ground cumin. Stir, then cover the pan and cook gently on a very low heat for 5 minutes. Stir from time to time to make sure nothing sticks.

Place a large piece of baking parchment or foil on a baking sheet and line with lemon grass leaves. Place the salmon on one half of the sheet, spoon the mixture over the fish and top with the lime slices, chopped coriander leaves and almond flakes. Cover with the other side of the sheet of foil or baking parchment, sealing the edges tightly by turning them over twice. Bake in the oven for 25 minutes.

Open the parcel (beware of the steam when you do this), return to the oven and bake, opened, for a further 10 minutes.

TROUT WITH LEMON GRASS STUFFING

I made this for one of my husband Mac's famous birthdays. We had friends for dinner and they were amazed at how succulent the lemon grass kept the trout and the flavour. Give it a go, it is brilliant. Accompany the fish simply with new potatoes and a crisp green salad or dwarf beans.

Serves 4

4 whole trout
50 g unsalted butter
1 tbsp lemon juice
1 lemon, quartered, to serve

For the lemon grass stuffing
50 g unsalted butter
175 g shallots, finely chopped
2 tbsp lemon grass leaves, finely sliced
2 lemon grass stems, peeled and finely sliced
175 g fresh breadcrumbs
sea salt and freshly ground black pepper

Make the stuffing first. Melt the butter in a frying pan and gently fry the shallots until golden. Add the lemon grass leaves and stems and fry for a further few minutes until they are soft. Add the breadcrumbs and stir around until well mixed. Remove from the heat, season with salt and black pepper to taste. Leave the stuffing to cool completely before using.

Clean and wash the fish. Make three shallow diagonal cuts on each side, then fill each with a little of the stuffing. Melt the butter in a small pan, add the lemon juice and use this liquid to baste the fish as they cook.

Pre-heat the grill to its highest setting. Put the pan under the grill for 5 minutes, turning and basting the fish after 2 minutes, then lower the heat to medium for a further 6–8 minutes, turning and again basting the fish halfway. Take care, as they can be fragile as they cook. Serve with the lemon quarters.

Excess lemon grass

Lemon grass oil

This oil is lovely for salad dressings, mayonnaise, stir-fry dishes and soups.

For more information about preserving and the risks of using herbs in oils, see page 36.

Makes 500 ml oil

5 swollen lemon grass stems
500 ml light olive oil
2 tsp lemon juice

Prepare the stems by removing the outer sheaths and revealing the white inner stem. Slice finely, then, using a pestle and mortar, add the stems and pound until you have a paste (you may have to do this in a few batches). Add a small amount of oil, mix, then spoon into a medium-sized bowl. Repeat until you have turned all the stems into paste. Once all the paste is in the bowl, add the remaining oil and the lemon juice and stir well.

Pour into a container with a sealing lid, and pop into the fridge. Use within 5 days; shake well before use as the lemon juice will separate.

Alternatively, after 2 days strain the oil through an unbleached coffee filter paper, pour into a clean sterilised container with a sealing lid and keep in the fridge. Use within 3 days; shake well before use.

LEMON VERBENA

(also known as Lippia, Vervain)
Aloysia triphylla syn. *Lippia citriodora)*

The scent of this herb transports me back down memory lane. Simply by rubbing its rough leaves and releasing its sharp lemon sherbet scent lifts the spirits and reminds me of my great-aunt Ann. She had this shrub growing against her back door, so as you entered the house from the garden, you automatically brought the scent of lemon verbena with you.

Description

This herb is tender, so it will need protection below 4°C. It is a deciduous shrub, which means that it drops its leaves in winter, leaving it looking like a dead twig, which it is not. The new leaves reappear late in the following spring. It has clusters of tiny white flowers tinged with lilac in early summer and rough, pale green lance-shaped leaves that smell strongly of lemon sherbets.

Plant it in a light free-draining soil in a warm sunny site, preferably against a wall. It makes an ideal container plant; use a soil-based compost with extra grit. Place the container in a warm, sunny, light and airy spot and water well throughout the growing season. Protect from frost in winter by either bringing it into a cold greenhouse or cold frame (if it is in a container), or covering it with a cloche or horticultural fleece (if it is planted out).

History in cooking

There is very little history associated with this herb; it originated in South America and arrived in Europe in the 18th century, where it was used to perfume finger bowls during banquets.

Harvesting and uses

Leaves:

These can be picked all summer, but the best-flavoured leaves are those picked in early summer while they are bright green and before they start to lose colour and curl in the autumn. The leaves can be used to flavour oils and vinegars, fruit puddings and jellies. They can transform home-made cakes, too: simply lay whole leaves on the base of a well-greased cake tin, pour in the cake mixture, then bake in the usual way.

Flowers:

Pick flowers throughout the summer. They have an intense lemon sherbet flavour and are lovely scattered over fruit or salads, or added to jellies.

Properties

The leaves contain vitamins A, B and C and they are digestive, antioxidant, antispasmodic and a sedative. A tea made from 3–5 leaves last thing at night helps the digestion, and as it is a mild sedative and calmative, it also aids a good night's sleep.

Different varieties   White Brush

Aloysia gratissima

This is a half-hardy deciduous shrub with delicate, small, slightly vanilla-scented, white or violet-tinged flowers and rough, lance-shaped leaves.

Its leaves are lightly minty, so great for making tea and adding a mint flavour to many dishes.

LEMON VERBENA CRÈME BRÛLÉE

My mother made the best crème brûlée. Alistair, my son, has inherited her passion for them and always rates restaurants and cooks on how well they make this pudding. This is a wonderful recipe; the flavour, with its hint of lemon sherbet, is unique, and makes this brûlée very special.

Serves 4

225 ml milk
1 handful of lemon verbena leaves, finely chopped (reserve a few whole ones to garnish)
7 egg yolks
100 g caster sugar
60 ml double cream
50 g demerara sugar

Pre-heat the oven to 140°C/275°F/gas mark 1.

Put the milk in a small pan with the chopped lemon verbena leaves, bring to simmering point, remove from the heat and leave to cool and infuse.

Place the egg yolks in a bowl with the caster sugar and whisk until pale and thick. Add the cooled infused milk and the cream and whisk well. Pass through a fine-meshed sieve.

Ladle the mixture into 4 ramekin dishes and set them in a roasting tin. Pour in enough water to come three-quarters of the way up the side of the ramekins, pop into the oven and cook for 1 hour or until set. Leave to cool, then refrigerate until ready to serve.

Just before serving, sprinkle the demerara sugar over the top of each pudding and caramelise with either a blow torch or by putting them under a hot grill. Decorate with some fresh lemon verbena leaves.

LEMON VERBENA SORBET

This is my favourite way of using lemon verbena; it is summer in a bowl.

Serves 4

150 ml water
150 g caster sugar
4 tbsp lemon verbena leaves, finely chopped, plus 8 whole leaves to garnish

Place the water in a small pan with the lemon verbena leaves, bring to a boil and simmer for 7 minutes to infuse the water. Add the sugar then bring to the boil for 5 minutes, and stir regularly so the sugar thoroughly dissolves and does not stick. Remove from the heat and cool for 30 minutes to allow the flavours to infuse.

If you wish to be posh, strain the infusion through a sieve, but if, like me, you love the leaves, simply pour the infusion into a freezerproof container and place in the freezer. Generally, sorbet takes 2 hours to set. Rather than have a solid block, stir it to break up the ice after the first 30 minutes and repeat 3 more times at 30-minute intervals.

If you are not serving the sorbet the same day, cover it and use within a month. Serve garnished with a couple of fresh lemon verbena leaves.

LEMON VERBENA AND RASPBERRY FOOL

I cannot put into words how lovely this late summer–early autumn pudding is. I am lucky enough to be able to grow autumn-fruiting raspberries, and this pudding was created because I am greedy about raspberries and passionate about lemon verbena.

Serves 4

10 lemon verbena leaves, plus 4 more, finely chopped, to garnish
2 tbsp vodka
500 g raspberries
100 g caster sugar
150 ml double cream

Place the lemon verbena leaves in a small bowl and add the vodka. Using a wooden spoon, crush the leaves in the vodka and leave to soak overnight.

The next day, crush the raspberries, using a fork, and add the caster sugar a spoonful at a time. Strain the vodka then add it to the raspberries. Whip the cream until it forms lines but not stiff peaks, then fold in the raspberries.

Serve in individual dishes, each decorated with 1 finely chopped lemon verbena leaf.

LEMON VERBENA AND PLUM CLAFOUTI

We tend to have a prolific crop of plums, and on alternate years they tend to appear when I have masses of lemon verbena leaves. The delicious combination of the slightly acidic plums and the sweet yet dry citrus fragrance of lemon verbena is just magical.

Serves 4–6

butter, for greasing
500 g plums (either Victoria or Marjorie), washed, halved and stoned
3 tbsp lemon verbena leaves, removed from the stem and finely chopped
4 eggs
60 g caster sugar
50 g plain flour
300 ml crème fraîche
3 tbsp brandy (optional)
2 tbsp icing sugar, for dusting

Pre-heat the oven to 180°C/350°F/gas mark 4. Butter a large gratin dish and arrange the plums on the base, cut-side down. Sprinkle over the lemon verbena leaves.

In a bowl, whisk the eggs, stir in the sugar, then slowly mix in the flour. Add the crème fraîche and brandy (if using), and stir until well mixed. Pour the egg mixture over the plums and lemon verbena and bake in the oven for 30–40 minutes until golden brown and firm to the touch.

Remove from the oven and let it stand for 5–10 minutes. Serve in slices dusted with icing sugar.

Excess lemon verbena

Drying lemon verbena leaves

I have to be honest, this is the only herb I dry; that is because, being a deciduous plant, it sheds its leaves in winter and I really do love a cup of lemon verbena tea, which the French call *vervain*, last thing at night to help me relax and sleep.

On a warm sunny day, pick the healthiest leaves you can from your lemon verbena, as they are the ones with the best properties. Try not to bruise the leaves, as this will not only damage the leaf but also impair the flavour. Do not be too greedy, for by picking in small amounts it is easier to control the quality.

The object of good drying is to eliminate the water content of the plant and at the same time retain the essential oil. Spread the leaves thinly on a wooden rack covered in muslin and place in a warm, dark, dry and well-ventilated room. If you have a spare room, this is ideal with the curtains drawn; alternatively use a cupboard with the door left ajar. Turn the herbs over by hand several times during the first week. The leaves should only take about 5 days to be totally dry; the test is that they crumble easily when crushed.

Ideally, store the leaves in a dark glass jar with a screw top that is labelled with the name and date. It is well worth checking the container during the first few days to see if any moisture has started to form on the lid. If so, this will show that the herbs have not been totally dried, in which case return them to the drying area.

The shelf life is approximately 1 year for dried herbs. They are usually 3 to 4 times more powerful in flavour than fresh, so you need to use less of them in recipes and for teas.

LOVAGE

(also known as 'the Maggi herb', Love Parsley, Sea Parsley,
Lavose, Liveche, Smallage, European Lovage)
Levisticum officinale

I cannot remember a time in my life when I have not been able to pick fresh lovage or harvest the seeds in autumn. My mother had a prolific plant in her garden and in both the houses where I have lived I have also had a productive plant. If you have the space, I do recommend this herb as it is so versatile.

Description

Lovage is a hardy herb that dies back in winter and reappears in the following spring. It will form a large plant in the garden – it can grow over 2 m high when in flower and spread to at least 1 m wide – so it is not recommended for a small plot. It has clusters of pale greenish flowers in summer that are followed by dark brown aromatic seeds. The leaves are dark green, deeply divided with toothed edges.

When planting lovage, prepare the site with well-rotted manure as it prefers a rich, moist, but well-drained soil in full sun or partial shade. You can raise it from seed sown in the garden in autumn or from plants created by the division of established clumps in early spring, just as the new shoots emerge. You can grow it in containers, but being a vigorous plant it will need repotting every year.

History in cooking

This herb has been cultivated for thousands of years. The Romans preserved the leaves in vinegar for year-round flavouring; the ancient Greeks chewed the seed to aid digestion and relieve flatulence; and the medieval monks grew it in the cloister gardens for many medicinal uses, including making a tea to treat nausea.

Harvesting and uses

Leaves:

Pick the leaves from spring until autumn. They are strong in flavour (it is rather like a mixture of celery and beef) and so need to be added sparingly to dishes or else the flavour can, when used too enthusiastically, destroy a meal. On the other hand, used carefully they can make a meal. The sweetest-flavoured leaves are the new spring shoots, the mature leaves are bitter. To maintain a supply of young leaves throughout the season, cut sections of the plant down to the ground and new shoots will appear. These can be added to stocks, stews, cheese and salads. Alternatively, crushed leaves can be rubbed over a chicken prior to roasting or round the edge of a salad bowl before adding the salad. Discard the spent leaves.

Flowers:

Pick in summer just when they open, divide into individual little flowers and scatter over tomatoes. They too have a strong flavour, so use sparingly.

Seeds:

The seed heads should be harvested when the seeds start to turn brown in autumn. On a dry day, cut them, tie a paper bag over the heads, and hang them upside down in a dry airy place. The dried seeds have a warm, meaty, celery flavour and can be crushed and used in soups, bread and pastries, or sprinkled over salads, rice and mashed potato.

Properties Lovage is a good carminative and digestive. It contains vitamins A, B and C and the minerals iron, sodium and magnesium. It is considered to be one of nature's antibiotics, with the ability to deal with bacteria and viruses. It has a cleansing effect on the body.

Different varieties None.

SAUTÉED CHICKEN WITH LOVAGE AND CIDER

A rustic meal packed with autumnal flavours. The dry apple of the cider and the Cox's apple, combined with the sweetness of the chicken and the celery-ish lovage seeds is delicious. Serve with creamy mashed potato or plain boiled rice.

Serves 4

500 ml vintage cider
8 chicken legs or thighs, skin removed
1 tsp lovage seed, ground
40 g unsalted butter
2 Cox's apples, cored and cut into wedges
250 g button mushrooms, washed and sliced
1 tbsp olive oil
2 tbsp lovage leaves, finely chopped (use young shoots)
4 tbsp double cream

Pour the cider into a medium pan, bring to the boil and simmer until reduced by about half.

Rub the chicken legs or thighs all over with the ground lovage seed. Melt half the butter in a large frying pan that has a well-fitting lid, add the apples and mushrooms and fry gently until golden brown. Remove with a slotted spoon and keep on a plate until required.

Melt the remaining butter in the frying pan with the olive oil, add the chicken pieces and fry on all sides – you may need to do this in batches. Once all the chicken has been cooked, return all the chicken pieces to the pan, add the reduced cider and bring to the boil. Reduce the heat to a simmer and cook gently for 20–25 minutes until the chicken is thoroughly cooked and beginning to fall off the bone. Add the apples, mushrooms and chopped lovage leaves and cream and cook gently for a further 5 minutes. Serve.

NEW POTATOES, SMOKED MACKEREL AND LOVAGE SALAD

This is a lovely early-summer meal; the saltiness of the mackerel against the lovage and minted new potatoes is mouthwatering.

Serves 4

350 g new potatoes
a pinch of salt
6 mint sprigs
100 g crème fraîche
1 tbsp young lovage shoots, finely chopped
juice of 1 lemon
2 smoked mackerel fillets, skinned and flaked
2 handfuls of young spinach leaves
1 handful of rocket leaves

Bring a large pan of water to the boil, add the new potatoes, salt and mint sprigs and cook for 15 minutes until tender.

While the potatoes are cooking, mix together the crème fraîche, young lovage shoots and the lemon juice in a large bowl – there is no need to add salt because there is enough saltiness in the lovage and smoked mackerel.

Once the potatoes are cooked, drain, halve, and set aside for a few minutes to cool down, then add to the crème fraîche mixture. Mix so they are well coated, then add the smoked mackerel and the spinach and rocket leaves.

LOVAGE, SORREL, CARROT AND PINE NUT SALAD

The biting sourness of the sorrel, mixed with the meaty celery flavour of the lovage and the sweetness of the carrot is an excellent combination. Do not think I have gone mad because I am only using 2 teaspoons of lovage, for, as I have said before, it is a very strong herb that can make or break a dish. This amount makes it. Serve with some fresh crusty bread.

Serves 2–4

3 carrots, grated
1 apple, grated
2 tsp chopped lovage leaves (use young shoots not mature leaves)
a handful of sorrel leaves, carefully washed then torn
1 cos or butterhead lettuce, washed and leaves separated
1 tbsp pine nuts

For the dressing
3 tbsp light olive oil
1 tbsp balsamic vinegar
salt and freshly ground black pepper to taste

Toss together the grated carrots, apple, lovage and sorrel leaves and the pine nuts in a large bowl.

Make the dressing by thoroughly mixing together all the ingredients. Pour it over the carrot and apple mixture and mix well.

Arrange the lettuce leaves on a serving dish and fill each of the leaves with a little of the mixture.

Excess lovage Lovage as a vegetable

In spring you can often have an abundance of young lovage shoots, and fortunately this is the best time of year to cook this herb as a vegetable. You can treat lovage the same way as spinach – by cooking all the young new growth of the plant – both stalks and leaves.

As I've already said, lovage does have a strong flavour, so I have found that in order to make it acceptable to all it is best combined with a white sauce. That way everyone is happy and the plates are clean. This is lovely with grilled smoked mackerel and mashed potato.

Serves 2–4

1 large handful of lovage stems and leaves
25 g butter
25 g plain flour
275 ml milk
freshly ground black pepper
grated nutmeg

Strip the lovage leaves from the stalks, wash, and cut the stalks up into segments. Bring a medium pan of water to the boil and add the young lovage leaves and stalks. Bring the water back to the boil, cover and simmer for about 3–4 minutes until tender. Strain the water.

Make a white sauce by melting the butter in a medium pan and stirring in the flour to make a paste. Add the milk a little at a time, whisking as you do so to avoid lumps. Season with a grating of black pepper and nutmeg.

When the sauce is made, add the lovage, stir and serve.

MARIGOLD

(also known as Pot Marigold, Calendula, Garden Marigold)
Calendula officinalis

Pot marigold has been a firm family favourite throughout the four generations of cooks; all of us have created or adapted recipes to incorporate this pretty herb. It is both interesting and important to note that throughout Europe pot marigold is a well-known medicinal and culinary herb. However, when lecturing further afield I discovered that when I mentioned marigold it was automatically assumed that I was talking about 'Tagetes', the African and French varieties which have insecticidal properties.

The flowers of these varieties can be very bitter, and in some cases toxic, so please check you have the calendula variety of marigold when making these recipes.

Description

Pot marigold is an attractive, jolly annual herb with daisy-like yellow or orange, single or double flowers from spring until the first frosts. The flowers are sensitive to variations of temperature and dampness. If they are open it will be a fine day, if closed, take your brollie with you. By dead heading the flowers when they are over you will encourage continuous flowering. It does self-seed abundantly but never seems to become a nuisance. The lance-shaped, lightly aromatic light green leaves are edible, fresh when young or cooked when mature.

This is a tolerant plant, for it will grow in any soil with the exception of waterlogged. It prefers a sunny position in the garden or a container, in which it will happily adapt to growing. Use a soil-based potting compost when potting it up. The seed is easy to handle and reliable to grow, so it is an ideal plant to sow when encouraging children to garden. Sow the seeds in late spring until early summer, direct into a prepared site in the garden or into a large container.

History in cooking

Pot marigold has been used as an edible plant for many years. The Indians and Arabs were the first recorded users of it, followed by the ancient Egyptians. The ancient Greeks garnished and flavoured food with the golden petals. In the 16th century in many countries, especially Holland, grocers and spice sellers had barrels filled with dry petals. These were sold in large quantities for use in drinks and broths, to flavour soups and stews, to colour butter and cheese, and also for medications.

Harvesting and uses

Leaves:

Pick young leaves in early spring to add to salads, while mature summer growth can be cooked like spinach – hence the name pot marigold, referring to cooking pots. However, be aware that the

leaves are not to everyone's taste, as they are bitter and hairy –
I have to admit to not liking them. The petals of the flowers, on the
other hand, are a different story.

Flowers:
Pick these just as they open from late spring until the first hard
frosts. The actual centre of the flower is bitter; it is the petals that
are used in many culinary ways. They have a light warm flavour
which combines well with cheese dishes, and are excellent in salads
and omelettes. They make an interesting cup of tea, too, and as
history indicates, they make a good food dye. Simply chop the petals
up very, very finely, or pulverise them using a pestle and mortar, and
add this paste to rice dishes, butter and, in fact, any foods that you
want to take on that lovely golden colour.

Properties

Pot marigold flowers are believed to help improve digestion
and stimulate bile production. The herb is also considered an
antispasmodic and is said to contain vitamins A, B and C.

Different varieties

Marigold Fiesta, Gitana
Calendula officinalis Fiesta Gitana Group
This is an attractive double-flowering variety of calendula; the
flowers can vary in colour or be mixed from apricot through to deep
orange. Use the petals in salads and to colour rice or butter.

FARFALLE AND POT MARIGOLDS

A simple and satisfying pasta dish that is quick to make and looks appetising scattered with the marigold petals. This is delicious served with salads and cheese.

Serves 2–3

a pinch of salt (optional)
185 g farfalle (or any pasta of your choice; flatter varieties are best in this recipe)
1 tbsp olive oil
1 garlic clove, crushed
2 tbsp pot marigold petals, removed from the flower head

Bring a large pan of water to the boil and add salt, if required. Add the farfalle slowly into the boiling water and stir. Boil for 10–12 minutes until al dente. Drain well.

Put the olive oil into the pan, gently heat and add the crushed garlic and the cooked farfalle and toss. Then add the marigold petals. Tip into a serving dish and serve either hot or cold.

POT MARIGOLD PIE

This is an old, traditional English recipe that I found on a piece of faded paper in my mother's notebook. I have tweaked it to suit today's palate and ingredients. The marigold petals give the pastry and the filling lovely golden flecks, and make this a unique dish.

Serves 4

For the pastry case
110 g wholemeal flour
¼ tsp salt
25 g unsalted butter, chilled, plus extra for greasing
25 g lard, chilled
1 tbsp pot marigold petals, removed from the flower head
1 tbsp cold water

For the pie filling
3 eggs
4 tbsp pot marigold petals, removed from the flower heads
3 heaped tbsp organic cottage cheese (plain)
1 tbsp icing sugar
a small pinch of salt
freshly grated nutmeg
zest of 1 lemon

Pre-heat the oven to 190°C/375°F/gas mark 5.

Sieve the flour and salt into a bowl. Using a knife, chop the butter and lard into small chunks then, using your hands, rub into the flour, lifting your hands several centimetres above the bowl with each movement so that the fat is cooled by the air as it falls into the bowl. (This is exactly how my mother taught me, because she said I had hot hands and would make heavy pastry!)

When it looks like fine breadcrumbs, add the marigold petals, then carefully add the water while you mix the pastry with your other hand until you have a light firm dough.

Knead lightly, then place the pastry in a bowl and cover it with or just wrap in cling film and pop into the fridge for 1 hour before rolling out. This will help prevent it shrinking when you cook the pie.

Grease an 18–20-cm, loose-bottomed flan tin. Roll out the pastry to a 5 mm thickness. Line the flan tin with the pastry, lifted into place on the rolling pin. Trim the edges generously. Prick the bottom with a fork, cover the pastry case with a round piece of greaseproof paper, spill baking beans (or I used dried baked pasta) over the base and put the tin in the oven for 15 minutes.

Take the tin out of the oven, remove the beans and the paper, then pop it back in the oven for a further 10 minutes, until the bottom is no longer soggy.

Lower the oven temperature to 170°C/325°F/gas mark 3.

Separate the eggs and mix the yolks with the petals. Mix the cottage cheese with the sugar, salt and the nutmeg. Add the petal mixture and lemon zest to the cottage cheese mixture.

In a separate bowl, whisk the egg whites to soft peaks then fold them into the cottage cheese mixture. Pour into the baked pastry case and cook in the oven for about 25 minutes or until the pie filling feels firm to the touch. Serve when completely cold.

POT MARIGOLD AND BAY LEAF BAKED CUSTARD

Baked custards and milk puddings were a major part of my childhood; some I hated because the consistency was slimy, and others tasted of nothing in particular. This, on the other hand, was one of my grandmother's standbys and simply delicious. The flavour of bay and nutmeg with the hint of the marigold, plus the visual impact of the petals, was always a delight.

Serves 4

600 ml full-fat milk
1 bay leaf
4 eggs
50 g caster sugar
240 g pot marigold petals, removed from the flower head and finely chopped
nutmeg

Pre-heat the oven to 140°C/275°F/gas mark 1.

In a medium pan, heat the milk with the bay leaf until very hot but not boiling.

In a large bowl, beat together the eggs and sugar. Remove the bay leaf from the milk and then slowly add the hot milk to the eggs and sugar, stirring with a whisk. Strain into a 7.5-cm deep ovenproof dish, stir in the marigold petals and grate some nutmeg over the surface.

Place in a roasting tin containing enough cold water to come halfway up the sides of the ovenproof dish. Cook in the oven for 1½ hours until firm.

MARIGOLD BISCUITS

These marigold biscuits are lovely on their own, or served with lashings of whipped cream and fresh greengages, if you are lucky enough to have them in midsummer.

Makes approx. 12

100 g butter or soft tub margarine, plus extra for greasing
50 g caster sugar
175 g self-raising flour, plus extra for dusting
4 tsp marigold petals removed from the flower head

Pre-heat the oven to 230°C/450°F/gas mark 8. Lightly grease a baking sheet with a little butter.

Cream together the butter and sugar until light, then add the flour and mix well until it forms a ball. Take this out of the bowl and knead it on a lightly floured surface.

Gently roll out the dough then scatter the marigold petals over, very lightly pressing them into it using a rolling pin. Cut out small rounds using a biscuit cutter and place them on the baking sheet. Bake in the oven for 10–12 minutes until gold and firm. Remove at once and cool on a wire rack.

Excess marigold

Marigold petal butter

The only way to save the petals of this herb for the kitchen is to either infuse them in oil or use them in a butter, the latter which I find useful for all forms of baking.

Makes 250 g

8 tbsp pot marigold petals
250 g unsalted butter, at room temperature

Finely chop the marigold petals. Put the butter in a bowl, add the chopped petals and mix well. Cover the bowl and let the mixture rest at room temperature for a few hours.

Transfer the butter mixture to a container with a lid, place in the fridge and leave for a few days to allow the flavour to develop. This butter will keep in the fridge for about 2 weeks, or you could freeze it and then it will keep for 3 months. If you are freezing the butter, do not forget to label it.

MINT

(also known as Liu Lan Xiang)
Mentha

Description

Before I started school I knew the difference between garden, spearmint and apple mint as they had been an essential part of my mother's kitchen, and in turn mine, for mint is, without doubt, one of the indispensable culinary herbs. I have a large patch of Tashkent mint, an excellent spearmint, just outside my back door which I use virtually every day from early spring until the autumn.

All the mints mentioned in this chapter are the hardy herbaceous varieties, i.e. they die back in winter and reappear in the spring. The flowers in summer can vary from white to mauve, and the leaves, which are all highly aromatic, especially when crushed, can vary from being pointed to smooth, hairy to crinkly, depending on the variety. Common to all is that they are, however, attractive to bees and butterflies, which is a plus. On the down side, they are all invasive in the garden, so their site needs to be chosen with care.

Being promiscuous plants (which is why there are so many different varieties), they are not good raised from seed. To get the best and most reliable flavour, grow the plants from root cuttings taken in autumn. The most flavoursome and healthiest plants are those that are grown so the plant can spread naturally, which can be difficult in a small garden, so allocate an area to them. Plant in rich well-drained soil in a sunny position. If you do not have sufficient space in the garden for them to stretch out, mint grows well in containers in a soil-based potting compost. However, to keep the plant productive, do repot every year in the autumn; this will prevent the roots rotting and enable it to produce abundant leaf in the following season.

History in cooking

Mint has been used in cooking for thousands of years. There are two stories of which I am particularly fond. The first is that the ancient Greeks believed that after nights of heavy drinking they could place a wreath of mint on their heads to exorcise an impending hangover. The second illustrates its long association with hospitality. Two strangers were walking in Asia Minor, no one had offered them food or drink for many days until finally an elderly couple invited them in. Before laying the food on the table the couple rubbed mint leaves over the table and plates and scattered it over the food. The strangers were so pleased with the hospitality shown to them that on parting they expressed their gratitude by transforming the couple's humble home into a mansion – for the strangers were none other than the two gods Zeus and Hermes.

Harvesting and uses

Leaves:

These can be picked to be used fresh from spring until early winter, but the ideal time for harvesting all forms of mint is before flowering, when they are at their most succulent and flavoursome. They are great not only with vegetables, but also with fruit, cheese, meat, poultry, yoghurt and to make a refreshing cup of tea.

Flowers:

Pick the flowers in summer. The very small flowers are amazing for they have the most wonderful mint flavour. After removing the green parts, scatter them over salads, strawberries, and other summer fruit, or use in puddings.

Properties

The beneficial properties of mint in cooking are well known; these being as a digestive, antispasmodic and carminative. In addition, it also has antioxidant and antiviral properties.

Different varieties

There are so many different mints that I have just chosen my favourites here and grouped them according to flavour.

Peppermints

These have the strongest flavour, and are the best for making a digestive tea at the end of a meal or for adding to puddings.

Peppermint, Menthe d'Angleterre, Menthe Anglaise, Pfefferminze and Englisheminze,

Mentha x *piperita*
This has pale purple flowers in summer with peppermint-scented darkish green leaves.

Basil Mint

Mentha x *piperita* f. *citrata* 'Basil'
This has purple–mauve flowers in summer and highly scented, oval leaves that are green with a reddish tinge. This mint goes well with tomato dishes, especially pasta.

Chocolate Peppermint

Mentha x *piperita* f. *citrata* 'Chocolate'
This has pale purple flowers in summer with peppermint-scented dark green leaves. This variety is amazing, it tastes just like expensive chocolates. Try using it in chocolate mousse.

Spearmints These have a mid-strength flavour and are known as the classic mint that is ideal for mint sauce, with yoghurt or dressings, and served with new potatoes and strawberries.

Spearmint, Garden Mint
Mentha spicata
This variety has small purple–mauve flowers in terminal cylindrical spikes in summer with mid-green, oval, lance-shaped, wrinkled, spearmint-scented and flavoured leaves.

Tashkent Mint and Moroccan mint
Mentha spicata 'Tashkent' and *Mentha spicata* var. *crispa* 'Moroccan'
Both of these have mid-green, crinkled spearmint-scented and flavoured leaves. They are difficult to tell apart in the kitchen, but in the garden 'Tashkent' is taller and the leaves are rounder.

Mint flavoured
These mints have an all-round mild flavour that is good for jellies and sauces.

Apple Mint
Mentha suaveolens
This variety has mauve flowers in summer and roundish, hairy, mid-green leaves.

Bowles' Mint
Mentha x *villosa* var. *alopecuroides* Bowles' Mint
This has mauve flowers and round, hairy mid-green leaves. This is considered by many to be the best culinary mint. Personally, I dispute that, but I do agree that it is good in cooking.

MINT AND AUBERGINE BRUSCHETTA

The flavours of the mint, aubergine and garlic combine wonderfully in these delicious bruschetta.

For those like me who like to know the meaning of words, 'bruschetta' is derived from the Italian 'bruscare', which means 'to roast over coals'. Alternatively, you could call this posh toast. This is a lovely appetiser, or first course, for an early autumn meal.

Serves 4

2 firm aubergines
sea salt and freshly ground black pepper
6 tbsp olive oil
2 tbsp balsamic vinegar
1 tbsp flatleaf parsley, leaves picked and finely chopped
2 tbsp spearmint (Tashkent, Moroccan or Garden mint), finely chopped
1 garlic clove, peeled and very finely sliced
zest and juice of 1 lemon
1 ciabatta

Slice the aubergines on the diagonal into slices 1 cm thick. Sprinkle with salt and set aside for about 40 minutes. Place the aubergine in a colander and wash well under cold running water, then pat dry using a clean tea towel or kitchen paper.

Heat a griddle pan until hot. Lay the aubergine slices on it side by side and, when they are charred on both sides, put them into a salad bowl. (You may need to cook the aubergine in several batches.)

While the aubergines are cooking, put the olive oil and the vinegar into a large bowl and mix thoroughly until amalgamated. Add the chopped parsley and mint, then the garlic and 1 teaspoon of the lemon zest. Season with salt and black pepper to taste.

When the aubergines are cooked, add them to the bowl and mix them around, then check the seasoning again.

Heat a grill to hot. Cut the ciabatta on the diagonal into slices 2–3 cm thick, then grill lightly on both sides. Once the toasted ciabatta slices have cooled, top them with the mint and aubergine mixture, pressing it down so that the juices seep into the toast. Serve immediately.

TRADITIONAL BORSCH

This recipe has been taken from my grandmother's book, *Food for Pleasure*. Apparently it originally came from *Recipes of all Nations*, by Countess Morphy. I have slightly modified it by adding the mint crème fraîche, which goes so well with the sweetness of the beetroot. Also, I do not strain the borsch but serve it with the grated beetroot, which, in my opinion, adds texture and flavour.

Serves 4

90 g unsalted butter
4 large raw beetroot
1 litre good chicken stock, hot
140 g crème fraîche
1 tbsp chopped spearmint (not peppermint)
2 tsp chopped parsley

Melt the butter in a large pan over a low heat. Peel and grate the beetroot and add to the pan, cover and cook for about 20 minutes, stirring regularly. Stir in a little of the hot stock, and when this is absorbed stir in more. Repeat this process until the beetroot is tender. Once the beetroot is cooked, add the remainder of the stock and simmer gently for another 30 minutes, then strain or not, as required.

Mix the crème fraîche with the spearmint. Serve in individual bowls, each with a tablespoon of the minted crème fraîche, and scatter a small amount of parsley over the top.

HAM, MINT AND PEA SOUP

Mint, peas and leftover ham are the basis for this simple, hearty summer soup. The use of mint cuts the saltiness of the ham and enhances the flavour of the peas. If you've cooked a ham or turkey from scratch, you can use the bones and any cooking liquid to make a batch of rich stock. Serve with fresh crusty white bread.

Serves 6

100 g peas, podded (reserve the pods), or frozen (but then you miss the pods)
1.5 litres ham or vegetable stock
1 tbsp olive oil
1 medium onion, finely chopped
2 celery sticks, thinly sliced
2 carrots, finely chopped
2 tbsp dry white wine
200 g white haricot beans, soaked overnight or 2 x 400 g cans white haricot beans, drained
250 g cooked ham, cut into small pieces
2 tbsp spearmint leaves, chopped, but not too fine
salt and freshly ground black pepper

Put the pea pods in a large pan with the ham or vegetable stock (this will add a delicious pea flavour to the stock). Bring to the boil, then simmer for 5 minutes and strain, discarding the pea pods.

Heat the oil in a large, heavy-bottomed pan over a medium heat. When hot, add the onion, celery and carrots. Cover, reduce the heat and cook for about 15 minutes, until soft. Add the wine to the pan. Stir once or twice and simmer until the alcohol has evaporated. Add the haricot beans to the pan, stir once or twice, then leave to cook for a few minutes so they start to soften and mush a little.

Pour the stock into the pan. Bring to simmering point and cook for 10 minutes; you can slightly mush the beans if you like a thick soup or leave them alone if you prefer. Add the peas and cook until the soup returns to a simmer, then add the chopped ham and mint. Stir well, allow to warm through and season to taste.

ATUL KOCHHAR'S CHUTNEY PULAO

This recipe was kindly contributed by Atul Kochhar, the wonderful Michelin-starred chef who can be found at the Benares Restaurant, in Berkeley Square, London, and Vatika, in Hampshire. He inspires me as a cook because he combines the best of the East with the best of the West and he is passionate about herbs. Atul wrote this recipe, and this dish can be served with a raita or plain yoghurt.

He says: 'This pulao is a winner. It can be served on its own or as a part of any meat dish – especially lamb and pork. There is no secret involved, except a sheer love for herbs. Mix in the chutney paste just before you serve, and that keeps the flavours alive. This rice can't be stored, it has to be made fresh and eaten on the same day.'

Serves 4–6

For the chutney
100 g spearmint leaves
50 g coriander leaves
¼ tsp chopped green chillies
½ tsp chopped fresh root ginger
2 tbsp lemon juice
salt, to taste
2 tbsp vegetable oil
a pinch of sugar
50 ml water

For the rice
1½ tbsp vegetable oil
½ tsp cumin seeds
2 green cardamom pods
1-cm piece of cinnamon stick
½ medium onion, sliced
250 g basmati rice, washed and soaked for 30 minutes
salt, to taste
500 ml water

Blitz together all the chutney ingredients, except the water, in a food processor or with a hand-held blender to make a thick paste. Add the water to bring the paste together. Transfer to a bowl and keep, covered, in the fridge until required.

To make the rice, heat the oil in a heavy-bottomed pan and sauté the spices until they splutter. Then add the onion and sauté until translucent. Add the rice and sauté for 1–2 minutes, then add the salt and water. Bring to the boil then simmer very slowly for 3–5 minutes. Cover the rice and cook until the rice grains are properly cooked.

Just before serving, mix the thick chutney paste into the rice and stir in well.

MARIAN'S SUMMER MINTED CHICKEN

Marian is my son's godmother and my old flat-mate. This is one of her delicious and easy summer recipes. It works extremely well when made for a large number, and I have known her to cater for as many as 80 for a special birthday party, but it is also brilliant for a few. I particularly like the combination of spearmint and mango chutney – they go together so well. Serve with a crisp green salad and some crusty French bread.

Serves 4–6

4 cooked chicken breast
150 ml mayonnaise
150 ml soured cream
mango chutney, to taste
4 tbsp spearmint, finely chopped

To serve
1 mango, peeled and sliced
1 tbsp spearmint leaves, finely chopped

Cut the chicken into strips.

Combine the remaining ingredients and, when mixed, fold in the chicken. Spoon into a serving dish, cover with cling film and pop into the fridge for a minimum of 12 hours prior to serving, to allow the flavours to develop.

Before serving, decorate with the mango and mint.

MINT AND CARAWAY MERINGUES

These meringues were an inspiration. I was sitting mulling over writing this book while cleaning my caraway seeds; I already add walnuts to meringues and other seeds, so why not caraway? Then I thought, what would it be like to add mint to the anise and sugar? Those thoughts led to this recipe, which is magic. Serve with fresh fruit and whipped cream.

Makes 12

oil and flour for the baking sheets (optional)
4 eggs, separated (save the yolks for making sauces)
225 g caster sugar
2 tsp caraway seeds, crushed in a pestle and mortar
2 tbsp spearmint leaves, finely chopped

Pre-heat the oven to 120°C/250°F/gas mark ½. Either line 2 baking sheets with non-stick baking parchment or brush them lightly with oil, dredge with flour, then bang the sheets to remove excess flour.

Whisk the egg whites until quite stiff – they should remain in shape when shaken from a spoon, or some say 'make stiff peaks'. Add the sugar slowly, beating all the time, and add the caraway seeds and the spearmint.

Using two spoons, scoop a spoonful of the meringue mixture from the bowl and then use the other spoon to place it on the baking sheets. Repeat 12 times or until you have used up all the mixture. Put the sheets in the oven, bake for 1 hour then change the trays around, the top shelf being warmer than the lower. Bake for a further 30–40 minutes.

When the meringues are set, carefully lift them off the baking sheets using a palette or sharp knife and transfer to cool on a wire rack. If you want them really crisp, turn them all over and return to the oven for a further 30 minutes.

If you do not want to serve them immediately they will, once cold, keep in an airtight container for a few days.

Excess mint

My mum's mint sauce

Before I had even started school, Mum had taught me to make this sauce. I used to kneel on a wooden chair and chop mint using a very sharp knife. I always had a great sense of achievement and participation when I had created the sauce that was served with our Sunday lunch, which was the highlight of the week.

1 bunch of mint (it must be a spearmint, not a peppermint, any of these make a good mint sauce: 'Moroccan', Garden, 'Tashkent', Apple or 'Guernsey')
caster sugar (enough to cover the leaves when chopped)
white wine vinegar (balsamic vinegar can be substituted; if so, use less sugar)

Remove the mint leaves from the stalks and chop them very finely. Add the sugar and keep chopping; this way the oils and flavours of the mint are amalgamated into the sugar.

Once you are happy that it is all mixed, transfer the mint and sugar to a small bowl. Stir in enough vinegar to just make it runny, but not so much that you have masses of vinegar. Check the sweetness and add extra sugar if required.

This will keep for 7 days, covered, in a fridge. Stir well before use, and if it has dried out a bit, add a little extra vinegar.

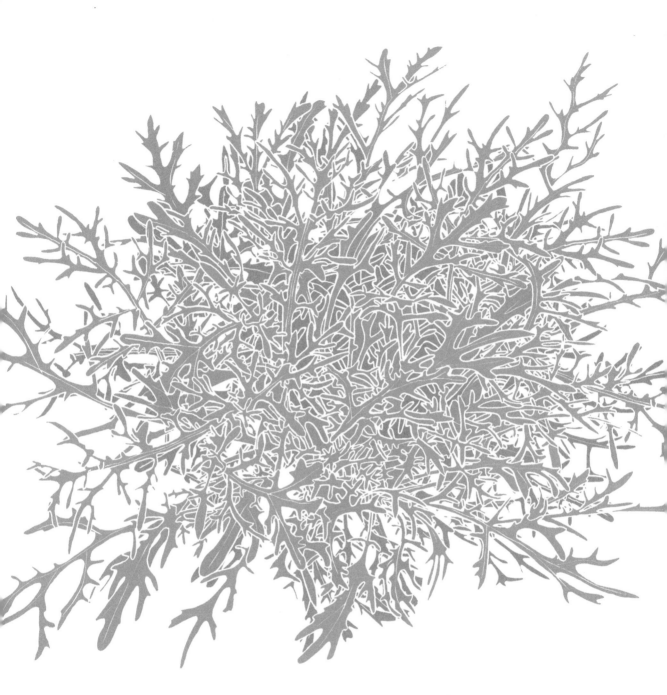

MUSTARD

(also known as Juncea, Indian Mustard, Mustard Greens,
Chinese Mustard)
Brassica juncea

I do not understand why this herb is not grown in every garden as it is easy, rewarding and amazingly useful. I grew it as a child and remember spending hours sitting at the kitchen table extracting the dried seeds from the pods so that Mum could make mustard. Home-made mustard makes a great Christmas present.

Description

Mustard is an annual herb with bright yellow flowers in summer which are followed by long narrow seed pods. The leaves can vary from oval to deeply lobed, and green, yellow or red with purple tint – all depending on the variety.

This is a satisfying herb to cultivate because it is fast growing and the seeds can be sown from spring until autumn. The plants produced from seeds sown in spring are ideal for both seed and leaf production, while plants from seeds sown in the autumn are ideal for a late salad crop. Choose a sunny site and prepare the soil the winter before sowing by feeding it with well-rotted manure.

History in cooking

Mustard has been used for thousands of years, both medicinally and in the kitchen. Historically the Romans used the brown, Juncea, mustard as a pungent salad vegetable, and the seeds of the black, Nigra, as a spice. The English name 'mustard' is said to derive from the Latin, 'mustem ardens', which translates as 'burning wine', a reference to the heat of mustard and the French practice of mixing unfermented grape juice with the ground seeds.

Harvesting and uses

Leaves:

Harvest Brown Mustard leaves from spring until late autumn – the young leaves have by far the best flavour, which is warm and peppery. Add to salads and stir-fry dishes, or use to transform a plain sandwich into a delight.

Flowers:

Pick for eating just as they open, from spring until early autumn. They have a mild mustard flavour that is great in salads.

Seeds:

The seed pods are harvested as they change colour, from summer until early autumn. Dry the pods in a light airy room until totally dried, then remove the seeds from the pods and store in clean dry jars with well-fitting lids. Mustard seeds only get their pungency when they are crushed and infused in a liquid. If you boil the crushed seed or overcook a sauce with crushed seed, it will become bitter.

The easiest and best way to use mustard seeds is to make your own mustard. (See page 204) The seeds are also great added to salad dressings or sauces. When adding mustard to food, remember that its pungency is destroyed by heat, so add it to sauces or stews at the end of cooking.

Properties

Mustard seeds, leaves and flowers are marvellous circulatory stimulants as well as being a noteworthy alkaline food. The alkaline content aids digestion, and mustards also have antispasmodic and diuretic qualities. Eating the fresh leaves and flowers in a salad is an excellent tonic because the leaves are rich in minerals, including high levels of phosphorous as well as calcium, iron, potassium and vitamins A, B and C.

Different varieties

White Mustard, Yellow Mustard

Brassica alba
This has pale yellow flowers in summer followed by long seed pods with pale yellow seeds and rough, bristly, oval, deeply lobed green leaves.

Brown Mustard

Brassica juncea
Clusters of pale yellow flowers in summer are followed by long seed pods with brown seeds and oval, lobed, olive-green leaves with pale green veins and crinkled edges.

Red Mustard

Brassica juncea 'Rubra'
This variety has yellow flowers in summer with oval, red, purple-tinted leaves with toothed edges and a pungent mustard flavour. Good in salads and sandwiches.

Mustard Red Frills

Brassica juncea 'Red Frills'
This has yellow flowers in summer with attractive, dark red, narrow indented leaves with a mild mustard flavour. Great for salads.

Black Mustard

Brassica nigra
The pale yellow flowers in summer are followed by long seed pods with dark brown seeds and rough, bristly, oval-lobed green leaves.

MUSTARD LEAF AND GREEN BEAN SALAD

Mustard leaves (especially the frilly varieties) have a unique flavour that starts off tasting of new potatoes then changes to being warm and spicy. This flavour is excellent with many vegetables, but my favourite combination is with the small French beans that appear in profusion in the summer. My mother often added them to salads, but I am sad that she did not know of this recipe, as I am sure she would have approved. You can add tuna fish or anchovies to make it into a complete meal.

Serves 2–4

200 g French beans, topped, tailed, then halved
3 tbsp olive oil or basil oil (see page 36)
1 tbsp balsamic vinegar
1 garlic clove, crushed
100 g mixed mustard leaves

Put the prepared French beans into a pan of boiling water and cook until just tender. Drain and set aside to cool.

Mix together the oil, vinegar and garlic. Wash, if necessary, the mustard leaves and shake dry. Place them in a serving bowl with the cold French beans, toss, add the dressing, toss again and serve.

WENDY'S MUSTARD AND FETA COTTAGE LOAF

For the past few years Wendy has been in charge of the show and garden plants on the herb farm. This is one of her favourite recipes. The aromatic mustard leaves go so well with the feta cheese and potato, enhancing all the flavours. Serve it with home-made tomato sauce and a crisp green salad.

Serves 4

175 g self-raising flour
1 tsp salt
a pinch of cayenne pepper
4–5 Welsh onions, finely sliced
1 tsp finely chopped sage
1 tbsp roughly chopped mustard leaves
115 g feta
1 largish potato, peeled and grated
1 egg
1 tsp French mustard
2–3 tbsp milk

Pre-heat the oven to 190°C/375°F/gas mark 5.

Sift together the flour, salt and cayenne pepper. Mix in the Welsh onions along with the sage and mustard leaves and two-thirds of the feta – which will need to be broken up into small pieces. Add the potato to the mixture, making sure it is well covered in flour.

In a separate bowl, mix together the egg, mustard and milk, beat well, then slowly add it to the flour and herb mixture to make a dough.

Remove from the mixing bowl and place on a greased baking sheet or one lined with baking parchment. Shape into a 15-cm round.

Break up the remaining feta into small chunks and push them onto the surface of the loaf. Sprinkle with flour and bake in the oven for 35–40 minutes or until golden brown. Serve warm.

MUSTARD-LEAF SAUCE

This is a lovely, spicy warm sauce that can be adapted by adding other ingredients. I often stir in hard-boiled eggs or breadcrumbs soaked in vinegar, which add different textures. Serve with fish, cooked meats, cheese and salads.

Serves 2–4

100 g mixed mustard leaves (red or yellow), washed and roughly chopped
1 garlic clove, crushed
2–3 tbsp white wine vinegar or herb vinegar
150 ml olive oil
salt and freshly ground black pepper

Put the mustard leaves and garlic into a food processor and blend with 2 tablespoons of the vinegar. With the motor running, add the olive oil in a slow stream, season to taste, then add the remaining vinegar, if required.

RABBIT IN MUSTARD SAUCE

Coney pie and Coney stew were part of my childhood, because where I lived in the West Country this was the name for rabbit. The name 'coney' originates, I believe, from the medieval French word 'connis', meaning wild rabbit.

I notice that rabbit is coming back into the kitchen. My wonderful butchers in Chipping Sodbury, Steve, Chris and John, often have it for sale and this is a delicious way to cook it. Serve with plenty of boiled potatoes, to mop up the sauce, and a crisp green salad.

Serves 4–6

575 g rabbit, removed from the bone (I admit the butcher does this)
seasoned plain flour, for dusting
40 g butter
225 g shallots, halved (or use 1 large, sliced onion)
1 garlic clove, sliced
300 ml vegetable or chicken stock
small handful of thyme leaves
salt and freshly ground black pepper
1 bay leaf
1 tbsp thyme mustard (or any herb mustard you have, see page 205)
150 ml double cream

Cut the boned rabbit meat into neat pieces then toss it in the seasoned flour. Set aside.

In a large pan or casserole, melt the butter and add the shallots or onion and cook until golden, not dark brown. Add the garlic for the last few minutes of cooking. Add the floured rabbit pieces, stir until lightly cooked all over, then pour over the stock and bring to a simmer. Turn the heat down and add the thyme and salt and black pepper. Cover and cook very slowly for 1½ hours until the meat is tender. Stir during the cooking to make sure nothing sticks.

Once the meat is tender, lift out the meat and onions, leaving the cooking juices behind, and place on a warmed serving dish. Remove the sprigs of thyme and re-heat the cooking juices, stirring well to remove any pieces stuck to the bottom of the pan. Add the thyme mustard and the cream, then stir until blended but do not boil, as this will destroy the mustard flavour. Check the seasoning.

Serve the rabbit with the sauce poured over.

Excess mustard

Mustards (as in the condiment) are increasingly popular and easy to make. The different-coloured mustard seeds – white or yellow, brown and black – are substantially different in character and produce a huge number of different tasting flavours depending on the combinations. Then when blended with other ingredients, such as wine, vinegar and herbs, you can create the perfect mustard for you, your friends and your family.

Herb mustards are particularly good when combined with crème fraîche or cream cheese as dips for vegetables or pretzels. They are also great added to salad dressings or sauces.

This is the basic mustard recipe to which you can add the herb of your choice. I mention some on page 205.

Quick and easy basic mustard recipe

My mother always made her own mustards, but her recipe took nearly 2 days to complete. With the advent of food processors and liquidisers I have found that I can make a good basic mustard in an hour. It is great fun and the herb combinations are endless: the final flavour can be sweet, hot, pungent, tangy or herby, depending on your personal taste. The whole process is surprisingly straightforward, and involves simply grinding and mixing mustard seeds with a few other ingredients. The seeds themselves are not hot until they are ground and moistened with some sort of cold liquid, but do be warned that freshly made mustard is searingly hot. It should be allowed to stand for 10–30 minutes to allow the flavour to develop and the heat to subside slightly. The longer it stands, the more mellow it becomes.

Makes 2 x small 100 ml jars

50 g white mustard seeds
30 g black mustard seeds
50 g light brown sugar
1 tsp salt
1 tsp turmeric
25–50 g herbs
(see herb list below; if using dried, use half the amount)
200 ml white wine vinegar, or white wine and cider vinegar, or a herb vinegar, or a combination of these

Put the mustard seeds, sugar, salt, turmeric and herbs into a liquidiser or use a pestle and mortar to blend them together until you have the consistency you require – this can be grainy or smooth.

Gradually add the vinegar, 1 tablespoon at a time, blending well between each tablespoon, and continuing to blend until you have a coarse paste.

Leave to stand for 10–15 minutes to thicken slightly. Spoon the mustard into sterilised small jars (see page 12). Seal, label and date the jars and place in a cool dark cupboard or old-fashioned pantry for 2 weeks before using, to allow the flavours to develop. Use the mustard within 6 months. Once opened, the flavour will start to deteriorate, so refrigerate it and use it within 1 month.

Herbs for mustards

Try any of the herbs mentioned below either singularly or mixed to make your own delicious condiment.

All the herb measurements are for 100 g of mustard.

Dill: Add 50 g of chopped dill leaves and 1 teaspoon of crushed dill seeds. This is particularly good served with smoked salmon.

Horseradish: Add 2 tablespoons of grated root. This is lovely with red meats.

Oregano: Add 25 g of chopped leaves. This is particularly good with goats' cheese and tomatoes.

Rosemary: Add 25 g of chopped leaves. This combines well with cold lamb – there is a saying that mustard with mutton is a glutton, but in this case it's worth it.

Thyme: Add 25 g of chopped leaves. Try this with cheese, meat and fish.

Winter savory: Add 25 g of chopped leaves. This is lovely used in a dressing for a bean salad.

Tarragon: Add 25 g of chopped leaves. This goes well with fish and cold chicken, and is also great for adding to sauces.

MYRTLE

(also known as Common Myrtle, Mirto)

Myrtus communis

I fell in love with myrtle after I had seen it being used as formal hedging at the Alhambra Palace in Granada, Spain, and then growing wild in the hills of Sardinia, where it can be found clinging to craggy rocks and smelling absolutely heavenly in the baking sun. Over the years myrtle has become one of my top must-haves for the herb garden, as it looks wonderful grown in the garden or in containers, and it is, in my opinion, a very under-rated and under-used culinary herb. It can transform an English summer barbecue into a Mediterranean feast.

Description

This lovely Mediterranean, aromatic, evergreen plant has leaves all year round, as well as pretty, fragrant white flowers throughout the summer which are followed by dark purple–black berries in late autumn. The dark green oval leaves are aromatic when crushed, smelling of sweet spice.

Being a Mediterranean herb, it will grow in a fertile well-drained soil in full sun. Where winters are borderline, plant it against a south- or west-facing wall, as this will not only protect it from cold winter winds but also cut the rainfall by 25 per cent, therefore restricting the amount of water the plant receives. Alternatively, if temperatures in your garden regularly reach below -5°C, grow myrtle as a container plant, using a soil-based potting compost, and bring it under cover for the winter months.

History in cooking

Myrtle has been used for over 2,000 years as a flavouring, a perfume and a medicine. The ancient Romans made myrtle wine by immersing the ripe fruits in mosto – fermenting grape juice. The fruits were also used in Roman cooking, especially with wild boar. In Chile, myrtle seeds and flower buds were dried and used to make a type of coffee.

Harvesting and uses

Leaves:

Being an evergreen the leaves can be picked all year round, but the best-flavoured leaves appear in midsummer on the new shoots that have started to change colour from light bright green to dark green. They have a warm, spicy, slightly bitter aromatic flavour. They need to be used carefully as they have a strong flavour that can overpower a meal, but when mastered they can transform soups, casseroles, stews, vegetable, poultry or meat dishes into feasts. Like bay, the leaves are not eaten but used to flavour and should be removed before serving. Foods flavoured with the smoke of myrtle leaves are common in rural areas of mainland Italy and Sardinia.

Flowers:

These can be picked throughout the summer and have a warm and spicy flavour. Add sparingly to rice and pasta dishes.

Berries:

The ripe berries can be harvested from late autumn to mid-winter. They have a dry, spicy flavour and go well with strong meat dishes, boar, duck and quail. The dried berries can be ground like pepper – it is known as 'Mursins' in the Middle East, where it is used as a spice.

Properties

Myrtle leaves and berries are an antiseptic; the buds and flowers contain vitamin C and citric acid. Medicinally, the leaves and berries have been used to treat diarrhoea and dysentery.

Different varieties

Variegated Myrtle

Myrtus communis subsp. *tarentina* 'Variegata'
This variety has fragrant white flowers with a hint of pink in summer, followed by dark purple–black fruits. The leaves are oval and dark green with silver variegation, developing a pink tinge in autumn.

Tarentina myrtle

Myrtus communis subsp. *tarentina*
This has small, fragrant white flowers in summer followed by small dark purple–black fruits. The leaves are small, oval, dark green and aromatic. The branches of this myrtle are very straight, making it ideal for using as natural barbecue skewers for grilling kebabs (both meat and vegetable), sausages, fish and peppers.

Variegated Tarentina myrtle

Myrtus communis subsp. *tarentina* 'Microphylla Variegata'
Small, fragrant white flowers with a hint of pink in summer are followed by dark purple–black fruits. The leaves are small, oval and dark green with silver variegation, developing a pink tinge in autumn.

ROAST BUTTERNUT SQUASH AND MYRTLE SOUP

The warm spice of the myrtle combined with the comforting sweetness of the butternut squash (especially when roasted) makes this a lovely winter soup –particularly when one has been working outside. Serve with sage rotis (see page 265).

Serves 4

800 g butternut squash
3 tbsp olive oil
4 myrtle sprigs
salt and freshly ground black pepper
4 whole and unpeeled and 2 finely chopped garlic cloves
2 onions, finely chopped
2 carrots, finely sliced
2 litres vegetable or chicken stock

Pre-heat the oven to 240°C/475°F/gas mark 9.

Cut the butternut squash in half, scooping out the seeds using a large spoon. Slice the flesh, including the skin, into 7-cm wedges and brush them with 1 tablespoon of the olive oil. Place the wedges in a roasting tin on top of 2 of the myrtle sprigs and season with salt and black pepper.

Place in the oven and roast for 45 minutes or until the squash is soft and caramelised. After 25 minutes of cooking, add the 4 unpeeled garlic cloves and the remaining sprigs of myrtle, which can be pushed under the cooking squash.

Meanwhile, heat the remaining olive oil in a large pan. Add the onions, carrots and remaining chopped garlic and cook gently for 10–15 minutes until soft but not brown. Pour in the stock, bring to the boil and simmer for 20 minutes or until the vegetables are tender.

Allow the squash to cool for 5 minutes when cooked. Using a large spoon, remove the flesh from the skin and add to the stock. Squeeze the roasted garlic from its skin into the stock and discard the myrtle. Simmer the stock and vegetables for a further 5 minutes or until the squash begins to break up.

Place the soup in a food processor or use a hand-held blender and whiz until smooth. Return the soup to the pan and gently reheat. Check the seasoning. Pour the soup into bowls and serve.

BEEF STEW WITH MYRTLE, CINNAMON AND RED WINE

There are two great tips in this recipe that I picked up from my mother. First: marinating meat not only makes it taste wonderful, it also tenderises it. Second: the salty flavour of pancetta adds another dimension to the dish. So combine these tips with the spicy myrtle and you have a great stew. Delicious served with noodles or mash.

Serves 4

500 g rump or braising steak, cut into 3–4-cm pieces
2 garlic cloves, crushed
2 cinnamon sticks, approx 4–6 cm long
2 x 8-cm sprigs of myrtle, plus 6 myrtle leaves
70 g cubed pancetta
30 g salted butter
6 small shallots, peeled but left whole
3 large carrots, cut into batons
1 tbsp plain flour
300 ml beef stock
300 ml red wine

Mix the prepared meat with the garlic, cinnamon sticks and myrtle sprigs in a large bowl, cover and leave in the fridge overnight.

The next day, pre-heat the oven to 150°C/300°F/gas mark 2. Drain the meat, reserving the marinade after removing and discarding the cinnamon and the myrtle sprigs.

Fry the pancetta in a casserole dish over a medium heat until it starts to brown. Add half the butter and all the shallots and carrots. Sauté until the carrots and shallots start to brown.

Pat the meat dry on some kitchen paper. In a separate pan, melt the remaining butter, add the meat to the pan and cook until brown, then transfer it to the casserole dish. Add the flour to this, stir well, then add the reserved marinade and the myrtle leaves. Bring to the boil. Add the stock and wine, return to the boil, cover, and put in the oven for 1 hour 20 minutes or until the meat is tender and the sauce has thickened.

Remove from the oven and stand, covered, for 20 minutes before serving.

HOT MEAD AND MYRTLE PUNCH

Although red wine is most popular for punches, mead blends well with sweet spice and myrtle berries, resulting in an unusual medium-sweet, full-flavoured drink. Excellent at Christmas or on a cold winter weekend when you have been for a long walk with friends.

Makes approx. 1.5 litres

700 ml bottle mead
575 ml dry cider
575 ml apple juice
2 oranges
12 cloves
12-cm piece of cinnamon stick
4 myrtle berries
60 g honey, or to taste

Put the mead, cider and apple juice into a large pan. Thickly slice the oranges and stick the cloves into the slices. Put them in the pan with the cinnamon stick and myrtle berries. Stir in the honey. Heat the punch to just below simmering point and keep it at that temperature for 20 minutes.

Strain the infused mead through a sieve. Serve hot, in warmed mugs or thick heatproof glasses.

MYRTLE BERRY, APPLE AND WALNUT CHUTNEY

I often make chutneys for Christmas presents. This is a particularly good one which is always popular as it goes well with cheese and cold meats.

Makes approx. 2.25 kg

900 ml malt vinegar
450 g light soft brown sugar
12 myrtle berries (fresh, if possible)
900 g cooking apples
450 g onions, chopped
225 g raisins
25 g English mustard powder
25 g freshly grated root ginger
2 tsp mild curry powder
20 g salt
110 g walnut pieces

Put the vinegar and sugar into a large pan and bring to the boil. Peel, core and roughly chop the apples and add to the pan with all the other ingredients, except the walnuts. Bring back to the boil. Cook, stirring more regularly as it thickens, until it is well reduced and thick (remember that it will thicken even more once cold).

Remove the pan from the heat and stir in the walnuts. Spoon the mixture into warm sterilised jars (see page 12) and seal with vinegar-proof lids.

This will keep for up to 1 year.

Excess myrtle

Myrtle salt

Being an evergreen herb which can be used for most of the year, a surplus of myrtle is something that occurs less than for the annual herbs. However, if you do not have a myrtle bush growing in your garden and you are given a branch, the best way to preserve the flavour of the leaves is to make myrtle salt, which is great with fish and barbecues.

Makes 250 g

250 g non-iodised salt
20 myrtle leaves

Using a pestle and mortar, pound together the salt and the myrtle leaves – the salt will pick up the flavour of the herb.
Bottle the salt and crushed leaves and keep in a dark cupboard.
It can be used immediately or stored, but it is best used within 3 months.

NASTURTIUM

(also known as Garden Nasturtium, Indian Cress, Large Cress)

Tropaeolum majus

This herb is recognisable in many gardens, but it is rarely acknowledged as the useful culinary and medicinal herb that it is. For me, it brings back many childhood memories, from using the flowers when creating miniature gardens, to astonishing school friends with the flavour of the leaves. Neither my grandmother nor my mother believed they were worthy of the kitchen. I, on the other hand, find them useful not only for the flavour but also for the flamboyancy that the flowers can add to a meal.

Description

Nasturtiums are half-hardy, meaning that they die as soon as there is any threat of frost and so only last one year. Despite this brevity, they are seriously worth growing for the wonderfully brazen flowers they produce all summer – the colours can vary from orange to amazing mahogany and deep crimson. The round mid-green leaves have a peppery flavour.

Sow the large, easy-to-handle seeds direct into small pots in early spring. Alternatively, sow the seeds in late spring into prepared well-drained soil in sun or partial shade. A word of warning; if the soil is too rich there will be an abundance of leaf and little flower, so be mean with your feed, fertiliser or compost if you want a profusion of flowers.

History in cooking

This herb was introduced into Europe from Peru in the 16th century. It was first known as Indian Cress (Nasturtium indicum) on account of the pungent watercress-like flavour of its leaves. The custom for eating its petals and using them for tea originated in the Orient, and from the early 17th century onwards there are references to nasturtium flowers being used in salads. Even the famous Mrs Beeton, in the mid 1800s, suggested that they should be used to dress a summer salad.

Harvesting and uses

Leaves:
Pick the young leaves from late spring until the first frosts or late autumn. Their peppery flavour combines well with salad leaves, especially when served with a vinaigrette dressing, potatoes, crème fraîche or cream cheese.

Flowers:
Pick from early summer until the first frosts or late autumn. These also have a light peppery taste that is ideal in all forms of salads, and served with mustard and fruit, especially strawberries.

Seeds:
The best-flavoured seed pods are those that are small and green, and they can be pickled or added to salads fresh; they are quite strong in flavour, so use sparingly. The seeds turning brown, which can be harvested from midsummer until early autumn, should be saved for drying and sowing in the following spring.

Properties

Medicinally all parts of the plant appear to be antibiotic. It also contains large amounts of sulphur and the leaves contain vitamin C and iron as well as an antiseptic substance, which is at its strongest before the plant flowers. Nasturtiums are reputedly good for the skin as an antiseptic wash.

Different varieties

There are many different varieties of *Tropaeolum majus*; some are bushy, some are trailing and some are climbing, but all have edible leaves and flowers. Here are just a few varieties that are easily available from good seed suppliers.

Nasturtium 'Alaska'
Tropaeolum majus Alaska Series
Red/orange flowers with variegated cream/white and green leaves.

Nasturtium 'Empress of India'
Tropaeolum majus 'Empress of India'
Dark red flowers with dark green leaves.

Nasturtium 'Peaches & Cream'
Tropaeolum majus 'Peaches & Cream'
Pale pink/orange/cream flowers with mid-green leaves.

Nasturtium 'Tom Thumb Black Velvet'
Tropaeolum majus 'Tom Thumb Black Velvet'
Deep red/scarlet flowers with mid-green leaves.

Nasturtium 'Double Gleam'
Tropaeolum majus 'Double Gleam'
Mixture of golden yellow, orange and scarlet flowers with mid-green leaves. This is a semi-trailing variety.

Nasturtium 'Jewel of Africa'
Tropaeolum majus 'Jewel of Africa'
Mixture of yellow, red, cream and pink flowers with variegated cream and green leaves. This is a climbing variety.

NASTURTIUM SALSA

This is a great way to serve nasturtium leaves and petals. The pepper flavour of the leaves goes so well with the fiery chilli, and the whole thing looks amazingly pretty in the serving bowl.

Serves 4

2 large tomatoes, skinned
1 small chilli, seeded and finely chopped
½ red onion, finely sliced then chopped
1 tbsp nasturtium leaves, chopped
1 tbsp balsamic vinegar
juice of ½ lime
salt
2 nasturtium flowers (petals only)

Cut the tomatoes in half, remove the seeds and discard them. Chop the tomatoes finely then place them in a small bowl. Add the chopped chilli, onion, nasturtium leaves, vinegar and lime juice and season with salt.

Scatter the nasturtium petals over the top and serve.

NASTURTIUM MUSHROOM BAKE

When I was growing up garlic mushrooms were considered de rigueur. I still have a soft spot for them. This dish combines the mushrooms and garlic with the peppery flavour of the nasturtium leaves, creating a lovely depth of flavours. It makes a good summer first course that can be served with crusty home-made bread or toast and a cold glass of cider.

Serves 2–4

6 tbsp olive oil
3 garlic cloves, crushed
20–30 fresh young nasturtium leaves
225 g fresh mushrooms, washed and sliced
1 tbsp thyme (common, French, Porlock or broad-leafed), leaves removed from the sprigs and finely chopped
salt and freshly ground black pepper
freshly grated nutmeg

Put the olive oil into a bowl and add the garlic to infuse for 1 hour.

Wash and dry the nasturtium leaves and add to the infused garlic oil.

Place the mushrooms in another bowl and cover with the thyme, salt and black pepper, and a grating of nutmeg. Gently stir the mushrooms well so they are all coated in the herbs and seasonings.

Remove the leaves one by one from the garlic oil, keeping the oil, and place one-third of the leaves on the bottom of a shallow 15-cm baking dish. Cover the leaves with half of the mushrooms, then cover these in turn with more leaves, followed by the remaining mushrooms and ending with a layer of leaves. Add a sprinkling of garlic oil, cover well and bake in the oven for 20 minutes. Serve.

GRILLED SALMON WITH NASTURTIUM BUTTER

The nasturtium butter is not only colourful but also packs a punch. Its piquant flavour enhances the flavours of the salmon, making this an attractive and appetising meal.

Serves 4

For the nasturtium butter
100 g unsalted butter
10 nasturtium flowers
juice of ½ lemon

For the salmon and salad
4 wild or organically farmed salmon steaks
1 red onion, finely sliced
1 sweet red pepper, seeded and finely sliced
1 iceberg lettuce, finely sliced

Salad dressing
3 tbsp olive oil
1 tbsp lemon juice
salt and freshly ground black pepper

Start by making the butter. Put all the ingredients in a food processor and whiz until totally mixed. Transfer to a small container with a lid and place in the fridge until required.

Pre-heat the grill to high. When hot, grill the salmon until it is cooked through.

Combine all the dressing ingredients and mix together well. Mix the onion, pepper and lettuce in a bowl and pour over the salad dressing. Arrange the dressed salad onto 4 plates and top each with a piece of grilled cooked salmon, then place a quarter of the nasturtium butter onto each and serve.

STUFFED NASTURTIUM LEAVES

This French recipe is lovely and unusual; the first time I had this I was 13 years old. I was staying with my Aunt Pippa, who then lived in La Garde Freinet in the hills above St Tropez. I was amazed to learn that I was eating nasturtium leaves. This recipe transforms them.

Serves 4

1 tsp capers, rinsed and chopped
1 small gherkin, finely chopped
1 tsp parsley, finely chopped
1 tsp chervil, finely chopped
24–30 nasturtium leaves
50 g can anchovy fillets, drained and cut into narrow strips
150 ml dry white wine
1 tbsp French tarragon vinegar (see page 316)
1 thyme sprig
1 bay leaf
2 tbsp olive oil

Pre-heat the oven to 150°C/300°F/gas mark 2.

In a bowl, mix together the capers, gherkin, parsley and chervil. Remove the stems from the nasturtium leaves. Place a little of the herb mixture into the centre of each leaf and cover with a strip of anchovy. Fold in the sides of the leaf and then roll it up, rather like a cigar, with the seam underneath.

Arrange the stuffed leaves in a shallow ovenproof frying pan and pour over the wine and vinegar. Add the thyme and bay leaf then transfer to the oven for 15 minutes.

Remove from the oven and transfer the stuffed leaves to a serving dish. Keep warm. Reduce the remaining wine and vinegar over a high heat until there are about 2 spoonfuls left. Put the olive oil in a small bowl and strain over the reduced warm wine, discarding the bay and thyme leaves. Whisk well then pour over the stuffed nasturtium leaves.

Chill until ready to serve.

Excess nasturtium

Pickled nasturtium seed pods

These pickled seed pods make a good substitute for capers. They have a light peppery flavour and add crunch to salads and sauces or are great with cheeses.

Enough nasturtium seed pods to fill a standard jam jar
2 tbsp salt to 1 pint water, repeated 3 times (see recipe)
2 tbsp French tarragon leaves, finely chopped
1 onion, finely chopped
425 ml white wine vinegar
12 black peppercorns
1 chilli, seeded and finely chopped
1 tsp salt
a generous grating of fresh nutmeg

Before putting the seed pods in the jam jar, place them in a bowl and cover with salted water. Leave them for 1 day, strain, then cover with clean salted water. Repeat this for 3 days. On the final day, drain, place in a dry tea towel and pat dry.

Place the dry seeds and seed pods in layers in the jam jar with the tarragon and onion.

In a pan, place the vinegar, peppercorns, chilli, salt and nutmeg, bring to the boil then simmer for 10 minutes. Allow to cool then strain and pour the liquid over the seed pods.

Seal with the lid and store in the fridge for at least 1 week before using.

OREGANO, MARJORAM

(also known as Maggiorana, Origano, Wild Marjoram, Mountain Mint, Oregano, Winter Marjoram, Winter Sweet, Marjolaine)
Origanum vulgare

I feel quite strongly about the subject – when is a plant oregano and when is it marjoram? In my understanding the only true marjoram is *Origanum majorana*, which is known as sweet marjoram, whereas oregano is *Origanum vulgare* (the *vulgare* part means common). Both are great in the kitchen and in the garden. Grandmother used oregano sparingly whereas my mother, who was enamoured with Mediterranean cooking, used sweet marjoram with gusto and at times rather too liberally.

Description

In summer this plant is a joy for the bees and butterflies which surround the flowers. All the varieties of *Origanum vulgare* are hardy, with clusters of tiny tubular mauve flowers in summer and dark green, aromatic hairy leaves, which, in winter, form a tight mat. Sweet marjoram, on the other hand, is an annual in cold climates. It has tiny white flowers which grow in a knot-like cluster and pale grey-green leaves that are highly aromatic.

The vigour and aroma of all forms of origanum does vary greatly depending on where it is planted and in which country. In the Mediterranean you can smell the oregano before you see it, but here in the damp, cool northern European climate you see it but only smell it when you either crush a leaf or cook with it. So for the best results, plant in full sun in a free-draining soil. Standard oregano and marjoram can both be grown from seed, however the seed is very fine, so mix with sand or flour before sowing so that you do not sow too thickly. Both varieties can be grown from cuttings taken from the new growth in summer and established plants of oregano can be divided in the spring or after flowering in late summer.

All oreganos can be grown successfully in containers. Use a soil-based potting compost mixed with additional sharp grit or sand and place the container in a sunny position.

History in cooking

In medieval times marjoram was combined with alecost to flavour ale – this was before hops were introduced into this country during the reign of Henry VIII (1491–1547). *The Englishman's Flora*, by Geoffrey Grigson (1905–1985), is illustrated with woodcuts from the 16th century, and one of these shows an Italian lady watering marjoram. Under the woodcut are the following words: 'confortat cerebrum et omnia viscera', which translates as 'comforts the head and all internal organs'.

Harvesting and uses

Leaves:
The leaves of oregano are available all year round, while those of marjoram are available, in the northern hemisphere, from spring

until early autumn. For both, the best-flavoured leaves can be picked either side of flowering. The summer leaves are much stronger flavoured than the winter mat-forming ones, because the warmth of the sun brings the oils in the leaf to the surface. The leaves can be used in salads, with eggs and vegetables, cooked with meat, in marinades, and they are also lovely with grilled fish.

Flowers:
Pick these just as they open throughout the summer and scatter over salads, soups, jacket potatoes and roast vegetables.

Properties

Marjoram and oregano have a soothing effect on the digestive system; they stimulate the digestive juices which help to break down rich and heavy foods. They are also highly valued for treating dyspepsia, loss of appetite, colic and nausea.

Different varieties

There are many varieties of oregano available' here I have simply chosen my favourites for the kitchen.

Greek Oregano
Origanum vulgare subsp. *hirtum* 'Greek'
This variety is a very strong-flavoured with hairy, dark olive green leaves and white flowers. Excellent with meat and casseroles.

Oregano Acorn Bank, Marjoram Acorn Bank
Origanum vulgare 'Acorn Bank'
This is a golden-leaved variety with clusters of tiny tubular pink flowers in summer. The leaves have a mild flavour and are good with vegetables and in salads.

French Oregano, French Marjoram
Origanum onites
The green leaves turn gold in the sun and it bears clusters of light pink flowers in summer. This oregano has a light spicy flavour which is good with vegetable dishes.

Sweet Marjoram, Knotted Marjoram
Origanum majorana
This aromatic marjoram is often grown as an annual. It has clusters of tiny white flowers with oval, pale green, soft aromatic leaves which have an excellent culinary flavour that goes well with tomatoes and tomato sauces, vegetables and meat dishes.

BAKED SWEET MARJORAM GOATS' CHEESE WITH ROAST VEGETABLE SALAD

This is a rustic summer salad. The marjoram and mint, being cousins, combine beautifully with the salty goats' cheese.

Serves 4

2 small courgettes or 1 large courgette, sliced into 1-cm rounds
2 red peppers, halved and seeded
4 tbsp olive oil, plus extra for drizzling
1 bulb of Florence fennel, halved and very finely sliced
1 bunch of rocket leaves
2 tbsp sweet marjoram leaves, removed from their stems
200 g goats' cheese, cut into 4 round slices
sea salt and freshly ground black pepper
juice of ½ lemon
10 spearmint sprigs, finely chopped (pick from the top so you have the new growth. Choose Moroccan, garden, or Tashkent mint, not peppermint)

Pre-heat the oven to 170°C/325°F/gas mark 3, and pre-heat the grill to hot. (If you have a combined oven, heat the grill first then pre-heat the oven once you have finished with the grill.)

Line the bottom of a grill pan with a piece of foil, lay the sliced courgettes and the pepper halves on the grill rack, drizzle with olive oil and place under the hot grill. Cook for about 3–4 minutes, turning the vegetables over halfway through. Remove from the heat. Place the peppers on a chopping board to cool and place the courgettes in a large bowl with the finely sliced fennel and the rocket leaves.

Chop the marjoram leaves finely and tip into a small bowl with 1 tablespoon of olive oil. Put the goats' cheese in the bowl with the marjoram and olive oil and season with black pepper. Make sure the goats' cheese is coated all over with the herby oil, then place on a baking sheet lined with baking parchment or foil. Pop in the oven and cook for about 10 minutes until golden brown. (The oven is better than the grill as the grill will burn the marjoram and destroy the flavour.)

Skin the peppers, slice into ribbons and add to the salad.

Make a dressing by combining the remaining olive oil with the lemon juice, salt and black pepper. Pour the dressing over the salad and toss well, then divide among 4 serving plates. Top with the goats' cheese, sprinkle with the chopped mint and serve.

SWEET MARJORAM, SPINACH AND TOMATO GALETTES

By using the aromatic sweet marjoram in both the pastry and with the tomato and spinach filling, the herb's wonderful warm spicy flavour permeates right through these small pastries.

This is a useful dish; you can make it for two then freeze the rest of the pastry raw, interleaved with foil. You can then use it at a later date to make a meal quickly.

I have to be honest, pastry and my gardening hands have never been a good mix, but recently I was introduced to a wonderful technique: you freeze the butter, grate it into the flour, then mix it with a palette knife, thus keeping warm physical touch to the minimum. Ever since adopting this tip these little tartlets (or, if you are being posh, galettes, as the pastry case has no sides) have been a great success.

Serves 3–6

For the pastry
110 g unsalted butter
175 g plain flour, plus extra for dusting
pinch of salt
1 tsp finely chopped sweet marjoram leaves
cold water

For the topping
225 g young leaf spinach
2 onions, peeled and thinly sliced
1 knob unsalted butter
1 tbsp chopped sweet marjoram leaves, plus a little extra to decorate
6 medium-ripe tomatoes, skinned and thinly sliced
1 tsp olive oil
25 g freshly grated Parmesan

Pre-heat the oven to 220°C/425°F/gas mark 7 and lightly grease 2 baking sheets.

To make the pastry, weigh and freeze the butter prior to use, wrapped in foil or cling film. Sift the flour into a large bowl with the salt. Remove the butter from the freezer, fold back the covering and grate over the flour using the coarsest side of the grater.

Once you finish grating, add the sweet marjoram leaves and fold in with the butter and flour using a palette knife. Once the butter is well covered, add 2 tablespoons of cold water – don't over-add the water, the dough should not be overwet. (I do use my hands for the last bit.) Having made the dough, remove it from the bowl, place it in cling film or in a plastic bag and put it in the fridge until you are ready to use it.

Wash the spinach and place it in a pan, cover with a lid, then cook on the hob over a medium heat. You only need the spinach to wilt down, which takes 2–3 minutes. Give it a turn, then drain all the excess liquid off through a colander, pressing the spinach with the back of a serving spoon to make sure all the liquid is squeezed out. Put to one side.

Fry the sliced onions in the butter until translucent. Add the sweet marjoram leaves and stir them into the onions. Remove from the heat and drain off any excess liquid.

To skin the tomatoes, simply place them in a bowl, cover with boiling water, leave to stand for 1 minute, then drain. The skins can now be removed easily – however they will be hot, so do protect your fingers.

Remove the pastry from the fridge, roll it out on a lightly floured surface to 3 mm thick. Cut out 6 x 15-cm circles and place them on the prepared baking sheets. Chop the spinach, then divide it between the 6 circles, leaving a narrow rim around the edge of the pastry. Scatter with the onion and marjoram mix, then cover with overlapping slices of tomato. Sprinkle over a little marjoram and olive oil.

Place the baking sheets in the oven for 10–12 minutes. If you are using 2, you will need to switch their position in the oven halfway through the cooking time. Remove from the oven, sprinkle with Parmesan and serve warm, or allow to cool and then serve.

FISH PIE WITH SWEET MARJORAM CRUMBLE

As a child I was always served fish on Fridays. Mum usually cooked a pie, as this made a small bit stretch a long way. As a treat she would buy smoked haddock, and today the aroma of this fish cooking transports me back to my childhood. I have added the marjoram crumble to augment the flavour of the pie. Serve simply with carrots and boiled new potatoes.

Serves 4

400 g smoked haddock fillets (try to get the un-dyed version)
1 onion, finely sliced
300 ml semi-skimmed milk
2 bay leaves
salt and freshly ground black pepper
45 g unsalted butter
75 g wholemeal flour
3 tbsp freshly grated Parmesan
2 tbsp sweet marjoram leaves, chopped
4 tsp cornflour
2 tbsp flatleaf parsley, finely chopped

Pre-heat the oven to 170°C/325°F/gas mark 3.

Put the fish in a roasting tin and add the onion, milk and bay leaves. Season with salt and black pepper to taste, then cover with foil. Place the tin in the oven and cook for 15–20 minutes.

Remove from the oven and check that when you touch the fish it is still firm but easily breaks up. Lift the fish out of the milk with a fish slice and put it onto a plate. Set aside the milk in the roasting tin and discard the bay leaf. Remove the skin from the fish and flake the flesh, discarding any bones.

In a mixing bowl, make the crumble by using your fingertips to rub the butter into the flour to make fine crumbs. Add the Parmesan and marjoram and seasoning to taste.

Mix the cornflour to a smooth paste with a little water. Put the infused milk in the roasting tin on the hob, on a low heat, add the mixed cornflour paste and bring to the boil, stirring until the sauce has thickened. Gently stir in the flaked fish and chopped parsley and season with salt and black pepper to taste.

Pour the fish mixture into an ovenproof dish. Spoon the crumble mixture over the top, press down with the back of a fork. Bake for 35 minutes or until the top is golden. Serve at once.

OREGANO COTTAGE PIE

In my grandmother's notebook I came across this description: 'Cottage pie is made with beef, shepherd's pie is made with mutton or lamb.' As soon as I read this it became an 'of course'; but I guess I had never stopped to think of the two names and why they had them.

When I was growing up this dish was a Wednesday meal and was made with what was left from the Sunday roast. Adding oregano to the dish spikes up the flavours of the pie. Serve with French beans, peas or Brussels sprouts.

Serves 4

15 g unsalted butter, plus extra for greasing and dotting
285–340 g cold cooked beef, mutton or lamb
180–225 g carrots, thinly sliced
1 small onion, finely chopped
1 tbsp oregano or sweet marjoram leaves, finely chopped
2 tsp plain flour
salt and freshly ground black pepper

For the topping
680 g potatoes (Desiree, Maris Piper or King Edwards)
4 tbsp milk
30 g unsalted butter

Pre-heat the oven to 190°C/375°F/gas mark 5 and grease an ovenproof dish.

First make the topping. Cook the potatoes in boiling water, drain, then mash with the milk and butter and set aside.

Prepare the meat by removing the fat, then either slice and dice it finely by hand, which makes nice chunky bits, or use a food processor to mince the meat. Do not over-process or it will become a mush.

Cook the carrots for 5 minutes, drain, reserve 150 ml of the cooking water and set aside. Fry the onion in the butter for 5 minutes until it is translucent, then add the meat and the oregano or sweet marjoram. Cook for a few more minutes, stirring all the time. Add the flour and cook for 1 minute to blend in any of the fat and juices. Add the carrot water plus any remaining gravy you might have, stir well until all is blended, then add salt and black pepper to taste.

Turn the contents into the prepared ovenproof dish. Lay the sliced carrots on the surface of the meat, then cover with the mashed potato. Using a fork, make lines in the mash then dot with a small amount of butter.

Cook in the oven for 30–35 minutes.

OREGANO AND LEMON PAN-FRIED CHICKEN

This is a simple, healthy meal that is quick to prepare and cook, only needing a little time to marinate. Using oregano and lemon as a marinade before cooking the chicken infuses it with their flavours. Delicious served with boiled rice and a crisp green salad.

Serves 2

2 chicken breasts fillets
zest and juice of ½ lemon
2 tsp oregano leaves, finely chopped
1 tbsp olive oil
1 tbsp parsley leaves, finely chopped
salt and freshly ground black pepper

Make shallow cuts in the chicken breasts. Mix the lemon zest and juice with the oregano leaves and rub into the chicken breasts. Leave in the fridge for 30 minutes to marinate.

Heat the olive oil in a small frying pan on a medium heat. When hot, remove the chicken from the marinade, fry for 8–10 minutes each side until cooked, then add the marinade and increase the heat until it is bubbling. Add the parsley leaves and turn off the heat. Toss everything around, season and serve.

OREGANO YORKSHIRE PUDDINGS

Adding oregano to Yorkshire-pudding batter transforms a family favourite into a treat. It also makes it ideal for vegetarians, for when I make the individual puddings I serve them with a rich, thick, home-made tomato sauce (see page 12) in the centre, topped with a slice of grilled goats' cheese.

Makes approx. 6–9 puddings, depending on the size of the tray

110 g plain flour
salt
2 eggs
275 ml milk
1 tbsp oregano leaves, finely chopped
2–3 tbsp vegetable oil or good dripping or lard

Pre-heat the oven to 230°C/450°F/gas mark 8.

Make the batter by sieving the flour and salt into a bowl, then make a well in the centre and add the eggs, breaking the yolks with a spoon before you start stirring. Add the milk gradually, stirring into the flour little by little until half the milk is added; keep going until all the flour is taken up and the mixture is smooth. Then add the rest of the milk and the oregano and beat for 5–10 minutes. Stand the batter in a cool place for 1 hour.

When the batter is ready, heat the oil or dripping in a roasting tin or Yorkshire pudding tray until it is just beginning to smoke and check that there is 1 cm of oil in each section. Pour the batter into the tin or into the individual sections. Cook for 5 minutes at 230°C/450°F/gas mark 8, then turn down to 200°C/400°F/gas mark 6 and cook for 35–40 minutes until crisp and puffy. Individual Yorkshire puds will take less time, about 15–20 minutes. Don't open the door of the oven too soon otherwise you will have flat puds.

Excess sweet marjoram

Sweet marjoram butter
This can be used to fry vegetables, to put on grilled tomatoes or for making pastry.

Makes 125 g

3 tbsp sweet marjoram leaves, finely chopped
125 g unsalted butter, softened to room temperature

Mix the chopped leaves with the butter. The simplest and easiest way of blending the herb and butter together is to use a fork. Once thoroughly mixed, pack the butter into a roll of greaseproof paper and place in the fridge for up to 24 hours before use. The longer you leave it, the better the flavour.

This can also be frozen. Place it in a freezerproof container, label it, and use within 3 months.

PARSLEY

(also known as Persil, Prezzemolo)
Petroselinum crispum

This is one of the most widely used herbs throughout the world. In the main it is used as a garnish, but it is also a great root vegetable and a brilliant leaf herb that can make bland food come alive. All four generations of my family that have contributed to this book have loved, respected and used this herb in the kitchen. I have deliberately chosen recipes from my grandmother and mother that show how this herb can make a meal.

Description

Parsley is a hardy biennial, which means that it produces leaf in the first year and flowers in the second. The flowers appear in creamy white clusters, while the leaves are a bright green (which can vary in depth of colour depending on variety) with toothed edges (again, this can vary according to variety, from being straight to amazingly tightly curled).

This herb has to be grown from seed. For the most productive crops, sow where you want to crop it as it hates being transplanted; so either sow seed direct into the garden once the soil has started to warm up, in mid-spring, or into a large deep container. Be patient, germination can vary from 10 days to 6 weeks. Parsley is a hungry plant, it likes a good deep soil, not too light and not acid. Always feed the chosen site well in the previous autumn with well-rotted manure.

If you wish to harvest parsley all year round, the ideal arrangement is to have two different sites prepared. For summer supplies, a western or eastern border is perfect because the plant needs moisture and prefers a little shade. For winter supplies, a more sheltered spot will be needed in a sunny position, like under a south-facing wall.

Remember to water well during hot weather. Hamburg or Turnip-rooted parsley differs only in the respect that it is a root not a leaf crop. The soil should be prepared in exactly the same way and the seed should be sown in shallow drills in mid-spring. Water well all summer. The root tends to grow more at this time of year and, unlike a lot of root crops, the largest roots taste the best. Lift the roots from the ground in late autumn until early winter.

History in cooking

Parsley has been popular since records began; the Romans ate it as a deodoriser, whereas the ancient Greeks believed that the plants grew from the blood of their heroes, so it was fed in abundance to their athletes. During the Middle Ages the monks grew parsley to treat the sick. John Gerard (1545–1612), the English herbalist and surgeon, said of parsley: 'It is delightful to the taste and agreeable to the stomache.'

Harvesting and uses

Leaves:

Pick the leaves from early summer of the first season to the early spring of the second. Parsley is a widely-used culinary herb, valued for its taste as well as its rich nutritional content (see properties, below). Cooking with parsley brings out the flavour of other foods and herbs. In bland food it is always best to add parsley just before the end of cooking to get the best flavour.

Seeds:

The seeds can be harvested from midsummer of the second season. They are hardly ever used in cooking but, like those of its cousin caraway, they are delicious ground and used to flavour soups, stews or casseroles.

Roots:

If you want to use the roots of parsley, grow separate plants for this purpose so you can get the seeds in the second year from the other plants. Dig up roots from autumn to early winter of the first season. The roots of the Hamburg parsley make a great alternative to carrots or celeriac; they are lovely cooked on their own, added to soups, stews or casseroles.

Properties

Parsley is a most beneficial culinary herb; it helps clear the toxins from the body and is also well known for its digestive properties and for being a diuretic, carminative, antispasmodic and a good antioxidant. It is renowned for its high vitamin and mineral content due to its long tap root; the leaves are high in beta carotene and vitamins A, B, B2, B3, C and E, plus the minerals calcium, iron, sodium, phosphorus and magnesium. So, all in all, this is a must-have culinary herb that should be eaten regularly.

Different varieties

French Parsley, Broad-leafed, Flatleaf Parsley
Petroselinum crispum French
This hardy biennial has umbels of small creamy white flowers in the second summer and flat, mid-green toothed leaves that are strongly flavoured.

Italian Parsley
Petroselinum crispum var. *neapolitanum*
This is a hardy biennial with umbels of small creamy white flowers in the second summer and flat, dark green, large toothed leaves that are strongly flavoured.

Hamburg Parsley or Turnip-rooted Parsley
Petroselinum crispum var. *tuberosum*

This is a hardy biennial that is usually grown as an annual with flat umbels of white flowers in summer, green leaves that are similar to French parsley and creamy white roots that have a similar flavour to celeriac. This variety was probably first developed in Holland, since it was once called Dutch parsley. It was introduced into England in the early 18th century, but it was only popular until the early 19th century. The plant is still frequently found in France and Germany in the vegetable markets.

FRIED PARSLEY

This is one of my grandmother's recipes from her handwritten notebook, which I have reproduced here with my comments in brackets. It is interesting that this dish has come right back into fashion as an appetiser. It is a wonderful way to use parsley, especially if you have a glut.

Get everything ready before you pick your parsley as this dish is useless once the parsley has started to wilt. Serve with freshly ground salt. This goes well with pâtés or with aperitifs.

Serves 4

1 large bunch of curly parsley
cooking oil, for deep frying

Unless it is absolutely essential, refrain from washing the parsley. If it is necessary do so, do it some hours beforehand and see that it is perfectly dry before lowering it into the hot fat, otherwise the fat splashes in a violent way and is dangerous.

Pick the sprigs from the main stalks of the parsley. Allow a really large handful of sprigs for 4 people. Set a pan of oil over a high heat. Put the parsley sprigs in a frying basket, and when the oil shows a faint blue haze, plunge it into the fat bath. Do not be deterred by the noise it makes. As soon as the hissing stops, lift out the parsley (it is ready in seconds) which should be bright green. (It should be crisp, bright green, not greasy, nor limp, nor brown.) Once cooked, place on kitchen paper to mop up the oil.

PARSLEY AND HERB SPREAD

The parsley enhances the spinach in this tasty spread which is wonderful served with toasted pitta bread, freshly baked crusty bread or cheese crackers.

Serves 4–6

450 g young spinach leaves
450 g flatleaf parsley leaves, roughly chopped
250 g coriander leaves, roughly chopped
250 g celery leaf, roughly chopped
4 garlic cloves, peeled and halved
50 ml extra virgin olive oil
1 tsp smoked paprika
¼ tsp cayenne pepper
1 tsp ground cumin
1 tbsp lemon juice
salt and freshly ground black pepper

Wash the spinach, parsley, coriander and celery leaf and shake dry, but do not towel dry.

Place all the washed herbs and spinach into a large pan with the garlic. Cover and heat gently until all the greens have sweated down. Drain in a colander and remove the garlic cloves; put them on a plate and squish into a purée using a fork.

When cool enough to handle, squeeze the excess water out of the herbs and spinach. In a medium frying pan, heat 1 tablespoon of the olive oil. Add the mashed garlic, paprika, cayenne and cumin to the pan and stir over a medium heat for 30 seconds or until fragrant. Add the spinach and herbs mixture and cook together, mashing and stirring at the same time until soft and smooth, for about 8 minutes.

Remove from the heat and transfer to a small bowl, add the remaining oil, mix well, and cover. Once cold, put the bowl in the fridge for at least 24 hours.

Just before serving, stir in the lemon juice and check the seasoning, adding extra salt and black pepper if needed. Serve as an appetiser or first course.

This spread will keep for 3 days in the fridge.

SALSA VERDE

Parsley comes into its own when used with salty dishes, and it is excellent when combined with anchovies. This is a useful summer sauce that goes well with so many dishes, particularly fish, boiled ham and new potatoes.

Makes approx. 250 ml

1 large bunch of flatleaf parsley
1 garlic clove, crushed
4 anchovy fillets, chopped
1 tbsp capers, drained and chopped
200 ml olive oil
salt and freshly ground black pepper

Wash and dry the parsley, cut off the bottom 1 cm of the stems but leave the rest. Check the leaves for any spoilt ones and remove.

Place the parsley in a food processor with the garlic, anchovies and capers. Process for a few minutes then, with the motor running slowly, add the oil in a steady stream. Season to taste.

PARSLEY AND LEMON ICE

Here is another interesting recipe from my grandmother's notebook (my notes are in brackets). I would never have thought of using parsley in a pudding, but it has a refreshing green flavour. We would call this sorbet, my grandmother called it ice. I find this a really good summer pudding.

Serves 4

Juice and pared rind of 1 lemon
425 ml water
50 g sugar
2 large handfuls of parsley

Put the lemon rind into a pan with the water and sugar, bring to the boil and infuse for 5 minutes (or until the sugar has melted, stirring with a wooden spoon). Add the lemon juice, strain and cool. (I don't strain it as I like the lemon bits, I simply fish the pared lemon peel out with a slotted spoon.)

Boil the parsley (bring a small pan of water to the boil and add the parsley) for 5–10 minutes (5 minutes is sufficient), then drain and press through a sieve. Add this to the lemon mixture and freeze. (I recommend you thoroughly stir this ice, using a fork, to form a slush. Do this twice during the first 2 hours of freezing; this way it will not be a solid lump when you come to serve it.)

PARSLEY HONEY

This recipe I found fascinating – it is one of my grandmother's recipes which she recommended during the Second World War when honey was difficult to obtain. It makes an interesting form of spread for bread! And, again, it is a unique way of using parsley as the flavour is, strangely, rather like honey, but perhaps that is word association. Great with yoghurt, crème fraîche and fruit.

Makes 2 x 450 g jars

175 g fresh parsley
850 ml water
juice of 1 lemon
450 g sugar

Wash and dry the parsley. Roughly chop, stems included, and put into a pan with the water. Bring to the boil and simmer gently for 30 minutes.

Strain through a jelly bag and measure the resulting juice. Put the juice into a clean pan with the lemon juice and 450 g of sugar for every 570 ml of parsley juice. Stir well over a low heat until the sugar has dissolved, then bring to the boil. Reduce the heat and simmer gently for 30–45 minutes until the mixture is clear and syrupy, very like thin honey.

Pour into warm, sterilised jars (see page 12) and cover and seal while hot.

Excess parsley

Frozen parsley

This is one herb that freezes well and it is an easy way to harvest an excess.

For a good harvest one needs to pick the leaf at its optimum flavour, which is in the first year in late summer and after the plant has been well fed. Pick the leaves as soon as the dew has evaporated, but before the height of the day. If the leaf is harvested late in the day, after it has been in the sun, all the essential oils will have evaporated. Freezing the leaves does destroy some of the beneficial essential oils, but it does not impair the flavour.

Pick the leaves with the stems. Wash, if necessary, dry well, then place in a freezer bag and pop in the freezer.

When you require the parsley, remove the bag from the freezer and crush the bag immediately; do not hesitate or leave the bag for a few minutes, because the parsley will thaw. By crushing the bag when the parsley is still frozen you will break it into small pieces giving you instant easy-to-use chopped parsley.

PURSLANE

(also known as Kulfa, Baql, Pigweed, Horse Money, Pussley)

Portulaca oleracea

This scrummy culinary and medicinal herb can be found growing wild throughout Europe and India. It is, in many countries, considered a pernicious weed. As a child it was one of the plants that my mother taught me to forage for when on holiday in France and Italy.

One of the funniest references I could find for this herb is a mention in Matthew Biggs's *Complete Book of Vegetables*, where I discovered that its name in Malawi translates as 'buttocks of the wife of a chief', obviously referring to its succulent round leaves and juicy stems! The mind boggles.

Description

Purslane is a hardy annual with small, yellow stalk-less flowers in summer which open in the sun and close in the shade. It has thick, fleshy, spoon-shaped mid-green leaves that, to me, taste of fresh mangetout with a hint of salt.

It prefers to grow in a sunny position in a moisture-retentive light soil which was not fed in the previous autumn. It is more attractive and more productive if grown in thick rows or clumps in the garden rather than as an isolated plant. It can be easily grown from seed sown in spring once the soil has warmed. It will adapt to growing in a container but it does not fare as well as when grown in the garden.

History in cooking

Historically this plant has been grown for culinary and medicinal use for over 2,000 years; it was used as an antidote to wasp stings and snake bites. Before the days of vitamin C pills, this herb was valued for its ascorbic acid properties and was used to treat and prevent scurvy.

Harvesting and uses

Leaves:
Pick for use fresh throughout the growing season – from summer until early autumn. Always pick from the top, not the sides, to encourage new growth. Purslane does not dry or freeze well, so preserve it by extracting its juice or pickling it in vinegar. In the Middle East, purslane is an ingredient of a traditional salad called Fattoush.

Flowers:
Pick flowers as they appear from summer until early autumn. The stems and flower buds add a delightful crunch to a mixed salad.

Properties

This is an important culinary herb as it is one of the few vegetable sources of omega-3 essential fatty acids. It also contains vitamins A, B and C and minerals such as magnesium, calcium and potassium.

It has anti-diarrhoeal and antibacterial properties and it is considered an aphrodisiac.

Different varieties

Golden Purslane
Portulaca oleracea var. *aurea*
This variety is a hardy annual. It also has small yellow flowers in summer with large, golden, disc-shaped succulent leaves. Golden purslane is ideal for container growing.

PURSLANE AND FLAGEOLET SALAD

Purslane transforms the texture of this salad as it adds crunch to the soft beans – a brilliant mix.

Serves 4–6

300 g dried flageolet or cannellini beans (or canned)
1 garlic head, cut in half horizontally
1 large lemon, cut in half
2 bay leaves
1 bunch of celery leaf (with stems)
2 handfuls of purslane leaves
5 tbsp olive oil
1 tbsp lemon juice
3 anchovy fillets
2 garlic cloves, finely chopped
1 tbsp finely chopped spearmint, Tashkent, Moroccan or Garden mint
1 tbsp chopped celery leaf
1 tbsp chopped flatleaf parsley

Soak the beans overnight in cold water, if using dried ones, then drain.

Put the beans in a large pan with lots of cold water, the garlic head, lemon, bay and celery leaves and stems, and bring to the boil. Simmer for 30–45 minutes until they are cooked, by which I mean soft with no hardness left. Do not add salt until they are cooked, otherwise you will make the skins very tough. As soon as they are cooked, add a pinch of salt, stir, then drain. (If you are using canned beans, skip this bit.)

Tip into a bowl and, while still warm, add the purslane leaves, the olive oil and lemon juice, anchovies, garlic and the chopped herbs. Toss and leave for 30–40 minutes before serving to allow time for the flavours to infuse.

PURSLANE AND SPINACH SALAD

This is an adapted French recipe. When on a barge on the Canal du Midi I found masses of purslane growing wild. The children and I used to forage for it for our lunch and add it to all forms of salad. This was our favourite recipe, especially when combined with the almonds, which were also abundant in all the local shops.

Serves 3–4

100 g purslane
100 g young spinach leaves
100 g feta
1 tbsp almonds, peeled
3 tbsp olive oil
1 tbsp white wine vinegar or herb vinegar
1 garlic clove, crushed
salt and freshly ground black pepper
a pinch of brown sugar

Wash and dry the spinach leaves and the purslane leaves and remove these from their stems. Mix together in a bowl. Break up the feta and scatter over the leaves.

Toast the almonds under a hot grill, shaking from time to time until they are golden but not dark brown.

Mix together the oil, vinegar, garlic, salt, black pepper and sugar in a jug and whisk until all amalgamated. Pour the dressing over the herbs and cheese, toss and scatter over the almonds, then serve.

PURSLANE, BREAD, TOMATO AND OLIVE SALAD

A hearty rustic salad which is an excellent way to use up any leftover bread. It is even better made with slightly stale bread. The purslane adds crunch and a clean flavour, which is lovely when combined with the tomatoes and bread. Accompany with a chilled glass of white wine.

Serves 4

100 g purslane (the succulent leaves removed from the stems)
500 g ripe tomatoes
salt
1 large red onion, halved and finely sliced
4 tbsp red wine vinegar
500 g stale, 2-day-old, white traditionally baked bread
4 tbsp flatleaf parsley, chopped
1 handful of lettuce or sweet basil leaves, torn
8 tbsp extra virgin olive oil

Wash and dry the purslane.

Cut the tomatoes into small chunks, put them in a colander, sprinkle with a little salt and leave for 10 minutes to allow the juices to be drawn.

Put the onion slices in a small bowl of cold water with a splash of red wine vinegar and a pinch of salt.

Break the bread up into chunks and place in a large bowl with just enough cold water to cover the bread. Set aside for 10 minutes. Drain the bread then, using your hands, squeeze out all the water. (If it is not squeezed well enough you will have a soggy meal.) Crumble the bread into a large serving bowl.

In a small bowl, add the purslane leaves, tomatoes, drained onions, parsley and the lettuce or basil leaves. Mix the oil and the remaining vinegar in a jug and check the seasoning, adding extra if required. Pour the dressing over the salad, toss well and then add to the bread. Mix all the ingredients well and serve.

Excess purslane

This is the only way I know of preserving purslane; it is a French delicacy which can be found in some markets in the south of the country. It is excellent with cold meats and cheese and in sandwiches.

Pickled purslane

1 kg purslane leaves and stems
3 garlic cloves, sliced
10 black peppercorns
1 litre apple cider vinegar

Wash and dry the purslane and cut it into 3-cm pieces. Fill a clean, sterilised (see page 12) glass jar with the purslane, to just below the rim. Choose a jar with a fitting lid that is not metal as this will be corroded by the vinegar. Add the garlic and peppercorns then pour over the vinegar, making sure that the leaves and stems are immersed in the vinegar.

Put in the fridge or a dark cold cupboard and leave for a minimum of 2 weeks before eating. It will keep for 3 months.

ROCK SAMPHIRE

(also known as Sea Fennel)
Crithmum maritimum

The first time I saw this herb growing in profusion was on the island of Gozo, near Malta, where it was often cooked with the local fish. Since then I have managed to happily grow it in containers so that I can use it in my kitchen at home.

A number of times I have read recipes for rock samphire to discover that the chef/cook is actually referring to marsh samphire (*Salicornia europea*), which is sometimes known as Glasswort or Pickleweed. This samphire grows on muddy flats or salt marshes at, or close, to standing water. The scale-like leaves of this plant are bright green in spring and lie flat on the succulent stems. Rock samphire, on the other hand, is related to fennel and grows, as its common name suggests, in the rocks.

Having cleared that up I must admit to being a fan of both, but I am more excited by rock samphire as it can be grown away from the sea.

Description

This hardy perennial has flat clusters of tiny pale yellow flowers in summer and aromatic, succulent, sea grey-green triangular leaves with long, rounded, linear lance-shaped segments which grow in small groups along the branch.

As this is commonly a seaside plant that grows literally in the crevices between rocks, it is essential, when growing it in a garden, to prepare the site well prior to planting. Make sure the soil is well drained and add extra grit if necessary. Plant rock samphire in a sunny position and protect from cold winds. In winter, cover the crown with straw, not mulch or compost which would cause it to rot. This herb can be raised from fresh seed sown under protection in the autumn.

History in cooking

Rock samphire was at one time cultivated in English gardens for its seed pods and sold in London, where it was called 'Crest Marine'. In John Gerard's (the 16th-century herbalist) time it was considered a very good condiment. He wrote in 1597:

'The leaves kept in pickle and eaten in sallads with oile and vinegar is a pleasant sauce for meat, wholesome for the stoppings of the liver, milt and kidneys. It is the pleasantest sauce, most familiar and best agreeing with man's body.'

Harvesting and uses

Leaves:

The best time for harvesting the leaves is in late spring and early summer before the plant flowers. They can be eaten fresh or cooked as a vegetable. Prior to cooking, remove any leaves that have begun to turn slimy and any hard parts of the stalk and soak in salt water for an hour. The leaves have an aromatic salty flavour which is delicious in salads or when cooked in butter. The leaves can also be used to make sauces and aromatic pickles.

Flowers:
The flowers can be picked throughout the summer, and the buds taste similar to fennel flowers but with slightly less anise. Add the flowers to salads, fish dishes or sauces.

Properties

This herb is high in vitamin C; it also has digestive and purgative properties. It is being used in current research to treat obesity and there are now a number of herbal products available using rock samphire which claim success.

Different varieties

None.

SHRIMP AND ROCK SAMPHIRE RISOTTO

Using rock samphire in this recipe adds not only the complementary aromatic, anise and salt flavours, but also texture.

Serves 4

750 g unpeeled, cooked pink shrimps or North Atlantic prawns
100 g rock samphire
75 g unsalted butter
½ onion, chopped
1 litre fish stock
1 blade of mace
2 shallots, finely chopped
1 garlic clove, finely chopped
350 g risotto rice
120 ml white wine
25 g Parmesan, freshly grated
salt and freshly ground black pepper

Peel the shrimps and set them aside, reserving the shells. Wash and clean the rock samphire, removing any hard woody bits or any soft slimy bits. Put the samphire into a bowl, cover with cold salted water and leave for 1 hour.

Melt 25 g of the butter in a large pan, add the onion and fry for 5 minutes, until soft and lightly browned. Add the shrimp shells and fry for 3–4 minutes, then add the stock and mace and bring to the boil. Cover and simmer for 20 minutes.

Pass the stock through a sieve into a clean pan, pressing out as much liquid as you can with the back of a ladle. Bring back to a simmer and keep hot over a low heat.

Melt the rest of the butter in a large pan and add the shallots and garlic and cook gently for a couple of minutes. Add the rice and stir until all the grains are coated in the butter. Pour in the wine and simmer, stirring constantly, until it has all been absorbed, then add a ladleful of the hot stock and stir until it has all been taken up before adding another. Continue like this for about 20 minutes, stirring constantly, until all the stock has been used and the rice is tender but is still a little al dente.

Before the risotto is ready, bring a large pan of water to the boil, drain the soaking samphire and wash under cold water. Add to the pan, simmer for 8 minutes until just tender, then drain well. Stir the shrimps, Parmesan and some seasoning into the risotto. Heat for 1 minute, then stir in all but a handful of the samphire.

Divide the risotto among 4 warmed bowls and serve, garnished with the rest of the samphire.

ROCK SAMPHIRE AND MUSSEL SALAD

Mussels equals summer holidays in Devon, where I was taught by my mother to collect and cook them; and in turn I taught my children the sheer delight of eating them. This they did with gusto one summer holiday in Brittany when they were only 7 and 8, much to the astonishment of the proprietor of the restaurant.

This recipe includes the sea from rock to shore; it is flavoursome and full of texture from the softness of the mussel to the crunch of the rock samphire. Serve it on a bed of crisp green lettuce with some fresh crusty white bread.

Serves 3–4 (depending on how greedy you are)

250 ml white wine
250 ml water
3 garlic cloves, finely crushed
1 small onion or shallot, finely sliced
1 bay leaf
900 g mussels, scrubbed and de-bearded
225 g rock samphire, washed, picked over, all tough old stems and slimy leaves removed, then soaked in cold salted water for 1 hour prior to use
60 ml olive oil
2 tbsp white wine vinegar
1 tsp French tarragon, finely chopped
salt and freshly ground black pepper

Combine the wine, water, garlic, onion and bay leaf in a large pan, bring to the boil, reduce to a simmer, then cover and cook for a few minutes. Add the mussels, increase the heat and cook for 4 minutes. Remove all the open mussels and discard any that have not opened. Strain the cooking liquid and return it to the pan. Remove the mussel meat from the shells and set aside.

Drain the soaking rock samphire and rinse it under cold water. Dry and lightly chop it, then add to the reserved mussel cooking liquid. Bring to the boil, reduce the heat and simmer for 4–7 minutes until the rock samphire is tender. Drain and set aside.

Whisk together the oil, vinegar and tarragon and season with salt and black pepper to taste. Mix together the rock samphire with the mussels, add some of the vinaigrette, toss and serve.

ROCK SAMPHIRE AND LAMB STEAKS

This is a great combination; the crunchy, salty, slightly anise flavours of the samphire work well with the sweetness of spring lamb.

Serves 4

2 tbsp olive oil
4 x 225 g lamb rump steaks
110 g unsalted butter
200 g young rock samphire leaves, washed and thoroughly checked, all tough old stems or any soft, slimy leaves removed
175 g young broad beans
salt and freshly ground black pepper
1 shallot or small onion, finely diced
1 garlic clove, finely chopped
3 tbsp flatleaf parsley, roughly chopped
2 tbsp balsamic vinegar
2 tbsp stock (preferably made from lamb bones)

Pre-heat the oven to 200°C/400°F/gas mark 6.

Heat an ovenproof casserole dish or frying pan until hot, add the olive oil and the lamb steaks and cook for 2–3 minutes on each side. Transfer the casserole dish or pan to the oven and cook for 12–15 minutes, uncovered, or for another 20 minutes if you prefer your meat well done. Remove from the oven and place the lamb on a plate to rest. Reserve the casserole dish or pan and its juices for later.

Meanwhile, heat a clean frying pan or pan that has a tight-fitting lid and add 25 g of the butter and the samphire leaves and gently fry, covered, for 4–7 minutes until the leaves become tender. Add the broad beans and stir well, then gently cook for a further 2–3 minutes. Check the seasoning and remove from the heat. Mix together the shallot, garlic and parsley in bowl and set aside until ready to serve.

Using the casserole dish or frying pan that the meat was cooked in, drain off any meat juices into a clean bowl and reserve. Place the dish or pan over a medium heat and add the balsamic vinegar. Bring to the boil and stir, scraping up the bits at the bottom. Add the stock and simmer for a further minute. Add the remaining butter and stir gently until melted and combined. Add the reserved meat juices and bring to a simmer. Check the seasoning, and add salt and black pepper if needed.

To serve, slice the lamb thickly and arrange on 4 serving plates. Place the rock samphire around the sliced lamb, then pour the sauce over the lamb. Finally, scatter over the parsley mixture.

Excess rock samphire

Pickled rock samphire

Raw rock samphire has a unique, salty aromatic flavour which, when cooked and pickled, changes into a more fennel-like flavour that is great with salads, cheese and cold meats.

Makes approx. 3 x 450 g jars

enough young rock samphire leaves to fill a standard colander
750 ml white wine vinegar
250 ml water

1 tsp salt
2 bay leaves
1 tsp ground mace
5 black peppercorns

Check through the rock samphire leaves, removing any hard main stems or any mangy soft pieces. Wash the leaves, then place in a large bowl of salted water and leave to soak for 1 hour or more.

Wash thoroughly in a colander to remove the salt. Place in a large pan with enough cold water to cover the leaves, bring to the boil and cook for 4–7 minutes. Drain.

In a separate pan, add the vinegar, water, salt, bay leaves and spices, bring to the boil, reduce the heat and simmer for 5 minutes. Strain into a jug, set aside and allow to cool.

Put the cooled rock samphire into sterilised wide-necked jars (see page 12), leaving a gap at the top and pour over the vinegar until it covers the leaves. Leave a small gap at the top of the jar.

Seal with a non-metallic lid and store for 4–5 months before using. Will keep for a minimum of 2 years if not opened. Once the jar is opened, keep in the fridge and use within a month.

ROCKET

(also known as Wild Rocket, Ruccola, Rucola, Rocquette)
Diplotaxis muralis

I love rocket. It is so versatile as it goes well with meat, fish and vegetables, and therefore I must have it in my garden. Well over a decade ago I had a large crop of salad rocket (see page 249) growing on the herb farm for a garden centre, but it ran to flower so I could not sell it. While I stood next to it, pondering what to do, I started eating the flowers. They were wonderful, so wonderful that they became the inspiration for my book *Good Enough to Eat*, which was all about growing and eating flowers.

Description

Wild rocket is a perennial herb that is often grown as an annual, especially in cold damp climates where it hates the winter. It has yellow, four-petalled flowers in summer with green, deeply divided aromatic leaves which form a rosette as the plant matures. It can be easily raised from seed sown in late spring, either direct into a prepared site in the garden when the air temperature at night does not fall below 7°C, or alternatively into a large deep container (as it has a long tap root) filled with a soil-based potting compost. When growing in the garden, for the ideal crop, plant it in light shade into a well-fed soil which does not dry out in summer.

History in cooking

For hundreds of years rocket has been collected in the wild and sold in markets in Southern France, Italy and Egypt. Both the leaves and seeds of rocket were used as flavouring by the Romans. In England the Elizabethans were extremely partial to it when used in salads.

Harvesting and uses

Leaves:
Pick leaves from early spring until early winter. The best culinary flavoured leaves are those that have reached full size but have not yet turned dark green – from spring to early summer and again in autumn. Summer leaves tend to be tough and bitter, especially if the weather is very hot. The peppery leaves are lovely when added to salads and are a common ingredient in the salad leaf mixtures that can be bought in Italian markets. Dress with salt, oil and vinegar, or simply serve on their own with a little fresh Parmesan.

Flowers:
These can be picked in summer as they appear. The whole flower is edible, although any excessive green should be removed. The swelling behind the flower, where the seeds are formed, adds the crunch when eating them, so you can use just petals, whole flowers, or whole flowers plus crunch depending on your taste or the recipe.

Both wild and salad rocket stimulate the appetite and digestion.

Properties   The leaves are high in sulphur, which is good for healthy skin, hair and nails. They also contain vitamins A, B, C and E.

Different varieties   ### Salad Rocket
Eruca vesicaria
This is a half-hardy annual with cream coloured flowers which, as they mature, become pale with purple veins. The leaves are oval and lance-shaped with a peppery/nutty flavour.

Sweet Rocket
Hesperis matronalis
This is a short-lived perennial herb with pink, white, purple or mauve sweetly scented flowers all summer. The leaves are lance-shaped, green and slightly hairy. This rocket can be eaten – the flowers are delightful in all forms of salad – however the leaves are only good for emergencies when one runs out of both salad or wild rocket. But then, if I am honest, there is no comparison, so change your recipe.

WILD ROCKET AND OMELETTE ARNOLD BENNETT

My grandmother, in her cookbook *Lovely Food*, credits this recipe to the Savoy Grill where this omelette, it is said, was created for the author Arnold Bennett. I, on the other hand, credit it to the Sloane Club, which to me is the most wonderful quintessential English club, where Mac and I stay during the RHS Chelsea Flower Show. It is within staggering distance of the show, and as we reappear each evening from building our display, exhausted, muddy, wearing our steel-toe capped boots and fluorescent dayglo safety jackets, no one bats an eyelid. To be able to come down to a bar which feels exactly like a comfy country sitting room, order a long cold drink and wild rocket and omelette Arnold Bennett with pommes frites (no, they don't serve chips), is sheer heaven.

The strong peppery taste of the wild rocket truly balances the flavours of the omelette and the smoked haddock.

Serves 2

wild rocket leaves, to serve
2 rounded tbsp crème fraîche
225 g smoked haddock, skin and bones removed and cut into 1-cm chunks
5 large eggs
½ level tsp cornflour
salt and freshly ground black pepper
10 g unsalted butter
1 tsp olive oil
50 g Gruyère, grated

Pour the crème fraîche into a medium pan and bring it to a simmer over a low heat, then add the smoked haddock and gently poach it for about 5 minutes.

Next, start making the sauce; this is what makes this dish, so don't skimp. Separate one egg and place the yolk into a small bowl and the white into another. Whisk the yolk with the cornflour.

When the fish is cooked, use a slotted spoon to lift it out of the pan and place it in a sieve over the pan. Using a wooden spoon, gently press the fish, allowing the juice to drip back into the pan. Place the fish on a plate. Bring the fish liquid back to simmering, not boiling, then pour it over the egg yolk and cornflour, whisking all the time. Return to the heat and simmer until the sauce thickens this should take only a few minutes.

Remove from the heat and add the cooked haddock. Check the seasoning and add black pepper and maybe salt, depending on the saltiness of the fish.

In a bowl, whisk the egg white to the soft peak stage and fold it into the haddock. Set aside while you make the omelette, for which you will need a 20-cm frying pan. However, before you start the omelette, turn the grill onto its highest setting.

In another bowl, beat the remaining eggs and season with salt and black pepper. Melt the butter and oil in the frying pan and, when hot, add the eggs and cook, drawing the sides slowly into the middle and tipping the pan to ensure all the juices are becoming cooked but the top is still soft. Add the haddock mixture, spreading it over the surface of the omelette, sprinkle with the Gruyère and place the omelette in the pan under the grill. Cook for 2–3 minutes until it becomes puffy and golden brown.

Remove from the grill and let it stand. Cut it in half and carefully slide each onto individual plates. Serve with the wild rocket leaves scattered on the top of the omelette.

FLORENTINE ROCKET AND FILLET OF BEEF

Hannah, my daughter, and I went on holiday to Florence where we ate some beautiful meals and this was one of them; so simple and so nourishing, so flavoursome and so attractive. Again, it is the peppery flavour of the rocket which is essential to this dish.

Serves 4

400 g beef fillet, left in one piece and trimmed
½ tbsp olive oil
sea salt and freshly ground black pepper
1 tbsp balsamic vinegar
4 tbsp extra virgin olive oil
60 g Parmesan
100 g salad or wild rocket, washed and roughly chopped

Pre-heat a ridged griddle pan, a grill or a barbecue.

Rub the beef with the ½ tablespoon of olive oil, season it, then cook on the heated griddle or under the grill for about 4–5 minutes for rare, turning it every so often so that it cooks evenly. If you prefer your meat medium or well done, cook for a further 3–5 minutes, depending on your taste and the thickness of the beef. Once cooked, place on a plate to cool. If there are any juices in the pan or grill pan, keep them for later.

Make the dressing by whisking together the balsamic vinegar and olive oil with any juices from the beef. Season with salt and black pepper to taste. With a potato peeler, shave slices of Parmesan as thinly as possible onto a plate. Slice the beef into ½–1-cm slices, dress the rocket leaves and arrange on a large plate, or individual serving plates, and arrange slices of beef on top. Scatter the Parmesan shavings on top and eat immediately.

ROCKET PASTA SALAD

A simple cold salad that is so useful, especially when one has guests who appear and need feeding. The salad rocket has a gentler flavour compared to its cousin, wild rocket. In fact, you could call it more nutty than peppery, but that is a matter of taste. What I do know is that this dish works because of the salad rocket.

Serves 4

320 g pasta (any of the following: fiorelli, cocciolette, farfalle or francesine)
3 garlic cloves, whole and peeled
500 g red cherry tomatoes
½ cucumber
1 tbsp pitted black olives
2 tbsp fresh chives
4 tbsp salad rocket leaves
sea salt and freshly ground black pepper
3 tbsp extra virgin olive oil
1 tbsp balsamic vinegar

Bring a large pan of salted water to the boil, add the pasta and garlic, bring back to the boil, then simmer until cooked and al dente. (This could be 5 minutes for fresh or 7–10 minutes for dried pasta.)

Drain in a colander and fish out the garlic, keeping it to one side for the dressing. While the pasta is still in the colander, hold it under cold running water tap to stop it sticking and to allow to cool down. Drain well then put the pasta in a large serving bowl.

Cut the tomatoes, cucumber and black olives into small pieces that are about the size of the pasta, then toss with the pasta. Using scissors, snip the chives over the pasta, roughly chop the rocket and fold it into the pasta.

Using a fork, mash the cooked garlic on a chopping board with a little salt. Make the dressing by combining the oil and vinegar and whisking well. Add the mashed garlic, whisk again, add salt and black pepper to taste, then pour over the salad. Toss well and serve.

Excess rocket

It is so easy to have a sudden glut of rocket leaves that you need to use up; you want to pick them to keep the plants productive but you do not want yet another rocket salad, so here is an easy and delicious solution.

Rocket pesto

This can be used to stir through cooked pasta, as a dip or added to potato salad.

Makes enough for a small jar

250 g wild or salad rocket leaves, washed, dried and roughly chopped
275 ml extra virgin olive oil
1 tbsp lemon juice
1 tsp lemon zest
30 g pine nuts
2 garlic cloves
salt
60 g Parmesan, grated

Blend the rocket leaves, olive oil, lemon juice and zest, pine nuts, garlic and salt until smooth. This can be done most easily in a food processor or blender, stopping a couple of times to push the ingredients down the sides of the bowl. Alternatively, you can use a large pestle and mortar.

When evenly blended, scrape into a bowl and stir in the grated Parmesan, check the seasoning and add extra to taste if needed. Cover the bowl and put into the fridge. Alternatively, if storing for some time, put into a screw-top jar and put a layer of olive oil on the top before sealing. This will then keep for 4–6 weeks in the fridge as long as the olive oil layer is maintained. You may need to top it up if you keep dipping into the jar.

ROSEMARY

(also known as Rosmarino, Rosmarin)
Rosmarinus officinalis

No herb garden should be without this plant; it is one of the most versatile and useful herbs in the kitchen, in the home and medicinally. It is associated with love, friendship and remembrance. Both my children took a large rosemary plant with them when they went off to university, to cook with and to drink as a tea – which, it is said, not only revives the memory but allegedly is also one of the best cures for a hangover!

Description

Rosemary is a hardy evergreen, so the leaves are available all year round, and has attractive, small pale blue flowers in spring and again in late summer. It has short needle-shaped, highly aromatic dark green leaves.

The most reliable way to grow this herb is from cuttings taken in summer from the new non-flowering growth. You can raise plants from seed, however they have a nasty knack of keeling over once they reach their first birthday. Rosemary prefers to be planted in a well-drained soil in a sunny position, however I have found, with patience, that it will adapt to growing in a heavy soil as long as it is in full sun. All forms of rosemary will happily adapt to being grown in a container in a soil-based potting compost.

History in cooking

This herb has been used for hundreds of years in the kitchen, as a preservative and medicinally. I love the story that in medieval times rosemary was used at banquets as an edible table decoration; large branches were dipped in egg white, sprinkled with grated tree resin to make it glisten, then placed on the table set in bread or lard.

Harvesting and uses

Leaves:

This is a useful herb because it can be picked all year round. The flavour is versatile and goes well with many forms of food, from roast vegetables, meat, soups, fish and eggs to all forms of bread.

Flowers:

Harvest the small flowers as they appear from spring to late summer. They taste of sweet rosemary and are lovely added to salads and scattered over cooked vegetables.

Properties

Rosemary is excellent for treating stomach cramps and flatulence. When used in cooking it helps to stimulate the appetite and the secretion of gastric juices. The leaves have antioxidant and antibacterial properties.

All forms of rosemary bearing the name *Rosmarinus officinalis* are edible. They can vary in flavour from the standard form, to very eucalyptus or to very pine. As there are so many different rosemaries available, I have limited the following list to my favourite culinary ones.

Different varieties

White Rosemary
Rosmarinus officinalis var. *albiflorus*
This is the very hardy form of rosemary that adapted to my heavy soil to produce a good round flavour.

Green Ginger Rosemary
Rosmarinus officinalis 'Green Ginger'
This variety is really worth looking for; the leaves have a rosemary ginger flavour, great with meat and vegetables.

Tuscan Rosemary
Rosmarinus officinalis 'Tuscan Blue'
This variety has a very straight habit, so the stems make ideal barbecue skewers.

Prostrate Rosemary
Rosmarinus officinalis Prostratus Group
This variety has a trailing habit, which is ideal for growing over walls or over the side of a container.

MEDITERRANEAN TOMATO AND ROSEMARY SOUP

My mother was a great soup maker and this is one of her recipes. Mum always used a pinch of sugar with tomatoes, even when making salads or a dressing to go over tomatoes, because she said it brought out their flavour. This is particularly true if you are using supermarket rather than home-grown tomatoes.

What transforms this soup from being run of the mill to good is the use of the rosemary; it truly brings out the flavours of the tomatoes. Serve with some fresh crusty white bread.

Serves 4

600 ml vegetable or chicken stock
50 g unsalted butter
1 tbsp olive oil
1 large onion, finely sliced
1 large red pepper seeds removed and finely sliced
1 garlic clove, finely chopped
675 g tomatoes, skinned and chopped
2 rosemary sprigs (each 3 cm long)
salt and freshly ground black pepper
a pinch of soft brown sugar
1 tbsp orange juice

Gently heat the stock in a pan over a medium heat.

In another large pan, melt the butter with the olive oil and gently sweat the onion and red pepper until soft (try not to colour it). Add the garlic, stir and cook for a minute. Add the chopped tomatoes, stir for a few minutes, then pour over the heated stock and add the rosemary sprigs. Simmer for 20 minutes, add the salt and black pepper to taste and, as my mother always said, a pinch of soft brown sugar.

Remove the rosemary sprigs – it does not matter if some of the leaves fall off. Either using a hand blender or a food processor, whiz for a few seconds. If you are being a purist you can sieve the soup over a large bowl so that it is perfectly smooth.

Return to the pan, add the orange juice and check the seasoning. Gently re-heat but do not allow it to boil. Pour into serving bowls.

ROSEMARY AND WINTER VEGETABLES

This is a most satisfying and comforting winter meal, which warms the cockles of one's heart. Rosemary infuses the vegetables and fills the kitchen with an appetising aroma. Serve with jacket potatoes and broccoli.

Serves 6–8

225 g dried red kidney beans or
400 g can, drained
2 tbsp light olive oil or sunflower oil
1 large onion, finely chopped
2 small turnips, sliced
2–3 parsnips
(depending on size), sliced
2–3 carrots
(depending on size), sliced
110 g button mushrooms, cut in half
1 tbsp wholewheat flour
425 ml hot vegetable stock
400 g can Italian tomatoes
2 tbsp parsley, roughly chopped
2 tbsp celery leaf, roughly chopped
1 tbsp rosemary leaves, removed
from the stem and finely chopped
salt and freshly ground
black pepper

Place the dried kidney beans in a large bowl and cover with boiling water, making sure you give an extra 2.5 cm of water so the beans are submerged. Leave for an hour to soak. Tip into a colander, rinse under cold water and place in a large pan. Cover with water (plus an extra 2.5 cm) and 1 tablespoon of oil to stop it boiling over. Bring to the boil and cook for 10 minutes, then simmer, covered, for 45–60 minutes or until the beans are tender. Alternatively, which is my preferred method, place the beans in a pressure cooker, add enough water to cover, with an extra 2.5 cm, bring to high (15 lb) pressure and cook for 8–10 minutes. (I do advise following your pressure cooker's instructions as they can vary.) Of course, if you are using canned beans, miss all this out!

Pre-heat the oven to 170°C/325°F/gas mark 3. Heat the oil in a large casserole dish, add the onion and cook for 5 minutes then add the sliced vegetables. Toss them in the oil so they are well covered, then add the mushrooms and stir well. Reduce the heat to low, stir in the flour and add the stock, a little at a time, stirring well. Once all the stock has been added, increase the heat to simmering point and cook for 2–3 minutes.

Tip in the tomatoes, cooked and drained kidney beans, the parsley, celery leaf and the chopped rosemary leaves, and cover and cook in the oven for 1½ hours.

ROSEMARY AND LAMB HOTCH POTCH

Rosemary is renowned for use with lamb; it is not only the flavour which suits the meat so well, it is also the fact that it helps one digest fatty meat. This warming lovely dish is equally delicious cold, in the unlikely event you might have some leftovers. Serve with some mashed potato.

Serves 4

6 tbsp olive oil
1 large onion, sliced
2 garlic cloves, finely chopped
8 lamb cutlets
2 carrots, diced
4 baby turnips, diced
2 bay leaves
3 rosemary sprigs
(approx 10 cm in length)
900 ml warm vegetable stock
salt and freshly ground
black pepper
500 g spinach, well washed and
torn into large bits

Pre-heat the oven to 170°C/325°F/gas mark 3.

Heat the oil in a frying pan, add the onions and gently cook until they are translucent. Add the garlic and cook for a few minutes. Remove from the frying pan. Add the cutlets and gently sauté on both sides to seal the meat.

Place the onion and sealed cutlets in a large casserole dish; add the prepared vegetables, bay leaves, rosemary sprigs and warm stock and season to taste. Place on the hob and bring gently to the boil.

Cover and place in the oven for 2 hours. Check the stock level occasionally; if it is beginning to look dry, add a little extra water. Twenty minutes before the end of the cooking time, take the casserole out of the oven, remove the bay leaves and the rosemary sprigs and add the torn spinach. Stir well, making sure that the spinach leaves are well covered with stock.

Return the casserole to the oven and cook for a further 20 minutes.

ROSEMARY DELUXE ROASTED POTATOES

These are known as Mum's posh chips, and are always very popular. I never seem to make enough of them.

Serves 4 after a day's gardening, or
6 for a dinner party

1 kg potatoes, washed
but not peeled
2 tsp sea salt
1 tbsp rosemary leaves, removed
from the stem and finely chopped
olive oil

Pre-heat the oven to 200°C/400°F/gas mark 6.

Cook the potatoes in a large pan of salted boiling water for about 12 minutes, or until your knife slides easily through them. Drain and leave for 5 minutes. Once cool enough to handle, slice the potatoes into large chips.

Put 1 teaspoon of sea salt into a pestle and mortar, add the chopped rosemary leaves and crush them together. (This will infuse the salt with the oil from the leaves.) Add the second teaspoon of salt and crush to mix together but not to make it fine.

Put a small amount of olive oil into a roasting tin and add the potatoes, toss well, add the salt and rosemary, toss again, add 2 more tablespoons of olive oil and place in the oven. Roast for 40–50 minutes until crisp and golden.

ROSEMARY BREAD

Until recently I have been very sniffy about bread machines. I have now used one and I am hooked. They are wonderful when you are running to stand still. This bread can be made by hand or in a machine, and it is lovely with soups or salads. The flavour of the rosemary leaves are gently infuses throughout the bread, so do not be tempted to use more than the teaspoon, as it would be overpowering. If you are using a bread machine, follow the manufacturer's instructions. This is a hand-made recipe, but I know that the ingredients happily adapt to being made in a machine.

Makes 1 large loaf, 2 small loaves or 6 bread rolls

25 g fresh yeast
a pinch of sugar
310 ml warm water
500 g white bread flour, plus extra for dusting
1 tsp rosemary leaves, stripped from the stems
2 tsp salt
60 ml olive oil

Pre-heat the oven to 200°C/400°F/gas mark 6.

Put the yeast in a bowl with the sugar, stir in the warm water and leave to activate.

Put the flour into a large wide bowl or onto your work surface. Make a well in the middle of the flour, add the yeast and most of the rosemary leaves, plus the salt and most of the olive oil. Mix well, then knead the dough for about 10 minutes until it is smooth, elastic and makes a compact ball.

Put the dough into a bowl, cover with a damp tea towel, and leave to rise in a warm place for approximately 1½ hours or until it has doubled in size.

Lightly dust the work surface with flour. Divide the dough in half, shape into ovals or rounds or small individual balls. Sprinkle the tops with the remaining rosemary and drizzle with the remaining oil. Dust a baking sheet with flour and place the loaves on it, leaving a space between each one for spreading. Cover loosely with a tea towel and leave in a warm place for a further 30 minutes to an hour until the loaves have risen.

Put into the oven and bake for about 35 minutes until the top is golden. Remove once cooked and place on a wire rack to cool before serving.

Once cold this bread can be placed in a freezer bag and frozen.

ROSEMARY, GARLIC AND LEMON MARINADE

To me, this sums up the Mediterranean. When you smell the food cooking that has been infused in this marinade you will be transported to the warmth of the sun, the clicking of the cicada, and the scent of the pine trees.

Makes enough for a joint of meat, a large fish or whole chicken

2 tbsp rosemary leaves, pounded in a pestle and mortar
6 garlic cloves, peeled and crushed
10 tbsp olive oil
zest and juice of 3 lemons
salt and freshly ground black pepper

Mix together all the ingredients in a large bowl, cover, and leave to infuse for 1 hour while you prepare your chosen meat or fish.

Rub the marinade into the meat or pour it over a fish that has had slices cut into the flesh. Cover and set aside for 1–3 hours; the longer the better for meat as the lemon will act as a tenderiser. Cook your marinated fish or meat accordingly.

Excess rosemary

Rosemary oil

I know that rosemary is an evergreen and that it is available all year round, but occasionally it is great to have oil infused with rosemary for making bread, or for using in stir-fries.

For more information about preserving and the risks of using herbs in oils, see page 36.

Makes 250 ml

3 good handfuls of rosemary leaves
250 ml light olive oil or sunflower oil
2 tsp lemon juice

Wash the leaves and dry on kitchen paper. Finely chop the leaves (this can be done in a food processor), add the oil and the lemon juice and mix well. Pour into a container with a sealing lid, and pop into the fridge. Use within 5 days; shake well before use as the lemon juice will separate.

Alternatively, after 2 days strain the oil through an unbleached coffee filter paper, pour into a clean dry container with a sealing lid and keep in the fridge. Use within 3 days; shake well before use.

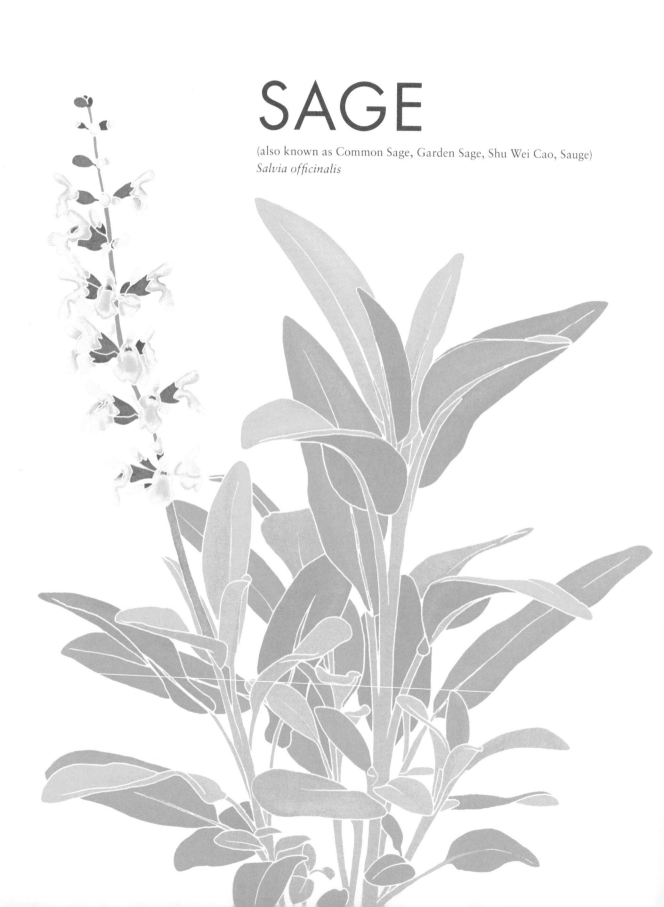

SAGE

(also known as Common Sage, Garden Sage, Shu Wei Cao, Sauge)
Salvia officinalis

Sage is one of those herbs that is so well known you think you can imagine the flavour. However, until you have had fresh pasta tossed in sage butter (see page 269), you have not known its true wonderful taste. It is also an archetypal herb for the cottage garden, especially when it is in full flower, when it becomes a magnet for bees and butterflies.

Description

Sage is a hardy evergreen herb with very attractive mauve–blue flowers in summer. The oval, grey-green leaves are textured and highly aromatic when crushed. Although predominately a Mediterranean plant, it is sufficiently hardy to withstand any ordinary winter outside without protection, as long as the site is warm, dry, well drained and the soil is not acid. The flavour of the leaf is more intense when grown in full sun in a free-draining, low-nutrient soil.

Sage can be grown from seed or from cuttings taken in late spring from non-flowering shoots. It does adapt to being grown in containers, but I do advise using a loam-based potting compost as it does not thrive for more than a few months in peat.

History in cooking

The generic name 'salvia' comes from the Latin 'salvere', which means to save, cure or to be in good health, which certainly reflects its historical reputation. Traditionally, before fridges were invented, sage was combined with salt and used to preserve meat, and before it became a culinary delight, in the Middle Ages, it was dried, powdered and scattered over food in a similar way to how we use pepper today.

Harvesting and uses

Leaves:
Pick fresh leaves from this evergreen herb throughout the year. In spring (before the plant flowers) the leaves have a mild warm flavour; after flowering the leaves have a stronger, tannic flavour.

Flowers:
Harvest flowers as they appear throughout the summer. The flavour of the flowers is similar to that of the leaves with a slight hint of sweetness, which makes them an ideal accompaniment for rice, meat, duck and stir-fry dishes where one wants extra zing.

Properties

Sage is a digestive, antispasmodic and carminative herb and it also eases flatulence and is a useful antioxidant. A tea made from 3–4 leaves can be used to alleviate upset stomachs and diarrhoea.

Different varieties

There are many different sages available so I have simply identified my favourites. If you want a quick guide as to whether or not your sage is edible, the most reliable check is to look at the name: if it mentions 'officinalis' you can be sure that the variety is safe to eat. Even so, there are some 'non officinalis' sages that are safe, such as the one identified below.

Narrow-leaved Sage, Spanish Sage
Salvia lavandulifolia
This hardy perennial evergreen has attractive blue flowers in summer. The small, narrow, oval, textured and highly aromatic leaves have an excellent and very strong culinary flavour. In my opinion this is the best culinary sage.

Purple Sage, Red Sage
Salvia officinalis Purpurascens Group
This is a hardy evergreen perennial that bears mauve–blue flowers in summer. The aromatic, oval, purple/red/grey textured leaves have a milder flavour than common or narrow-leaved sage and are good with vegetable dishes, such as stuffed peppers and courgettes.

Greek Sage
Salvia officinalis 'Greek'
This variety is a hardy evergreen perennial with very attractive pale mauve–blue flowers in summer. The aromatic, oval, grey textured leaves have a unique extra lobe at the base. When grown in full sun this sage has a strong flavour, which goes well with meat and tomato dishes.

CRISPY SAGE, APPLE AND WALNUT SALAD

This is an old family recipe, the origin of which I am unsure. What I am certain about is that the combination of sage, apple, walnut and lettuce has everything a salad should have.

Serves 2

100 g walnuts, coarsely chopped
5 sage leaves, torn into small pieces
1 Cox's apple, cored, cut into small slices
3 tbsp walnut or olive oil
1½ tsp white wine vinegar
1 sage leaf, finely chopped
salt and freshly ground black pepper
1 shallot, finely minced
a good mix of lettuce leaves

Place a small non-stick frying pan over a low heat and toast the walnuts, shaking the pan often. After the first 5 minutes, add the torn sage leaves and apple slices and keep shaking the pan gently, so that nothing sticks, until the walnuts and sage become gently cooked. Tip out into a bowl and set aside.

In a large bowl whisk together the oil, vinegar, finely chopped sage and enough salt and black pepper to taste. Once amalgamated, add the shallot and mix well.

Tear the lettuce leaves into bite-sized pieces and add them to the bowl. Using a spoon, gently toss to coat the lettuce well with the dressing. Arrange the salad on a plate and sprinkle with the toasted sage, apple slices and walnuts.

SAGE ROTIS

These small unleavened bread rolls are quick to make and extremely useful. They are ideal with soups or for filling with salad and popping into a lunch box. The sage subtly infuses the bread and is not overpowering.

Makes 6

100 g strong brown or wholemeal flour, plus extra for dusting
a small pinch of salt
2 tsp finely chopped sage leaves (narrow-leafed sage has the best flavour but either purple or common sage can be used)
1 tsp sunflower oil
60 ml warm water
unsalted butter

Sift the flour and salt into a large bowl and add the sage. Make a well in the middle of the flour, add the oil, then the warm water and, using your hands, blend into a pliable dough. Remove from the bowl and knead, on a floured work surface, for about 2 minutes or preferably 5 minutes; the more you knead the dough the softer the rotis.

Divide the dough into 6 portions and roll into balls. Dust the work surface with plenty of flour and roll out the dough into flat discs of 10-cm diameter.

Heat a griddle or a frying pan. Cook the discs on a high heat until the surface becomes bubbly. Turn over and press the edges down with a fish slice to cook evenly. As soon as brown spots appear, the roti is done.

Remove the roti from the pan and smear with butter. Keep warm by enclosing in a tea towel or foil. Cook all the rotis in the same way. Serve warm or reheat under a hot grill, taking care not to burn them.

LAMB AND SAGE STEW

The aroma of this warming winter dish as it permeates the house brings the family to the table without any extra shouting that lunch is on the table. Sage adds an earthy flavour to lamb and it is particularly good in this recipe – while also stopping me continually using rosemary, which in winter is my herb of choice. Serve with mashed potatoes and purple sprouting broccoli.

Serves 4

2 tbsp olive oil
8 meaty lamb chops
(about 1.3 kg in total)
2 sage sprigs, leaves removed from the stems and chopped
3 garlic cloves, finely chopped
salt and freshly ground black pepper
2 tsp plain flour
120 ml white wine vinegar
120 ml water
4 salted anchovy fillets

Heat the olive oil in a large casserole dish over a medium–high heat When hot, add the lamb chops and brown them all over.

Add the sage, garlic, salt and black pepper. Stir to release the flavours and coat everything in the oil. Sprinkle the flour over the meat, stir well then continue to cook over a medium heat, stirring from time to time until the meat is quite dark (8–10 minutes). Be careful not to burn the garlic. Add the vinegar and water, scraping up the bits at the bottom of the casserole. Bring the liquid to a simmer, then reduce the heat to low, cover the casserole, and cook for 40 minutes or until the meat is tender.

Just before serving, take a ladleful of juices from the casserole and mash the anchovy fillets in it until quite dissolved before pouring it back over the meat.

SAGE TOAD

This is the best form of comfort food and appeals to all ages. Using the sage in the batter brings this dish alive. Serve with home-made gravy, or simply as it is with a crisp green salad.

Serves 4

2 eggs
125 g plain flour
150 ml milk
150 ml cold water
1 tbsp sage leaves(either narrow-leaved, purple or common), finely chopped
salt and freshly ground black pepper
6 large pork sausages (preferably 70–85 per cent meat)
100 g streaky bacon
3 tbsp dripping or lard

Pre-heat the oven to 220°C/425°F/gas mark 8.

Mix together the eggs, flour, milk, water, sage, salt and black pepper and whisk well, making sure there are no lumps of flour. The final consistency should be similar to that of double cream, not the extra thick but double. Leave to rest at room temperature for at least 15 minutes to give the flour time to expand.

Remove the skins of each sausage by using a sharp knife, slicing the side then peeling the skin off. Wrap each sausage in a slice of streaky bacon. Put the dripping or lard in a roasting tin (I use my meat roasting tin which is 28 cm x 32 cm) and place in the oven until the lard/dripping begins to smoke.

Pour in the batter – it will sizzle, but don't panic – arrange the sausages and bake for 25 minutes. Check that it has risen and is beautifully golden, if not, leave for a further 5 minutes.

SALSICCE E FAGIOLI

The title for this recipe when written in Italian sounds so wonderful compared to sausages and beans. I ate this in Tuscany on holiday with my daughter. It was a cold February and the wind was bitter; this dish was so nourishing and warming and such a brilliant use of sage that I asked for the recipe. Admittedly, we cannot get the same sausages, however one can buy great 80 per cent plus meat content sausages in any good supermarket and they make perfectly good substitutes.

Serve with fresh pasta or fresh bread, a crisp green salad and a glass of good red wine.

Serves 4

500 g dried cannellini or other white beans, soaked for 12 hours or overnight in cold water
3 garlic cloves, peeled and left whole
2 sage sprigs
2 tbsp olive oil
6 large pork sausages, Italian or 80 per cent plus meat content
400 g can chopped tomatoes with juice
salt and freshly ground black pepper

Rinse the soaked beans in cold water, put them into a large pan, cover with cold water and bring to the boil. Skim the surface of the water to remove the scum while boiling. Add 2 of the garlic cloves and 1 sage sprig and cook for 1–1½ hours until the beans are tender.

In another large pan, heat the olive oil. Prick the skin of the sausages with a fork to stop them splitting. Fry on a medium heat to brown on all sides, add the remaining garlic clove and the remaining sage sprig. As soon as the herbs begin to sizzle, add the tomatoes and simmer for about 15 minutes to allow all the flavours to combine.

Drain the cooked beans, reserving a couple of cups of the cooking liquid. Add the drained beans to the sausages and tomatoes, check the seasoning and add salt and black pepper, if needed. Simmer for a further 10 minutes; if the sauce is becoming too thick, dilute with the reserved bean water.

SAGE AND POTATO BAKE

This is another of my culinary accidents; I started making roast potatoes then friends turned up so the potatoes would not stretch in time. So I took the potatoes out of the roasting tin and put them in with the herbs, milk and egg and turned it into a bake. The trick with this dish is to keep the potatoes poking above the milk mix so that they become crispy, which is wonderful when combined with the herb custard mix. Serve with roast chicken or as a vegetarian meal with grated cheese sprinkled over the top.

Serves 4–6

900 g boiled potatoes, peeled and diced
2 tbsp light olive oil or rapeseed oil
25 g unsalted butter, plus extra for greasing
110 g double cream
200 ml semi-skimmed milk
1 egg
1 tbsp sage leaves, finely chopped
1 tbsp flatleaf parsley, finely chopped
1 garlic clove, crushed

Pre-heat the oven to 170°C/325°F/gas mark 3.

In a frying pan, sauté the potatoes in the oil and butter until golden. Grease a large dish (I use a lasagne dish) and add the potatoes.

In a jug, mix together the cream, milk, egg, sage, parsley and garlic and pour over the potatoes. Bake in the oven for about 1 hour until golden.

MUM'S SAGE BREAD SAUCE

Mum always made the best bread sauce; it was thick, creamy, fragrant and scrummy. Her use of sage was in those days original. We enjoyed this sauce with many dishes, from roast chicken to baked onions.

Serves 4–6

570 ml milk
10 cloves
1 small onion or ½ large onion
nutmeg
salt and freshly ground black pepper
10 fresh sage leaves, torn
110 g fresh white breadcrumbs
25 g unsalted butter (optional)
2 tbsp double cream

Pour the milk into a pan, press the cloves into the onion and add it to the pan. Grate some nutmeg onto the surface of the milk with some black pepper, turn the heat on to very, very low and slowly simmer, uncovered, for 30–40 minutes to allow all the flavours to infuse.

Remove the onion and take out the cloves, then put it to one side. Add the sage leaves and stir. You will find that there is a layer on the bottom of the pan, so stir well, scraping the bottom of the pan, then increase the heat slightly, add the breadcrumbs, stir well, turn the heat down and gently simmer for 10 minutes, stirring to make sure nothing sticks. If the sauce is too thick, add the butter. Stir well.

Finely chop the infused onion, add to the sauce, stir, then check the seasoning. Serve in a warmed bowl, adding the double cream just before serving.

Excess sage

Sage butter

This is incredibly useful. One of the best ways to use it is to toss it, melted, with cooked fresh pasta; serve it with no other sauce, just some Parmesan and a crisp salad. Heaven.

Makes 125 g

handful of sage leaves
125 g unsalted butter, slightly softened

Remove the sage leaves from their stems. Once removed, tear into pieces, then chop with the butter to release the oils. You do not need the sage leaves to be fine, just small enough not to overpower the taste of the food it is being combined with.

Finish the blending with a fork. When it has been thoroughly mixed, pack it into a roll of greaseproof paper and place in the fridge for up to 24 hours before use. The longer you leave it the better the flavour.

This butter can be frozen; put it into a freezerproof container and label it. It will keep for up to 3 months.

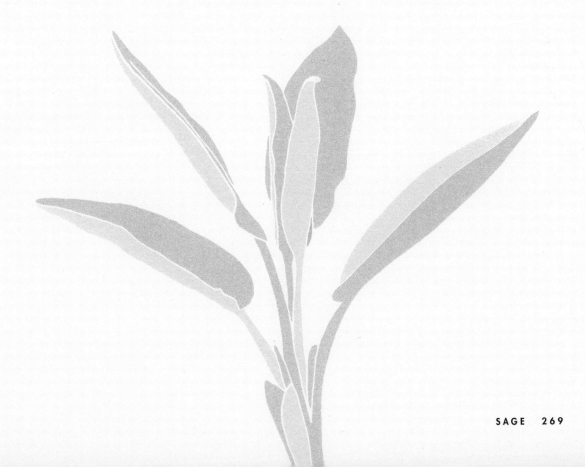

SALAD BURNET

(also known as Meadow Pimpernel, Garden Burnet)

Sanguisorba minor syn. *Poterium minor*

At the primary school I attended in the village of Chew Magna there was only one teacher, Miss Woods, and she was formidable. I have mixed memories of that school, for when I started I was left handed, however, as Miss Woods did not like an untidy classroom she changed me over to being right handed. On a happier note, what I do remember with fondness and gratitude were the nature walks; she taught us to recognise bird song, trees and wild plants. One of the many plants we saw was salad burnet, which used to grow on Dundry Common, which was part of our weekly walk. We used to pick the young leaves and chew them as we marched along in single file.

The leaves have a bitter yet cooling, cucumber flavour, and today, when I eat them in salads, I remember those walks.

Description

This is one of the most useful herbs because the soft grey-green leaves, which are divided into neat ovals with toothed edges, belie their strength. They are evergreen; surviving most winters in the UK, and in hard ones will only die back for a short time before reappearing in early spring. This makes them useful in the kitchen, especially in winter when all other salad herbs have finished. In summer tiny magenta flowers appear around small, compact thimble-shaped flower heads that stand about 30 cm above the leaves. Interestingly, these flower heads are male at the bottom, bisexual in the middle and female at the top.

Plant salad burnet in a well-drained soil in partial shade; semi-shade is important when growing this plant for culinary use because the leaves become very bitter in summer when grown in full sun.

History in cooking

Traditionally this herb was used in the Mediterranean to flavour wine which was drunk as a tonic. Nicholas Culpeper (1616–1654), the herbalist, wrote that 'it was a most precious herb, the continual use to of it preserve the body in health and the spirit in vigour'. Salad burnet was taken to the New World by the Pilgrim Fathers. In 1865 Matthew Robinson, in *The New Family Herbal*, wrote, 'The continual use of it preserves the body in health and the mind in vigour. Pick two or three of the stalks, with leaves put into a cup of wine, especially claret, are known to quicken the spirits and drive away melancholy'.

Harvesting and uses

Leaves:

These can be picked all year round, but the best seasons for harvesting are spring and early autumn (after the summer growth has been hard cut back to encourage the plant to produce new growth). Mature leaves are bitter and drying to the mouth and not of much culinary merit. Use young leaves in salads, with egg dishes, with cream or cottage cheese and in drinks. One of the best dishes I ever created with this herb was poached salmon dressed with the salad burnet leaves, which I made for my mother's 60th birthday.

Properties Salad burnet reputedly gives relief from indigestion simply by eating a few leaves after a meal or when one has indigestion. It is known to be a carminative, digestive and antioxidant; it also contains vitamins A, B and C and is rich in calcium, potassium, iron and magnesium.

Different varieties None.

SALAD BURNET EGG SALAD

A delicious weekend lunch or a light supper as suggested by my wonderful Aunt Kate, who loves simple food served well. The cool, dry cucumber flavour of the salad burnet leaves combines well with the eggs and mayonnaise. Serve with some fresh chunky wholemeal bread.

Serves 2

6 eggs
150 ml mayonnaise
55 ml plain yoghurt
2 tbsp salad burnet leaves, finely chopped
salt and freshly ground black pepper
1 crisp green lettuce, broken into whole leaves

Place the eggs in a large pan, fill it with water and place it on the hob on a high heat. When the water comes to a boil, turn the heat down to medium and cook the eggs for 8 minutes.

Remove the pan from the hob, drain the water and run cold water over the eggs until they have cooled down. Remove the shells, chop up the eggs and place them in a large bowl. Add the remaining ingredients and mix well. Serve on a whole piece of crisp lettuce.

SALAD BURNET AND SWEET CICELY SPRING SALAD

This should be made at the start of the season when one can go out into the garden and pick young salad burnet and sweet cicely leaves. The flavour combination of the cool, dry cucumber with the sweet anise is magic.

Serves 2

4 young sweet cicely sprigs
8 salad burnet sprigs
1 endive, radicchio, chicory or chicory frisée, leaves separated, washed and dried
4 rashers smoked streaky bacon, cut into small squares
1 tsp pine nuts
2 tbsp olive oil
1 tsp balsamic vinegar
salt and freshly ground black pepper

Mix the sweet cicely and salad burnet with the endive, radicchio, chicory or chicory frisée leaves in a large serving bowl.

In a large frying pan, dry-fry the bacon pieces, then add the pine nuts and cook until golden.

Mix together the olive oil and vinegar to make a dressing, check the seasoning and add salt and black pepper to taste, then add the bacon and nuts.

Sprinkle the dressing over the salad leaves, toss and serve.

SALAD BURNET AND DILL BUTTER

The cool, dry nutty flavour of salad burnet with the aromatic unique taste of dill is a wonderful combination.

Use this versatile butter in sandwiches filled with fish, cold ham, or grated carrot and apple. Alternatively, you can use it to cook baked fish or simply dotted over steamed asparagus.

Makes 225 g

6 salad burnet sprigs
6 dill sprigs
225 g unsalted butter, slightly softened

Remove the leaves from the stems of the salad burnet, then chop them with the leaves and stems of the dill and the unsalted butter to release their oils. Finish the blending with a fork.

When the herbs and butter have been thoroughly mixed, pack the butter into a roll of greaseproof paper and place in the fridge for up to 24 hours before use. The longer you leave it, the better the flavour.

This butter can also be frozen in a freezerproof container. It will keep for up to 3 months.

SALAD BURNET SUMMER COCKTAIL

Here I have gently converted this old recipe to suit today's tastes.

Makes approx. 1 litre

12 whole salad burnet leaves
1 bottle of hock
(German white wine)
300 ml amontillado sherry
1 lemon, cut into slices
2 litres soda water
crushed ice

Bruise the salad burnet leaves then place them in a large jug and add the hock, sherry and the lemon slices. Cover and leave to stand for 2 hours.

Just before serving, add the soda water and crushed ice.

Excess salad burnet

Salad burnet vinegar

This is a useful vinegar for salad dressings and mayonnaise and a great way to use lots of new growth, which will encourage the plant to produce more.

Makes 450 ml

10 tbsp chopped salad burnet leaves
450 ml white wine vinegar

Crush the salad burnet leaves using either a pestle and mortar or a wooden spoon and a bowl.

Bring the vinegar to boiling point in a pan and pour a small amount over the burnet in the mortar, pound together for a minute or two, then allow to cool.

Add the cooled, infused vinegar to the remaining vinegar and pour into a sterilised (see page 12) bottle or jar with a non-metallic lid. Keep for 2 weeks, shaking thoroughly every few days. After the 2 weeks, strain the vinegar through an unbleached coffee filter paper and rebottle. This will keep for at least 2 years.

SAVORY

(also known as Winter Savory, Mountain Savory, Timo, Sajolida, Throumbi, Sarriette)
Satureja montana

My mother only grew summer savory, *Satureja hortensis*, the annual savory, which she used liberally with broad beans to make an excellent summer dish. It was not until I started the herb farm that I found out that there are many other varieties which are all just as delicious to cook with.

Description

Winter savory is a southern Mediterranean herb that in cool climates becomes a partial evergreen; which means that some leaves can be picked in the winter months. It has attractive small white flowers that are similar to those of thyme and small, dark green, oval pointed leaves that are highly aromatic when crushed and taste strong with pepper overtones when eaten straight from the bush.

All types of savory prefer to be planted in a well-drained poor soil in a sunny position that has not been fed with well-rotted manure or compost the previous autumn. Winter savory can be used as a low edging plant, as it is pretty in the summer, especially when in flower. However, it can look a bit sparse in winter.

As winter savory grows naturally in hot climates in rocky conditions, in cold or damp climates they are ideal container plants. Use a mix of equal parts soil-based compost and coarse horticultural grit, and place the container in a sunny, dry sheltered spot.

History in cooking

This ancient herb has been used as a food flavouring for over 2,000 years. The ancient Romans used it to flavour sauces and vinegar. Traditionally in southern Italy, where it grows wild, it has been used not only with grilled fish and lamb but also to swill out the wine barrels before refilling with the new season's harvest. Bunches of winter savory were then attached to each barrel to deter the fruit fly from entering the barrels while the grapes fermented.

Harvesting and uses

Leaves:

Harvest leaves from early spring until late autumn. However the best leaves from all the varieties come from the new tip growth, as they are the most pungent and succulent. Savory, being known as 'the bean herb', combines well with all forms of bean, from green vegetable beans, such as broad beans, to dried pulses. The leaves have a sweet aroma and pungent flavour and can be used as a substitute for black pepper. Note, though, that the flavour is lost when the herb is boiled.

Flowers:

Pick as they appear throughout the summer. The small flowers pack a powerful flavour which goes well with cheese, salads, and with plums and pears.

Properties The leaves aid and stimulate digestion, and they also ease colic, flatulence and feelings of fullness.

Different varieties

Summer Savory, Bean Herb
Satureja hortensis
This is an annual herb with small, white, mauve-tinged flowers in summer and mid-green/olive, linear, pungent small leaves. This is a favourite in Europe and the USA, where it is widely used in bean dishes.

Savory Illyrica, Dwarf Winter Savory
Satureja montana subsp. *illyrica*
This semi-evergreen perennial has small mauve flowers in summer and dark green, linear, pungent leaves. Like winter savory this has a strong flavour, which makes it excellent for marinades, grilled meat, vegetables and pulses.

Creeping Savory
Satureja spicigera
This variety is an herbaceous perennial with tiny white flowers in late summer and bright green, linear, highly pungent leaves. This can be found growing wild in Sardinia where it is used as one of the ingredients in salami.

Greek Savory
Satureja thymbra
This is a semi-evergreen perennial with lovely small purple flowers and dark green linear leaves that are very aromatic. This herb has had many names, and has even been grouped with thymes. It is excellent with grilled fish, lamb and mushrooms.

African Savory
Satureja biflora
This semi-evergreen perennial has small white flowers and mid-green linear leaves that have a spicy lemon flavour. African savory goes well with pulses and vegetable dishes.

BROAD BEANS WITH SUMMER SAVORY CREAM

Peppery savory is delicious with broad beans. This is my mother's recipe. I have only changed one ingredient: she used double cream and I prefer crème fraîche. If you have the time and patience you can remove the bean skins after cooking, as the vivid green underneath looks striking and the flavour is sweeter. Serve with cold ham.

Serves 2 as a main course, 4 as an accompaniment

340 g young broad beans, shelled
2 summer savory sprigs
30 g unsalted butter
1 tbsp summer savory leaves, finely chopped
150 ml crème fraîche
1 egg yolk
salt and freshly ground black pepper

Bring a pan of water to the boil, but do not add salt at this stage as it will toughen the skins of the broad beans. Add the beans and the summer savory sprigs. Cook until tender, then drain and remove and discard the savory.

Melt the butter in another pan, turn the heat to low then add the beans and the finely chopped savory leaves. Mix the crème fraîche with the egg yolk and add to the pan. Cook, stirring all the time, over a moderate heat, for a few minutes until the cream thickens. Do not allow the sauce to boil or it will curdle. Season to taste.

Pour into a warmed serving bowl and serve straight away.

SAVORY, HAM AND JERUSALEM ARTICHOKE BAKE

Jerusalem artichokes are renowned for causing flatulence; by cooking them with savory you will find that not only is the flavour enhanced but they are much easier to digest.

Serves 4–6

225 ml crème fraîche
juice of 1 lemon
2 garlic cloves, finely chopped
1 good handful of savory (winter, creeping or summer), leaves picked and chopped
3 handfuls of Parmesan, grated
salt and freshly ground black pepper
4 slices of cooked ham, cut into squares
1 kg Jerusalem artichokes, peeled and cut into long thin slices
2 good handfuls of fresh breadcrumbs
olive oil

Pre-heat the oven to 220°C/425°F/gas mark 7.

In a bowl, mix together the crème fraîche, lemon juice, garlic, half of the savory and three-quarters of the Parmesan and season well to taste. Throw in the ham and sliced Jerusalem artichokes. Mix well and place everything in an ovenproof baking dish.

Mix the breadcrumbs with the remaining savory and Parmesan and some salt and black pepper. Sprinkle the flavoured breadcrumbs over the artichokes and drizzle with a little olive oil.

Bake in the oven for around 30 minutes until the artichokes are tender and the breadcrumbs are golden.

WINTER SAVORY WITH BRAISED RED CABBAGE

Red cabbage is something I have grown to love. As a child I found the flavours too strong, but as my palate has matured I really enjoy this dish and find it useful, as it can be served hot or cold and will keep well in the fridge for several days.

Mum used to add raisins to encourage us to eat it; I have added savory as I find the piquant pepper flavour combines well with the caraway and cabbage.

Serve hot with cold meats and roast chicken, or cold with Cheddar and fresh crusty bread.

Serves 4–6

1 medium red cabbage
25–50 g butter
1 large cooking apple, peeled and sliced
2 medium onions, peeled and sliced
2 garlic cloves, crushed
zest and juice of 1 orange
3 winter savory sprigs
1 bay leaf
1 bunch of flatleaf parsley
1 tsp caraway seeds
¼ tsp freshly grated nutmeg
¼ tsp ground cinnamon
salt and freshly ground black pepper
2 tbsp brown sugar
1 glass of red wine (preferably a glass from the night before's bottle)

Pre-heat the oven to 150°C/300°F/gas mark 2.

Remove the large, damaged outer leaves of the cabbage. Quarter it, discard the central core, then shred as finely as possible. Melt the butter on the hob in a heatproof casserole dish, add the cabbage, cover and cook gently for 5 minutes. Add the apple, onions, garlic, orange zest and juice, savory sprigs, bay leaf, parsley, spices, and salt and black pepper to taste. Mix everything together, add the sugar and wine, stir again then cover and put in the oven for 3 hours. Check half-way through that it is not drying up; if it is, add a little hot water.

SAVORY, GARLIC AND MUSHROOM BAKE

In Greece savory is often combined with mushrooms. Here is a simple recipe for a light lunch or supper that highlights the flavour of this herb.

Serve with a mixed herb salad and some fresh crusty bread to mop up the mushroom juices.

Serves 2

25 g unsalted butter,
plus extra for greasing
12 large field mushrooms
(preferably freshly picked),
or cap mushrooms
2 tbsp olive oil
6 tbsp coarse dry breadcrumbs
2 garlic cloves, finely sliced
1 heaped tsp savory leaves,
finely chopped
salt and freshly ground
black pepper
nutmeg (if using shop-bought
mushrooms)

Pre-heat the oven to 170°C/325°F/gas mark 3. Grease an ovenproof baking dish.

If you have been lucky enough to pick field mushrooms in mid autumn, these will need to be washed, peeled, then sliced and patted dry. Alternatively, you can use cap mushrooms which will need to be washed, dried, then sliced in half; there is no need to peel.

Heat the olive oil in a frying pan, add the breadcrumbs and stir. As soon as they start to brown, add the garlic, savory leaves, salt, black pepper and nutmeg (if you are using fresh field mushrooms, omit the nutmeg). Cook until the garlic becomes translucent but not brown.

Place the mushrooms in the prepared dish, sprinkle over the herby breadcrumbs, pop in the oven and bake for 25 minutes.

Excess savory

Summer savory butter

Being an annual herb, one can have a glut of summer savory, so this is a good way of preserving it for use later in the season. I use this butter for grilling fish or lamb instead of rosemary.

Makes 125 g

125 g unsalted butter, slightly softened
handful of savory leaves

Remove the savory leaves by gently rubbing your fingers up and down the stems. Once removed, gently chop to release the oils, then mix the chopped leaves with the butter. (The easiest way of blending the herb and butter together is to use a fork.)

When thoroughly mixed, pack it into a roll of greaseproof paper and place in the fridge for up to 24 hours before use. The longer you leave it, the better the flavour.

This can also be frozen – put into a labelled freezerproof container. It will keep for 6 months.

SHISO

(also known as Perilla, Chinese Basil, Wild Sesame,
Rattlesnake Weed)
Perilla frutescens

Until recently this Far-Eastern herb was relatively unknown as a culinary delight in Western countries. Even in the early 1980s, purple perilla was being used in the UK as a spectacular spot bedding plant rather than in the kitchen.

I discovered its culinary prowess about 15 years ago while I was exhibiting it at one the RHS's London flower shows. News of perilla being at the show obviously spread throughout the Japanese community, because during the two days of the show, I sold out of plants and I learnt from my customers all about this unique and delightful herb. Interestingly, it is now a chef's designer herb, being served as a cress herb – or seedlings – where the flavours of the leaves are more concentrated and intense.

Description

Shiso is a hardy annual, with pale pink/mauve flowers in summer and large, deeply cut, textured, aromatic cumin-flavoured leaves. This herb is grown from seed sown in late spring when all threat of frost has passed. When growing in the garden, plant in a fertile well-drained soil that has been well prepared with well-rotted compost or leaf mould in the previous autumn, in sun or partial shade. One word of warning, though; do not plant near where horses or cattle might eat it because it can cause respiratory failure in such animals.

History in cooking

The leaves and seeds of shiso have been widely used in China since 500 AD, both in the kitchen and medicinally. It has also been used in Japanese cuisine for hundreds of years.

Historically the oil extract from the seeds was used across Asia to cover biscuits, and this practice continues today in rural areas of Korea. Whereas in Nepal and parts of India, traditionally the seeds were ground with chilli and tomatoes to make a savoury dip or side dish. Again, they are still prepared this way in rural parts now.

Harvesting and uses

Leaves:
The leaves can be picked fresh as required from spring until the first frosts. Picking the growing tips will keep the plant more productive than taking the side leaves. Also, the growing tips have the most intense flavour so they can be eaten raw or are ideal for stir-fry dishes. If using mature leaves, they should be cooked.

Flowers:
Pick the flowers as they appear in summer. They have a sweet flavour and are great added to all forms of salad or scattered over cold fish dishes.

Seeds:

Harvest seeds from late summer until early autumn. The seed has an interesting, rather sweet flavour. I have not cooked with it, but I do know that perilla is grown as a seed crop in Japan and northern India. It is then crushed and the oil is extracted, which is said to be rather similar to linseed and is used equally for both culinary and medicinal purposes. However, in parts of Asia perilla oil is valued more for its medicinal benefit than its flavour, as it is a very rich source of the omega-3 fatty acid and alpha-linolenic acid.

Properties

This herb is one of the strongest natural antioxidants; it has been under research at Osaka University in Japan where they have found that it is more powerful than ascorbic acid. Another noteworthy benefit is its ability to dissolve cholesterol.

Different varieties

Zi Su, Egoma
Perilla frutescens var. *frutescens*
A hardy annual with mauve flowers in summer and large, aromatic, green leaves with a hint of brown and a deep purple underside. It is an important culinary and medicinal herb from Korea.

Green Shiso, Aoshiso and Perilla
Perilla frutescens var. *crispa*
This hardy annual has pink flowers in summer and aromatic, anise-flavoured, deeply cut, bright green leaves with crinkled edges. Green shiso is the variety most commonly seen in Japanese markets, and it is used there as a vegetable. The leaves can also be used as a wrapping for rice cakes, and in salads and tempura. The seeds from this variety are used as a condiment and with pickles. The essential oil extracted from the leaf and flowering parts contains a substance that is a thousand times sweeter than sugar, and which is used in confectionery.

Purple Shiso, Akashiso, Beefsteak Plant
Perilla frutescens var. *purpurascens*
This is a hardy annual with pink flowers in summer and deeply cut, aromatic, dark purple leaves with crinkled bronzed edges. There can be considerable variation amongst seed-raised plants; the flowers can be red and the leaves smoother. Purple shiso is used as a dye for pickling fruit and vegetables, as a dried powder in a side dish with rice, as an ingredient in cake mixes and as flavouring in beverages. The flower heads are used as a condiment with sushi.

VEGETABLE AND SHISO TEMPURA

Shiso is brilliant cooked this way, as you keep all its unique cumin-like flavour which combines so well with the other vegetables.

The art of good tempura is to have everything ready before you make the batter; aside from the ingredients, have next to you a bowl of flour for dunking the vegetables, a wire draining rack, kitchen paper, plus a couple of serving bowls so that as soon as a batch is made it can be served.

Cook the vegetables in small batches and have everyone ready to eat as soon as the vegetables are cooked.

Tempura is a very sociable dish, as it is eaten in batches rather than all in one go. However, if you would rather serve it all in 'one go', pre-heat the oven to 180°C/350°F/gas mark 4 and place a serving bowl in the oven once it has heated up. Put the batches of tempura in the bowl as they are removed from the oil.

Serves 4

100 g mushrooms, cut into bite-sized pieces
100 g courgettes, cut into bite-sized pieces
100 g red peppers, seeded and cut into chunks
100 g broccoli, broken into small florets
20 shiso leaves (red, green or a mixture), stems removed

For the dipping sauce
3 tbsp soy sauce
3 tbsp dry sherry
1 tbsp sugar
zest of 1 lemon

For the batter
85 g plain flour, plus extra for dusting
1 tbsp cornflour
1 tsp sea salt
200 ml ice-cold sparkling mineral water
some ice cubes
vegetable oil, for frying

First wash and prepare the vegetables and the shiso leaves.

Make the dipping sauce by combining all the ingredients. Pour into a serving bowl.

Make the batter in two batches – that way it will not have to stand before using. Mix quickly; it does not matter if you have a few lumpy bits, for if you overmix the batter will be heavy.

Heat the oil in a wok or wide frying pan to 170–180°C/325–350°F. Test by dropping a small amount of batter in it: if it sinks then rises to the surface, the temperature is right.

Do not overcrowd the pan, just fry a few pieces at a time. Dip the vegetables in the flour, shake off any excess, then coat them in batter and slide them into the oil. The shiso leaves do not need to be dunked in flour first; simply dip in the batter, shake off the excess, pop into the oil and cook for 1 minute, then remove from the oil and drain. Cook the vegetables for 2–3 minutes, turning frequently with long chopsticks or a slotted spoon until the batter turns a light gold and the pieces rise to the surface.

Remove the cooked vegetables from the oil and place on the draining rack or kitchen paper and serve immediately with the dipping sauce.

Repeat until all the vegetables and shiso leaves are cooked.

STIR-FRIED SHISO AND CUCUMBER

The combination of the cool cucumber and the cumin sweetness of the shiso is delightful, and this makes a tasty (and quick) light supper. Serve with boiled rice.

Serves 2–3

1 cucumber, peeled to make stripes
3 tbsp light olive oil
1 fresh red chilli, seeded and finely chopped
2 garlic cloves, finely chopped
1½ tsp light soy sauce
1 tsp white wine vinegar
6–8 leaves of purple or green shiso, finely chopped
1 tsp sesame oil

Cut the cucumber in half lengthwise. Holding the knife at an angle, slice each half into 3-mm thick semi-circles.

Heat a flat-bottomed wok or a deep frying pan over a high flame until it smokes, then add the olive oil. Add the cucumber, stir and spread the slices out so they cover as much of the surface of the pan as possible. Turn them carefully from time to time until they brown slightly on both sides. Add the chilli and garlic and stir fry until fragrant. Pour in the soy sauce and vinegar and mix well. Add the shiso leaves and stir. Remove from the heat, stir in the sesame oil and serve immediately.

SPICY TUNA AND SHISO BURGERS

Fish, especially tuna, combines well with the spicy flavour of shiso. These burgers are delicious and very spicy – so go steady on the wasabi paste.

Serves 6

700 g fresh, skinless tuna steaks or 2 x 200 g cans of tuna steak
6–8 green shiso leaves
2 spring onions, trimmed
1 tsp wasabi paste or mustard
3-cm piece of fresh ginger, grated
salt and freshly ground black pepper
60 ml teriyaki sauce
2 tbsp honey
1 tbsp vegetable oil
3 ciabatta or burger buns
2 tbsp sweet chilli sauce, plus extra to serve
1 cucumber
1 crisp lettuce, washed and dried
pickled ginger, to serve

Break up the tuna, then chop it and place it in a mixing bowl. Finely chop the shiso and spring onions and add to the tuna with the wasabi or mustard, and ginger. Mix thoroughly, check the seasoning and add salt and black pepper to taste, if needed. Alternatively, use a food processor: add the tuna, shiso, spring onions, wasabi and ginger to the mixing bowl and pulse to mix all the ingredients together, but do not over process.

Shape the mixture into 6 burgers and put on a plate or baking sheet. Cover with cling film and chill in the fridge for 1 hour.

Mix together the teriyaki sauce and honey and set aside.

Heat the vegetable oil in a non-stick frying pan. When the pan is hot, add the tuna burgers and cook for 3–4 minutes each side, brushing with the teriyaki and honey glaze as you go.

Pre-heat the grill. Cut the bread or buns in half and lightly toast the cut side under the grill. Cut the cucumber into ribbons using a vegetable peeler and shred the lettuce. Spread the bread halves with the chilli sauce and top with the cucumber ribbons and the shredded lettuce. Add the burgers and spoon over the juices from the pan. Arrange on a serving plate alongside small bowls of pickled ginger and sweet chilli sauce.

Excess shiso

Shiso marinade for raw fish

This marinade is lovely with many forms of meaty white fish. You do need a good crop to be able to harvest 2 tablespoons of growing tips. Serve with a crisp green salad and vinaigrette or sticky rice.

Makes approx. 250 ml

500 g cod fillet or other meaty white fish

For the marinade:
200 ml white wine vinegar
2 tbsp shiso growing tips (green or purple)
juice of 1 lemon
juice of 1 lime
1 tbsp sea salt
2 garlic cloves, sliced

Mix together all the ingredients to make the marinade. Slice the fish into 2.5-cm pieces and place in a shallow dish. Pour over the marinade, cover the dish with a lid or foil and refrigerate for 3 hours, turning the fish every half-hour so that it is completely saturated in the marinade. Leave for a further 24 hours, covered, in the fridge.

Remove the fish from the marinade and slice very thinly to serve.

The marinade on its own will keep in a sealed container in the fridge for 48 hours prior to use without losing flavour.

SORREL

(also known as Bread and Cheese, Sour Leaves, Tom Thumbs,
A Thousand Fingers, Sour Sauce)
Rumex acetosa

When my children were at the local infant school, their class used to walk over to the herb farm where we would talk about plants relevant to what they were learning at school. One year they came over and I had been talking about how the Romans, as they marched along, used to eat a sorrel leaf to stop themselves feeling thirsty as they did not have bottles of water. One little boy asked if he could eat a leaf. I gave him one, he ate it and proclaimed 'it's like a Granny Smith apple'. After that remark, I was deluged with requests for leaves.

One word of caution; you should not eat fresh, raw sorrel (cooked is fine) if you suffer from gout or have kidney stones. Equally, avoid overeating this herb in its fresh form while breastfeeding.

Description

This herb looks very like its cousin, dock; the leaves are longer and lance-shaped but the dull and inconspicuous flowers are similar. The difference comes in the taste of the young leaves, which have a refreshing lemony flavour. It is an herbaceous perennial, meaning that it dies back into the ground during winter, reappearing in the following spring.

Sorrel prefers a rich acid soil that retains moisture, although, it will happily adapt to any soil that does not dry out in summer. If you want to crop this herb for use in the kitchen I do recommend planting it in partial shade, because once the heat of summer sets in, the leaves become tough, bitter and inedible. A leaf or bark mulch keeps the soil cooler and, once the temperature falls, the flavour will improve. In the summer the plant tends to run to flower and seed quickly, therefore, to keep the leaves fresh, succulent and productive for the early autumn, remove the flower heads as they appear.

History in cooking

The historical use of sorrel as a food dates back to 3,000 BC. It is said that eating sorrel leaves cured Julius Caesar's soldiers of scurvy.

The ancient Egyptians and Romans ate sorrel to offset their rich food. The Tudors considered it to be one of the best vegetables and in Lapland sorrel juice has long been used instead of rennet to curdle milk.

Harvesting and uses

Leaves:

Young leaves are tender and not as sour or tough as mature leaves, so pick these from spring until early autumn. A few young leaves added to salads gives a refreshing sharp flavour, and they make great sauces, which can be served with fish or meat. The leaves can also be used as a natural meat tenderiser by wrapping them around tough meat while it is cooking, or can be added to stews and casseroles or combined with eggs and cheese.

Properties Sorrel is high in oxalic, tannic and tartaric acid as well as vitamins A, B1, C, and the minerals calcium, potassium, iron and sulphur. Sorrel leaves stimulate the salivary gland, and for this reason eating a small leaf is beneficial to the digestion.

Different varieties Sheep's Sorrel
Rumex acetosella
This variety has small inconspicuous flowers which turn greenish brown as the fruit ripens in early summer. The mid-green leaves are shaped like a barbed spear. It grows wild on heaths and grassy places, and where it grows indicates that the soil is acid. Use young leaves in salads and sauces.

Buckler Leaf Sorrel, French Sorrel
Rumex scutatus
This has small inconspicuous flowers that turn greenish brown as the fruit ripens in early summer. The mid-green leaves are shaped like squat shields. Use the young leaves in salads and sauces.

GRANDMOTHER'S SORREL SOUP

I have reproduced this recipe for *Potage a l'oseille* just as my grandmother Ruth wrote it, including her notes which were written under each recipe. It is a lovely way to use sorrel. This is taken from her book *Food for Pleasure*, published in 1950. Inside my copy is written: 'To Clare, with love from Mummy'. Clare was my mother.

If you don't grow sorrel or can't buy it, let someone who knows what it is gather the tiny leaves from the wild sorrel, as it is easy to make a mistake and get the wrong leaves. Sorrel has a bitter, lemony taste and makes a smooth soup. I use chicken stock instead of water.

Serves 2

3 large handfuls of sorrel
butter or margarine
salt and freshly ground
black pepper
300 ml chicken stock or water,
previously warmed
bread, sliced, 4 very thin slices
(stale bread is excellent)
2 egg yolks
1 tbsp milk

Pre-heat the oven to 150°C/300°F/gas mark 2.

Clean the sorrel leaves, remove the stalks and centre ribs, and wash them well. Wilt them in a pan with a piece of butter the size of an egg; add the black pepper and salt and sufficient water or stock to make a good soup.

Toast a few very thin slices of bread in the oven. Using this toasting method rather than a toaster means the bread becomes hard and crisp rather than just toasted on the outside.

Beat the egg yolks with the milk, and add this to the cooked sorrel and stock. Stir well. Break 2 slices of toast into a few pieces, divide these between 2 bowls then pour the soup over and serve, putting the remaining dry toast on a plate so that it can be eaten with the soup.

BATAVIA FRAPPÉ

This is another wonderful soup made by my grandmother and appears in two of her books: *What's cooking?* and *Food for Pleasure*. I have only slightly adapted it to suit today's ingredients. The combination of cucumber and peas with sharp sorrel is great; it is difficult to believe that this recipe was written over 60 years ago.

Serves 4

2 handfuls of peas in their pods
2 handfuls of sorrel
2 cucumbers, peeled and grated,
then left to drain for 30 minutes
300 ml cold water
850 ml vegetable stock
300 ml white wine
salt and freshly ground
black pepper
single cream, to serve

Bring two small pans of water to the boil. Add the peas to one and the sorrel to the other and cook until tender. Drain, saving the pea cooking water to use with the vegetable stock. Purée the peas and sorrel. Drain, and remove as much of the liquid as possible from the cucumbers, and combine with the 2 purées.

Put the water, vegetable stock and white wine together in a pan and bring to the boil to remove the alcohol from the wine. When cool, stir in the purées and drained cucumber. Stir well then pass through a sieve – do not be tempted to liquidise as this will give the wrong texture.

Check the seasoning. Pour the soup into a container and place in the fridge for at least 2 hours before serving. To serve, add a dash of single cream.

SORREL AND ANCHOVY TART

The sharpness of the sorrel with the saltiness of the anchovy fillets makes this tart delicious. Serve with a fresh tomato salad and new potatoes.

Serves 4–6

185 g ready-rolled plain
shortcrust pastry
350 g sorrel, washed
and stalks removed
25 g butter
2 tbsp olive oil
3 onions, thinly sliced
10–12 anchovy fillets, chopped
½ tsp freshly grated nutmeg
freshly ground black pepper
2 eggs, plus 2 egg yolks
350 ml double cream

Pre-heat the oven to 200°C/400°F/gas mark 6.

Line a shallow 24-cm loose-bottomed flan tin with the pastry, prick the base with a fork and bake blind in the oven for 20 minutes. (For those of you not sure of the term 'bake blind', this is when you line your pastry with a circle of greaseproof paper slightly larger than the pastry case. Then place some ceramic baking beans, or in my case some dried baked pasta, inside to weigh the pastry down.)

Take out of the oven, remove the baking beans and greaseproof paper, then return the pastry case to the oven and bake for a further 5 minutes. Remove from the oven and allow to cool slightly while you cook the sorrel.

Put the sorrel in a pan with a little water. Put the lid on and let it simmer over the lowest possible heat for 5 minutes. Drain it in a colander, using a saucer to squeeze out as much liquid as possible. Set aside.

Melt the butter and oil in a frying pan and gently fry the onions for about 10 minutes or until they are soft and beginning to caramelise, stirring occasionally. Remove the pan from the heat and stir in the drained sorrel, anchovies, grated nutmeg and black pepper.

In a large bowl, beat the eggs, egg yolks and cream together, then add the sorrel mixture to the egg mixture and give it a really good stir. Pile the mixture into the pre-baked pastry case and bake in the oven for 25–30 minutes or until the filling looks set and the edges are turning golden brown. Remove the tart from the oven and allow it to cool before serving.

SORREL AND RHUBARB SAUCE

This is an early summer recipe when the rhubarb is at its best and the sorrel is young and tender. The combination of the fruit and the sour leaf of the sorrel is very good and goes well with all smoked fish, especially mackerel.

Serves 4

450 g rhubarb, cut into
2.5-cm pieces
150 ml melted butter
½ tsp grated ginger
½ tsp lemon zest
a pinch of grated nutmeg
2 tbsp caster sugar
2 handfuls of sorrel,
washed and chopped

Boil the rhubarb in a pan with a splash of water until tender, then pass it through a sieve.

Return to the pan, add the melted butter with the heat on low and bring to simmering point. Add the ginger, lemon zest, nutmeg and sugar, stir well and cook very gently for about 10 minutes, then fold in the sorrel and cook for a few more minutes until the sorrel has broken down. Serve.

Excess sorrel

The best way to cope with a glut of this herb is to pick the young leaves, wash and dry them, then pop them into a freezer bag, seal, then freeze. Once removed from the freezer, the leaves become very limp as they thaw, but they do retain their flavour so are great for making sauces and soups.

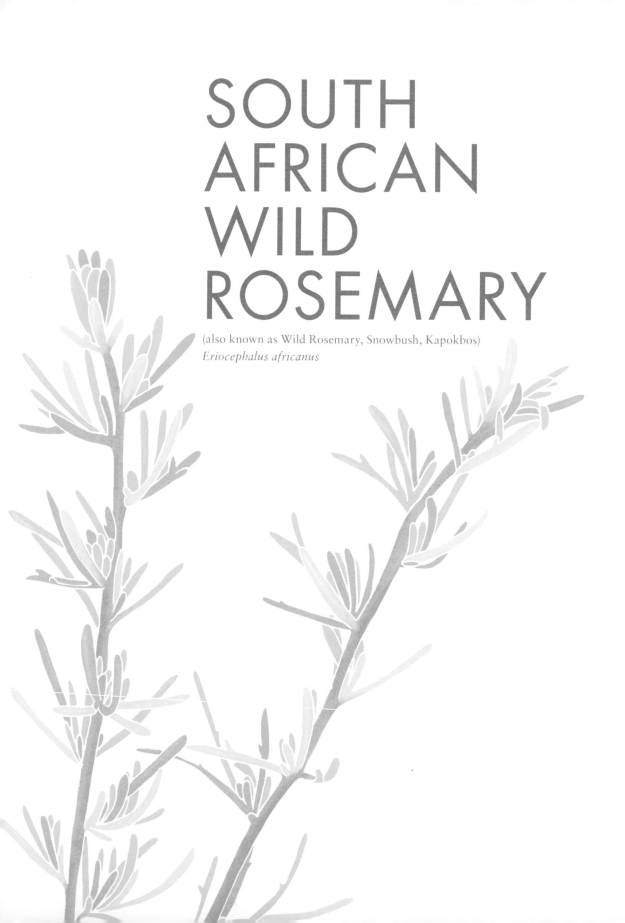

SOUTH AFRICAN WILD ROSEMARY

(also known as Wild Rosemary, Snowbush, Kapokbos)

Eriocephalus africanus

I am lucky enough to have seen this graceful plant growing wild in South Africa although, to be honest, it does not stand out as it is surrounded by hundreds of other fantastic flora and fauna. It is not until you rub the leaves that you realise the culinary potential of this herb. I am surprised that it is little known or used, as I find it a great alternative to the standard rosemary.

Description

This herb was much used by the early Cape people and the Khoi. It is a half-hardy evergreen with small, needle-like, silver-haired, oval, slightly succulent aromatic leaves which grow in tufts along the branch. The attractive clusters of small white flowers, with magenta centres, are followed by seeds covered in masses of tiny white hairs which make them look fluffy. The whole plant has a spreading arching habit, so when the plant is in seed it looks rather like a wave crashing in to shore.

South African wild rosemary can be raised from seed, but that can be a bit hit or miss, so it is much easier to take cuttings in late spring. Amazingly drought-tolerant, it will adapt to most soils, with the exception of heavy cold clay and marshy types of soil. The ideal conditions are full sun and a well-drained soil, and it is a good coastal plant as it likes the sea spray and wind. In warm climates it can be grown as a hedge or clipped into ball shapes. In cool climates it is a tolerant and attractive container plant. Protect from frost.

History in cooking

I do not know of any recorded history of this herb being used in cooking. However, I am sure that the indigenous South African Khoi will have recipes and uses dating back for hundreds of years.

Harvesting and uses

Leaves:

As an evergreen the leaves are available all year round. They have two distinct flavours: mild in the spring from the new growth, and intense after the long hot summer when the leaves are small and the flavour is more concentrated. These leaves should be cooked and not eaten raw, making them ideal for dishes that require a long cooking time, such as stews and casseroles, both with meat and vegetables.

Properties

Wild rosemary has traditionally been used as a medicine for many ailments, such as coughs and colds, flatulence and colic, and also as a diuretic and a diaphoretic. It is said to have similar qualities to rosemary (*Rosmarinus officinalis*).

Different varieties

There are different forms of *Eriocephalus*, however I can find no record of them being used in the kitchen.

SOUTH AFRICAN WILD ROSEMARY POT-ROASTED CHICKEN

A simple dish that can be quickly prepared and is a pleasure to eat. The flavour of the wild rosemary combines so well with the chicken, and the cooking juices produced make the most lovely flavoured gravy or sauce.

Delicious served with mashed potato.

Serves 6–8

1.5 kg whole chicken
330 ml dry cider
2 large onions, sliced
4 leeks, white bit only, sliced and well washed
4 South African wild rosemary sprigs, leaves removed from the stems
salt and freshly ground black pepper
142 ml pot double cream

Pre-heat the oven to 170°C/325°F/gas mark 3.

Put the chicken in a large casserole, pour over the cider and stir in the onions, leeks and wild rosemary sprigs. Season, cover and roast for 45 minutes.

Uncover the chicken and roast for a further 45 minutes, until it is golden on top and cooked through. Transfer the bird to a plate to rest for 5 minutes.

Put the casserole on the hob over a low heat and pour in the cream to warm through. Season to taste.

Carve the chicken and serve with the leeks and pan juices.

SPECIAL LAMB STEW WITH SOUTH AFRICAN WILD ROSEMARY

This flavoursome autumn meal was the first dish I cooked with this herb. I included it in *Jekka's Complete Herb Book*, and as it has proved so popular, it had to be included in this book, too. We all know standard rosemary goes well with lamb, but this wild version adds another dimension. Serve with rice and a salad or green beans.

Serves 4–6

100 g dried chickpeas (or canned)
4 tbsp light olive oil
1 large onion, finely chopped
500 g lean lamb, cubed
salt and freshly ground black pepper
juice of 2 lemons
2 bay leaves
3 South African wild rosemary sprigs, roughly 10 cm long
3 leeks, cleaned and chopped
250 g spinach
200 g flatleaf parsley
1 lime, sliced

Soak the dried chickpeas overnight. The next day, drain, then cook them in fresh unsalted water for 15–20 minutes. Drain, rinse under fresh cold water and set aside. Alternatively, drain the contents from the can, rinse, and set aside.

Heat 2 tablespoons of the olive oil in a large, heavy pan and slowly sauté the onion. Add the lamb and brown on all sides, then season with salt and black pepper. Pour over the lemon juice, add enough boiled hot water to just cover the meat, then add the bay leaves and the wild rosemary. Cover and simmer for 30 minutes.

Heat the remaining olive oil, sauté the leeks, spinach and parsley until just cooked. Add this to the meat with the chickpeas and lime slices. Check the liquid just covers the lamb and add extra if needed. Simmer all the ingredients for a further hour, checking from time to time that nothing is sticking.

Just before serving, remove the wild rosemary sprigs and the lime slices, which can be used to decorate the serving plate.

WILD ROSEMARY TORTILLAS

These tortillas are exceedingly versatile; they can be served with soups, or filled with spicy mince, or cheese and salad, or served for lunch filled with tomatoes, cheese and lettuce. Wild rosemary is more subtle than standard rosemary, so when baked in these breads it adds a delicate flavour.

Makes 6–8

250 g plain flour, plus extra for dusting
2 tsp salt
2 tsp finely chopped South African wild rosemary leaves (or you can use standard rosemary)
4 tsp baking powder
2 tbsp lard, margarine or shortening
150 ml warm water (more if needed)

In a large bowl, stir together the flour, salt, wild rosemary leaves and baking powder. With your hands, gradually work in the lard, margarine or shortening until it is all incorporated. Add enough warm water to make a soft but not sticky dough. Leave to rest, covered with a clean tea towel, for 30 minutes.

Turn out onto a lightly floured board and knead for 5 minutes. Divide the dough into 8 and shape into round balls using your hands. Roll each one out to a 2–3 mm thickness.

Place a heavy frying pan or a griddle onto a medium–high heat and add the tortillas one at a time. Cook each one for 30 seconds until brown patches form, then turn over and cook on the second side. Place the cooked tortilla in a clean tea towel to hold the steam in. Repeat until all are cooked.

Serve warm.

Excess South African wild rosemary

I have yet to have a glut of this herb and, being an evergreen, I can pick it fresh when required, so there has been no need to preserve it.

STEVIA

(also known as Honeyleaf, Caá-ehe)

Stevia rebaudiana

This is a truly amazing herb; take the smallest piece of leaf and put it on the end of your tongue and you will realise that the claim that it is 30 times sweeter than sugar is true. In fact, records show that a quarter of a teaspoon of dried leaf is equivalent to 225 g of sugar!

I have read many arguments regarding the safety of stevia, all of which leave me confused. The situation at the moment is that the Japanese, who have banned all artificial sweeteners, have been using stevia as a commercial sweetener for over 30 years with no adverse reactions. However, agencies in the USA and Europe have banned it for sale as a food or food ingredient, but it can be sold as a dietary supplement, not as a sweetener, in the USA. Research is ongoing, with no definitive conclusions as yet drawn. So it is up to you. I will always adhere to science when a fact is proven, but so far nothing has been proven, so for now I will continue to cook with it.

Description

Stevia is a subtropical evergreen herb often grown as an annual in cold climates. It has clusters of small white flowers and green, oval, serrated leaves with an intense sugary taste with a hint of liquorice.

You can grow stevia from seed, but germination is erratic, so I recommend growing it from cuttings taken in early summer. This herb can only be grown outside in the tropics, but will happily grow in a container elsewhere, if put in a frost-free position over winter.

History in cooking

This herb has been used in South and Central America for hundreds of years. In the 16th century the invading Spaniards noticed that the Guarani Indians of Paraguay were using this herb not only to sweeten their drinks, but also to make herbal remedies and snacks.

Harvesting and uses

Leaves:

Outside the tropics the leaves can be picked from late spring to mid-autumn. Young leaves provide the best flavour, and it truly does mean that you can cook without sugar. The most important point to remember is not to use too much, or you will ruin your dish. Stevia is excellent with any recipe using fruit, juices or dairy. It can withstand high temperatures, which will not destroy its sweetness, but it is not good for home baking, with a few exceptions such as carrot cake (see page 301). This is because it lacks sugar's abilities to add texture, caramelise, or feed the fermentation of yeast.

Properties

Stevia is a digestive tonic and a natural sweetener. The leaves contain vitamins B and C, and the minerals calcium and potassium.

Different varieties

None.

TO MAKE A STEVIA SOLUTION FOR EVERYDAY USE

Many factors can alter the sugar content in the leaves of this herb; for example it could be the time of year, the temperature at which it is grown, or the soil conditions in which it is grown, so there is no exact way to know the sweetness of what you are picking. To overcome this I have devised a general all-purpose way of making a stevia solution which is good for everyday use.

Always start with a few leaves because you can add but you cannot take away sweetness once you have created the solution.

Stevia leaves
300 ml boiled water

Take one leaf and place it in a measuring jug. Add the boiled, but not boiling, water and leave to stand for 10 minutes.

Taste the water with a teaspoon; if it is not sweet enough for your taste or recipe, add another leaf.

Pour the water and leaves into a small pan and re-heat to just below boiling point. Let it stand, covered, for a further 10 minutes then taste again. If it is not sweet enough, keep adding leaves one by one and heating until you achieve the flavour you require.

STEVIA LEMONADE

A lovely, cold refreshing drink for the summer, in which stevia sweetens the lemon perfectly.

Makes 825 ml

zest of ½ lemon
275 ml freshly squeezed
lemon juice
550 ml cold water
2 tsp stevia solution
(see recipe above), or to taste
3 lemon slices, plus extra to garnish
2 mint sprigs, plus extra to garnish
1 lemon verbena sprig
ice cubes

Combine all the ingredients in a large jug and stir well.

Place an ice cube in each glass, pour the lemonade over and garnish each with a slice of lemon and a sprig of mint.

CARROT CAKE

Stevia works well in this cake because it is used with ripe bananas, meaning the caramelising action of the sugar is not missed.

Serves 8–10

butter, for greasing
275 g plain flour
1 tsp salt
1 tsp bicarbonate of soda
2 tsp baking powder
1 level tsp dried stevia leaves,
crushed to a powder
25 g walnuts, finely chopped
25 g blanched almonds,
finely chopped
150 g carrots, grated
3 large eggs
180 ml salad or corn oil
2 ripe bananas, peeled and mashed

For the topping

75 g unsalted butter, softened
150 g rich cream cheese
½ level tsp dried stevia leaves,
crushed to a powder
½ tsp vanilla essence

Pre-heat the oven to 180°C/350°F/gas mark 4. Grease a 20-cm round cake tin.

Into a large mixing bowl, sift together the flour, salt, bicarbonate of soda and the baking powder. Add the crushed stevia leaves, the walnuts, and the carrots and stir well so that everything is amalgamated.

In a separate bowl, beat the eggs and add the corn or salad oil and the mashed banana and whisk again. Then, slowly stirring all the time, add this mixture to the flour mixture.

Turn the mixture into the prepared baking tin and bake in the centre of the oven for about 65 minutes, until golden brown and slightly shrinking from the sides of the tin and a skewer pierced into the centre comes out clean. Turn out onto a wire rack to cool.

Make the topping by mixing together all the ingredients. Unlike when you use icing sugar, this topping will not set hard, but it is still delicious.

Once the cake is cold, spread the icing over the cake and use the prongs of a fork to make a pattern in the icing.

BANANA CAKE

This is an old trusty family favourite that I have adapted to include dried stevia as this herb combines so well with bananas. If you have a food processor this recipe takes seconds, alternatively it is a good workout for your beating arm.

Serves 8–10

2 bananas
100 g soft margarine
1 level tsp dried stevia leaves
2 eggs
225 g self-raising flour
1 level tsp baking powder
2 tbsp milk

Pre-heat the oven to 180°C/350°F/gas mark 4. Grease a 20-cm round cake tin.

If you are using a food processor, add the bananas and process for 10 seconds, remove the cover and add the margarine, stevia, eggs, flour, baking power and milk. Replace the cover and mix for 10 seconds.

Alternatively, for those making this recipe by hand, in a large mixing bowl, mash the bananas until fine, then add the margarine and stevia and mix well. Beat the eggs in a small bowl and gradually mix them into the banana, margarine and stevia. Slowly add the flour and baking powder and mix carefully so as not to get lumps. Add the milk and stir to combine.

Pour the mixture into the prepared cake tin and bake in the centre of the oven for about 1 hour until well risen and golden brown.

Turn out of the tin and cool on a wire rack. Serve just as it is or with unsalted butter.

Excess stevia

Dried stevia leaves

The object of good drying is to completely eliminate the water content of the plant and, at the same time, retain its essential oils and flavour. These leaves will be three to four times sweeter than the fresh leaves, so do use them carefully and sparingly. The dried leaves can be used ground or in a liquid solution.

Spread out the leaves in a thin layer on a wooden rack covered in muslin and place in a warm, dark, dry and well-ventilated room. If you have a spare room, this is ideal, with the curtains drawn; alternatively, use a cupboard with the door left ajar.

Turn the herbs over by hand several times during the first week. When the leaves are totally dry and crumble easily when crushed, they can be stored.

Put the leaves into a dark glass jar with a screw top and label with the name and date. The shelf life of the dried herb is approximately 1 year.

SWEET CICELY

(also known as Anise, Myrrh, Roman Plant, Sweet Bracken,
Sweet Fern, Switch)

Myrrhis odorata

I did not discover sweet cicely until I started the herb farm. I found it growing at one of the herb gardens I was restoring and became fascinated by its history and by the fact that it is hardly used today. With the current culinary trend for eating what our ancestors ate, I foresee this herb coming back into 'vogue'.

Description

This attractive, hardy perennial herb is one of the first to emerge after the winter. In spring you can literally sit and watch it grow. The finely divided, fern-like green leaves smell of sweet anise when crushed and it bears clusters of small white flowers. The attractive long seeds start green and ripen to black in the autumn, and they too have an anise flavour when eaten in the green.

Sweet cicely prefers a humus-rich, well-draining soil in light shade. It is renowned for self seeding, so if the seed is not wanted, either to reproduce the plant or for winter flavouring, the whole plant should be cut down immediately after flowering. This will encourage a new batch of leaves to develop which are great for late-summer salads or puddings. The plant can be raised from seed sown in the autumn, as it needs a frost to germinate, or from division of well-established plants in autumn when the plants start to die back.

History in cooking

An ancient herb, sweet cicely can be found growing wild throughout Britain. There are records of the herbalist John Gerard, in the 16th century, enjoying the roots boiled like parsnips. The seeds are known in the countryside as a wayside nibble.

Harvesting and uses

Leaves:

Pick the leaves from spring until early autumn. The flavour of the leaf is sweet aniseed. Chop finely and stir into salads, dressings and omelettes. Add to soups, stews and to boiling water when cooking cabbage. Add to cream for a sweeter, less fatty taste.

Flowers:

The whole flower is edible and can be harvested as it appears from early to mid-spring. Detach each individual flower from the cluster making sure all green bits are removed. The sweet anise flavour is lovely with tart fruit dishes, or try it mixed with apple purée, plum fool or rhubarb tarts.

Seeds:

Harvest ripe seeds from late summer. Toss unripe seeds, which have a sweet anise flavour and a nutty texture, into fruit salads or chop into ice cream. Ripe seeds have a nutty anise flavour and can be used whole in cooked dishes such as apple pie, or crushed to flavour soups and sauces.

Roots:

Dig up from early autumn. The roots can be cooked as a vegetable and either served with butter or a white sauce, or allowed to cool, then chopped up and added to salads. Alternatively, they can be eaten raw, peeled and grated, and served in a French salad dressing. The best description as to the flavour is to think of parsnip with an added hint of aniseed. The root, I know from first-hand experience, makes a very good wine – so good it won first prize for a root wine at the local wine circle.

Properties

Sweet cicely contains a volatile oil that includes anethole, which is also found in fennel. This produces the sweet anise flavour of the leaves, flowers and seeds which aids the digestion of acid, spicy and fatty foods.

Different varieties

None.

PASTA WITH SPRING HERB SAUCE

The most wonderful spring meal; fresh pasta tastes delicious with the anise of the sweet cicely, the sourness of the sorrel, the onion aroma of the chives and the fresh flavour of the parsley.

Serves 4

120 ml extra virgin olive oil
1 onion, finely chopped
4 tbsp fresh breadcrumbs
6 sweet cicely leaves, washed, dried, thick stems removed and coarsely chopped
6 baby sorrel leaves, washed, dried, thick stems removed and coarsely chopped
a handful of chives, cut with scissors
a handful of parsley leaves, finely chopped
500 g fresh pasta
salt and freshly ground black pepper
Parmesan, grated, to serve

Heat 2 tablespoons of the oil in a deep frying pan and fry the onion and breadcrumbs until crisp.

In a large bowl, add all the herbs to the remaining oil.

Fill a large pan with salted water and bring to the boil, then add the pasta. Once the pasta is al dente, drain well then toss it in the oil and fresh herbs mixture. Season with black pepper, fold in the onion and breadcrumbs, and serve immediately with the Parmesan.

SWEET CICELY AND RHUBARB PUDDING

This pudding is based around an old Yorkshire recipe. Historically the county was famous for its rhubarb. For those of you that have walked the Yorkshire Dales you will have seen sweet cicely growing in profusion along the sides of the roads and at the edges of the fields, so this pudding is a true Yorkshire celebration. Traditionally this is served with custard, however clotted cream is also great.

Serves 4–6

4 egg whites
120 g plain flour
180 ml milk
75 g raisins
350 g young rhubarb stems
3 tbsp butter
1 tbsp light oil (grape or sunflower)
120 g sweet cicely leaves, finely chopped
2 tbsp brown sugar

Pre-heat the oven to 200°C/400°F/gas mark 6.

Lightly beat the egg whites then incorporate the flour, milk and raisins. Leave the batter to settle while you prepare the other ingredients.

Wash the rhubarb, remove the leaves and the white part at the end of the stem, then slice into 2.5-cm lengths. Place the rhubarb in a bowl, cover with boiling water and leave for 5 minutes. Drain.

In a deep-sided roasting tin, put 1 tablespoon of the butter with the oil. Place the tin in the oven until the oil bubbles but does not brown. Pour the batter, with the raisins, into the base of the hot tin. Immediately sprinkle the rhubarb and sweet cicely into the centre of the batter, leaving a 3 cm border around the edge. Return to the oven and bake for 20 minutes, or until the top has browned.

Melt the remaining butter in a pan and stir in the sugar. Allow to cook until syrupy, then drizzle over the top of the pudding.

SWEET CICELY SODA BREAD

As a child I visited Southern Ireland regularly as my father was brought up in Tipperary. There we often had soda bread; it was the first bread I was taught to make because, unlike standard bread, you do not have to knead it for hours.

Many herbs can be added to soda bread, but sweet cicely imparts a lovely anise flavour to the bread which, when eaten with a good potato soup, is superb.

Makes 1 large or 2 small loaves

50 g butter, plus extra for greasing
50 g porridge oats
1 tsp bicarbonate of soda
1 tsp cream of tartar
(don't skip this, it is important)
250 g plain flour,
plus extra for dusting
125 g wholemeal flour
1 tsp salt
2 tbsp sweet cicely leaves, removed from the stems, finely chopped
250–275 ml sour milk or, if you can, buttermilk

Pre-heat the oven to 220°C/425°F/gas mark 7 and grease a baking sheet or line it with non-stick baking parchment.

Combine the oats, bicarbonate of soda, cream of tartar and both the flours in a large bowl. Add the salt and rub in the butter until it resembles breadcrumbs. Add the sweet cicely, mix, then pour in the sour milk or buttermilk, adding just enough to form a soft but not sticky dough. If you have made it too wet, add a tiny bit more flour.

Combine the ingredients, then turn out onto a lightly floured board and knead gently, and I mean gently, for a few minutes. Shape into a round and place on the baking sheet. Flatten slightly with your hand and then, using a sharp knife, mark a cross in the surface of the dough. Bake for about 25–30 minutes until cooked.

Remove from the oven, place on a wire rack, cover the hot bread with a clean tea towel and allow to cool. Serve barely warm. This bread only keeps for a day, but on the plus side it does freeze, in an airtight freezerproof container, for 1 month.

Excess sweet cicely

The seeds are the most prolifically produced part of this plant, and they are ideal for drying. Once dried, they can be used throughout the autumn and winter to add a light, nutty anise flavour to soups, stews, sauces and apple pies.

Harvesting sweet cicely seeds

The seeds are ripe for harvesting when they turn black and start falling from the plant. It is important to harvest seeds on a dry, still, sunny day. Always collect seeds after midday so that any morning dew has dried off.

The seeds are easily large enough to handle, so take a paper bag or a seed tray lined with newspaper so that you can collect as much as possible and prevent it spreading around the garden. Also, especially if you intend to collect other seeds, take a plant label to put in with the seeds so you do not forget what you have collected.

Once you have collected enough seeds, clean them by removing them from the stems. Spread them out thinly on some muslin or kitchen paper, place in a dry, airy room and leave for a few days until totally dry. Check them before storing as there is no point in keeping damaged or eaten seeds.

Store the seeds in a labelled dark glass jar, cardboard box or paper envelope for up to 2 years.

TARRAGON

(also known as French tarragon, Estragon, Little Dragon)
Artemisia dracunculus

Both my grandmother and mother used this herb profusely in the kitchen and, it is fair to say, it was this herb that was the key to my starting the herb farm. It all came about because a girl friend of mine asked me for some tarragon as she was cooking an Elizabeth David recipe. I realised that it was not possible to buy fresh French tarragon anywhere in the UK, so I started propagating it, then selling it on to shops and garden centres. The demand for French tarragon and other fresh herbs we were growing meant that we quickly grew out of our garden in Bristol and, 23 years ago, we moved to our present site.

Description

French tarragon is an elegant, hardy, herbaceous perennial which dies back in early winter, reappearing in early spring. It has tiny yellow flowers in summer, however it rarely flowers in cool climates. The long, mid-green aromatic leaves are smooth in texture and have a lovely anise flavour when eaten.

This form of tarragon can only be raised from cuttings taken from growing tips or roots in spring. Russian tarragon, on the other hand, is also a hardy herbaceous perennial with vigorous growth, can be grown from seed sown in spring. When planting French tarragon in the garden, choose a well-drained site in a sunny position and protect from excessive wet and cold in winter. Russian tarragon will grow in any conditions. Either tarragon will grow well in containers; use a soil-based substrate and protect the herb from excessive wet and cold. Cut watering down in the winter to minimal and place the container in a frost-free environment.

History in cooking

In ancient times the mixed juices of tarragon and fennel made a favourite drink for the kings of India. This Rolls-Royce of the kitchen has been attributed with causing the divorce of Henry VIII from Catherine of Aragon, because of her excessive use of it in cooking.

Harvesting and uses

Leaves:
Pick the leaves from early spring to early autumn. Their flavour varies as the season progresses. The sweetest anise flavour comes in early spring, so this is the ideal time for making tarragon vinegar as one can use both the leaf and stalk. In summer the leaves become coarser and have a more intense, slightly bitter anise flavour, so these are well suited to any long cooking, such as stews, casseroles or baking.

Properties

Tarragon is a very good digestive, antioxidant, diuretic and sedative. It also contains vitamins A, B and C, and with calcium, magnesium and potassium it is beneficial for the liver as well as for easing heartburn and gastric upsets.

Different varieties

Russian Tarragon
Artemisia dracunculoides
A hardy herbaceous perennial that has tiny, insignificant yellow flower heads in summer. The long, narrow mid-green leaves are slightly coarse in texture and the flavour is similar to grass with a hint of anise. This plant originates from Siberia, hence the name Russian tarragon, and which also explains why it is so hardy.

Winter Tarragon, Mexican Tarragon
Tagetes lucida
This variety is a tender herbaceous perennial with yellow marigold flowers in late summer and narrow, lance-shaped, aromatic, mid-green toothed leaves, which have strong aniseed/liquorice scent and flavour. In cool climates this herb dies back in early spring, reappearing in early summer, hence one of its common names, winter tarragon.

CONSOMMÉ À L'ESTRAGON

One of my grandmother's friends, Lady Jekyll, whose sister-in-law was the famous gardener Gertrude Jekyll, gave this recipe to my grandmother. Apparently when Lady Jekyll made this soup the tarragon would have cost 6d – i.e. 6 old pennies from the market. My grandmother recommends this soup for those who are trying to lose weight. Personally I think it is simply a great summer soup, and the French tarragon in it makes it a good digestive at the start of a dinner party.

The soup is by far the best when made with a home-made stock, made either from a chicken carcass or a clear stock made from vegetables.

Serves 6

1.5 litres good chicken or vegetable stock (see page 13)
8 French tarragon sprigs (approx. 15 cm long)
2 egg whites
1 tbsp French tarragon leaves, finely chopped
salt and freshly ground black pepper

Pour the stock into a large pan, add the French tarragon sprigs and simmer on a very low heat for 30 minutes.

Ten minutes before serving the soup, fill a deep-sided frying pan with water, place on the hob and bring to the boil. In a bowl, whisk the egg whites to stiff peaks and fold into the tarragon leaves. Drop 6 small tablespoons of whipped egg whites into the boiling water to poach for 3 minutes. Turn each one over after 1 minute to cook on the other side.

Pour the hot soup into individual mugs or bowls. Drain each poached egg white and let them float like islands on the top of the soup. Serve.

RUTH'S VERSION OF PANNA (1931)

This recipe is taken from my grandmother's cookbook, *Lovely Food* (1931). She suggested cooking this as, 'A short dinner for people one really likes, who often come to one's house, and whose conversation is too good to allow it to be disturbed by many courses'. Serve with fresh toast.

Serves 6–8

1 handful of spinach leaves
1 onion, finely chopped
1 French tarragon sprig
1 bunch of flatleaf parsley
2 hard-boiled eggs
3–4 sardines, from a can
some anchovies, from a can
30 g butter
salt and freshly ground black pepper

Place the spinach, onion, French tarragon and parsley in a large pan over a medium heat and, using a wooden spoon, gently stir until the spinach has wilted down.

Press out all the water from the boiled vegetables and herbs. Have ready the eggs, sardines, anchovies and butter. Pound everything together and pass through a sieve.

Season well and spread on a baking sheet. Place this on ice until you are ready for it to be sent to the table.

To serve, the panna should be cut with a cutter into round pieces about 4 cm thick and 1 piece given to each person.

Serve on crushed ice in a silver dish.

MY VERSION OF PANNA (2008)

My mother inherited this dish from her mother who passed it onto me. Until I wrote this down I have never followed a particular recipe; it is one of those dishes that once you have the main ingredients – fish, spinach, egg and French tarragon – you can adapt to suit your palate or to work with what's in your cupboards. If you prefer, you can use 150 g of smoked mackerel instead of the sardines and anchovy. The French tarragon goes so well with the fish that it is the one ingredient I would not miss off.

This is a versatile dish which can be served as a first course with toast or some oatmeal biscuits or is great for lunch served with salads. Or, if there is any left over (which is rare) it can be used in sandwiches.

300 g spinach leaves
1 onion, finely chopped
2 French tarragon sprigs
(approx. 15 cm long), leaves
removed and chopped
1 bunch of flatleaf parsley, chopped
2 hard-boiled eggs,
peeled and quartered
1 can sardines in olive oil
(88 g drained weight)
1 can anchovy fillets in olive oil
(30 g drained weight)
60 g unsalted butter
freshly grated nutmeg

Place the spinach in a large pan over a medium heat and, using a wooden spoon, gently stir until the spinach has wilted down.

Remove from the heat, put in a colander and press out all the excess moisture.

Add all the remaining ingredients to a food processor, except the nutmeg, then add the warm spinach. Whiz, stop, and whiz again. Do not over process, as this is much better if it is not too fine.

Once mixed, grate in the nutmeg to taste, stir well, then put into a small dish. Cover and keep in the fridge until needed.

CHICKEN AND TARRAGON ROULADE

The first time I cooked this recipe from my Aunt Anthea, I was serving a cold lunch to the Fruit, Vegetable and Herb committee of the RHS; I had been told 18 were coming but 26 turned up. This amazing roulade managed to stretch magnificently.

The French tarragon makes this dish; the anise flavour combines well with the cream cheese and chicken which is then offset by the smoked bacon. A great combination. Serve with a fresh, crisp green salad and new potatoes covered in mint.

Serves 6–8

6 chicken breast fillets
10 rashers of traditional smoked streaky bacon
200 g cream cheese
1 tbsp French tarragon leaves, finely chopped
500 g spinach, cooked and well drained
salt and freshly ground black pepper

Pre-heat the oven to 170°C/325°F/gas mark 3.

Place a large rectangle of cling film on a board and cover with the chicken breasts, their thicker bits opened out. Don't overlap them and don't worry if there are small gaps. Cover with another sheet of cling film and bash with a wooden kitchen hammer or a rolling pin.

Take off the top layer of cling film and cover the chicken breasts with the rashers of bacon, laying them up and down, not across. On top of the bacon spread a moderate layer of cream cheese, then sprinkle over the French tarragon leaves. Finally, add a layer of spinach, having squeezed out any excess water.

Then comes the fiddly bit. Lightly oil a baking sheet and put it in front of the board. Take the far edge of the cling film and roll the chicken towards you into a Swiss roll, removing the cling flim as you go. Roll the chicken straight onto the baking sheet. Cover the roulade loosely with foil just across the top and slightly down the sides, but not so it is airtight. Place in the oven for 50 minutes.

Remove from the heat and allow to cool. Once cold, cover with clean foil and place in the fridge for 1 hour prior to serving. Serve cold, cut into thin slices.

FRENCH TARRAGON AND CHICKEN BREASTS

This is my mother's recipe, which is very simple and shows off the wonderful flavour of the tarragon. Serve this dish with jacket potatoes and a crisp green salad for a lovely summer meal.

Serves 2

25 g unsalted butter
light olive oil or sunflower oil
2 chicken breast fillets
1 shallot, finely chopped
1 garlic clove, finely chopped
1 tbsp French tarragon leaves, removed from the stem and finely chopped, plus a few whole leaves to garnish
2 tbsp crème fraîche

Heat a large frying pan with a lid and add the butter and a good glug of olive oil. Once the butter has melted, add the chicken breasts and cook on both sides until golden brown to seal the meat. Lower the heat, cover and cook for about 10 minutes until cooked through.

Remove the cooked chicken and add the shallot and garlic to the pan. Increase the heat and cook, stirring, until soft. Add the crème fraîche and cook for 1 minute.

Return the chicken breasts to the frying pan and toss them in the sauce for 1 minute. Serve garnished with some tarragon leaves.

TARRAGON ICE CREAM

Jonray and Peter Sanchez-Iglesias, who with their parents run the Michelin-starred restaurant Casamia in Bristol, gave me this recipe. They are two of the most creative young chefs who use herbs well and originally; they instinctively understand the flavours. This tarragon ice cream is no exception – it is wonderful.

Serves 4–6

300 ml double cream
300 ml whole milk
1 bunch of French tarragon (reserve a few sprigs to garnish)
1 sheet of leaf gelatine
6 egg yolks
150 g sugar

In a pan, heat the cream and milk to simmering point, then add the tarragon. Remove from the heat and leave to infuse for a minimum of 4 hours.

Strain the tarragon cream/milk through a fine sieve and return to the heat until it is just warm.

Add the leaf gelatine to a bowl of cold water and leave to soften. Whisk the egg yolks and sugar until thick and creamy, then pour the milk/cream mixture onto the egg yolks, whisking continuously.

Cook the tarragon mixture over a medium heat, stirring all the time with a wooden spoon. When the liquid is slightly thick on the back of a cool spoon, take off the heat straight away, stir in the gelatine sheet, and then pour into a bowl set over iced water to cool it right down.

Once cool, strain through a sieve then pour it into an airtight container and leave in the fridge for 2–6 hours before churning in an ice-cream machine. If you don't have an machine, put the ice cream in a freezerproof container in the freezer for 4 hours, removing it every hour to give it a good stir to break up the ice crystals.

CARROT, TARRAGON AND WALNUT BREAD

Soda bread always reminds me of my early childhood in Ireland where I used to get in the way while helping to make it. This recipe is an adaptation of an Irish soda bread recipe. Tarragon combined with toasted walnuts makes this a tasty loaf.

Makes 1 large loaf or 2 small ones

350 g plain flour,
plus extra for dusting
150 g wholemeal flour
1 tsp salt
2 tsp bicarbonate of soda
150 g carrots, grated
1 tbsp toasted walnuts, chopped
1 tbsp French tarragon leaves,
removed from the stems
and roughly chopped
300 ml low-fat yoghurt
125 ml semi-skimmed milk

Pre-heat the oven to 230°C/450°F/gas mark 8.

Combine the flours, salt and bicarbonate of soda in a large bowl, then stir in the carrots, walnuts, French tarragon, yoghurt and enough milk to make a soft and fairly sticky dough.

Remove the dough from the bowl and place onto a floured surface. Form it into a flat ball – there is no need to knead it. Put the dough on a baking sheet lined with baking parchment, slash the top with a cross and bake for 30 minutes until risen and cooked. To check if it is cooked enough, tap the bottom of the loaf – it should sound hollow.

Excess tarragon

French tarragon vinegar

One of the most useful vinegars, this recipe is also a great way to use a glut of French tarragon leaves in early summer. The vinegar can be used for salad dressings, marinades or mayonnaise.

Makes 500 ml

500 ml white wine vinegar
enough French tarragon leaves to fill a 500 ml bottle

Fill a clean empty bottle full of French tarragon leaves. Top up with white wine vinegar and seal. (Use a plastic or plastic-lined lid as vinegar corrodes metal.) Leave on a sunny windowsill for 4 weeks, shaking it gently from time to time. Strain through an unbleached coffee filter paper and return to a clean, sterilised bottle (see page 12). Add a sprig of tarragon for identification and decoration.

If you cannot wait 4 weeks for the vinegar to infuse with the herbs, try this quick method: Put the herbs and vinegar into a covered, heatproof china bowl set over a saucepan of cold water. Bring the water to the boil, then remove the bowl from the saucepan. Leave the mixture to cool for about 2 hours before use.

THYME

(also known as Serpillo, Tomillo, Garden Thyme)
Thymus vulgaris

Thyme is one of the great European culinary herbs whose use spread with the ancient Egyptians and Greeks. When it is used in cooking its wonderful smell fills the kitchen with a mouthwatering aroma. For me, this is particularly noticeable in winter, as the smell of thyme as it cooks brings summer into the kitchen. This is because it seems to radiate the warmth and sunlight that it has absorbed over the hot summer months, which is sublimely uplifting on grey winter days.

Description

Thyme is a hardy evergreen that can be found growing wild throughout many countries of the northern and southern hemispheres. It is an attractive herb, not only to the human eye, but also to bees and butterflies. It grows in two forms: upright and creeping. Both habits have small aromatic leaves which can vary in colour from dark to bright green, and tiny aromatic flowers which can also vary in colour from white through to deep red and violet.

All varieties of thyme should be planted in a well-drained soil in a sunny position. Thymes hate being wet in winter and, even worse, they hate sitting in water. Make sure the soil has adequate drainage and, if necessary, dig in extra horticultural grit. All thymes are ideal for growing in containers; use a soil-based potting compost mixed with extra grit and place in a sunny position.

To maintain a good healthy plant it is essential to trim all thymes after flowering; this not only encourages it to put on new growth but also prevents it from becoming woody and from sprawling in the wrong direction.

History in cooking

Historically thyme was used with meat dishes, especially rabbit (which was traditionally called 'cony') and to make infusions, either with wine or water. A tea was also made by pouring boiling water over wild thyme leaves, and this was drunk as a tonic to revive and refresh people who had had a period of sickness.

Harvesting and uses

Leaves:

As thyme is an evergreen the leaves can be picked fresh all year round as long as you are not too greedy. There are two methods for picking leaves for culinary use: either as whole sprigs or just leaves. Sprig length is determined by the age and type of the thyme plant. For example, if it is common thyme a sprig length, from the tip, would be on average 6–8 cm and it would certainly have some woody section. If, on the other hand, it was a creeping variety (for example, 'Jekka's'), the sprig length will be shorter, about 4–6 cm and, in the main, it would be green growth. If you just require the leaves, the simplest method of removing them from the stem is to

hold the stem at the tip and gently run your fingers down it.
The best time for preserving the leaves is before flowering, because
they have the strongest flavour then. This is in spring for the early
varieties and early summer for the remaining varieties.

Flowers:
Pick the flowers as they open from late spring until late summer.
All thyme flowers are edible. They are best used sprinkled over
cooked vegetables or rolled into pastries prior to cooking.

Properties

A valuable property of thyme is its oil, which is extracted from the
leaves. This oil contains a constituent called thymol, which is a
strong antiseptic and muscle relaxant. The antiseptic properties help
to kill any minor bugs that might be in the food prior to cooking.
Thyme oil also helps break down fatty foods like beef, therefore
aiding in the digestion of heavier dishes. In the past 10 years
research has indicated that thyme is also a strong antioxidant.

Different varieties

All thymes are edible, but in my opinion the following thymes have
good culinary flavours which combine well with a range of dishes.

Bertram Anderson Thyme
Thymus pulegioides 'Bertram Anderson'
Mild flavour, good with vegetables.

Broad-leafed Thyme
Thymus pulegioides
Strong rounded flavour, excellent with meat, especially for roasting.

Caraway-scented Thyme
Thymus herba-barona
Original caraway flavour that goes well with chicken and meat, and
works well in both marinades and dressings.

Common Thyme, Garden Thyme
Thymus vulgaris
Ideal for bouquets garnis and with meat, chicken, fish, cheese
and in sauces.

Compact Thyme
Thymus vulgaris 'Compactus'
The leaf has a stronger flavour than common thyme. Good with
meat, duck and in marinades.

Creeping Lemon Thyme
Thymus 'Creeping Lemon'
This has a true lemon scent and flavour. Perfect with chicken, fish, vegetables and for making marinades and dressings.

French Thyme
Thymus vulgaris 'French'
This has the most pungent flavour of the thymes listed here. Use with tomatoes, fish and chicken, and in dressings and sauces.

Golden Lemon Thyme
Thymus citriodorus 'Golden Lemon'
This has a pungent flavour and scent that is lemon with a hint of spice. It works well in marinades, dressings and with chicken dishes.

Golden thyme
Thymus pulegioides 'Aureus' AGM
This has a lovely warm flavour and is good with vegetable dishes and tomatoes.

Jekka's Thyme
Thymus 'Jekka'
Well, what can I say? This is a seedling that appeared on the farm, and it grew and grew. It has a wonderful robust habit, surviving all weathers. It is great with vegetable and meat dishes.

Lemon Thyme
Thymus citriodorus
This has a strong lemon flavour and scent. Delicious with fish and chicken, and in dressing and marinades.

Orange-scented Thyme
Thymus 'Fragrantissimus'
I am a real fan of this thyme. The flavour is warm and spicy with a hint of orange. Excellent with strong meats and adds flavour to spicy puddings. It is also good in sauces, marinades and dressings.

Pine-scented Thyme
Thymus longicaulis
This thyme has a unique flavour which should be used sparingly. Ideal for marinades.

Porlock Thyme
Thymus 'Porlock'
An early-season thyme that has a warm mild flavour in comparison to French thyme. Goes well with all forms of food: meat and vegetables alike. Excellent in bread, too.

Silver Posie Thyme
Thymus vulgaris 'Silver Posie'
This has a mild flavour reminiscent of garden thyme but softer. Good with vegetables, chicken and in sauces.

Silver Queen Thyme
Thymus x *citriodorus* 'Silver Queen'
An interesting lemon-flavoured and scented thyme. Good with fish, vegetables and puddings. Good in pastry.

THYME SOUFFLÉ

I always thought soufflés were for sophisticated cooks, so I was delighted to find that they were not, and I vividly remember creating this dish with much pride when we lived in our first house. My tips are to whisk the egg whites until they form stiff peaks, not to open the oven door while the soufflé is rising, and to have everyone sitting at the table before you take the soufflé out of the oven.

The fresh thyme leaves combined with the cheese makes these little soufflés extra special.

Serves 6

50 g unsalted butter, plus extra for greasing
40 g plain flour
300 ml milk
a pinch of cayenne pepper
¼ tsp mustard powder
a little freshly grated nutmeg
1 heaped tbsp French, common, or compact thyme leaves, removed from the stems and finely chopped
salt and freshly ground black pepper
75 g Parmesan, freshly grated, or any other strong-flavoured cheese (it needs to be strong to balance the thyme)
3 medium eggs, separated, plus one extra egg white

Pre-heat the oven to 190°C/375°F/gas mark 5. Butter 6 x 8 cm ramekins.

Melt the butter in a pan and stir in the flour. Cook for 1 minute, stirring all the time. Remove from the heat and gradually blend in the milk. Return to the heat and cook for a few minutes, stirring constantly until the mixture thickens and is very smooth.

Remove from the heat, stir in the cayenne pepper, mustard and nutmeg. Add the thyme, salt and black pepper and mix vigorously until blended. Allow this mixture to cool a little before stirring in the Parmesan. In a bowl, beat the egg yolks thoroughly then stir them in. Set aside.

In an immaculately clean bowl, whisk the 4 egg whites until they are stiff. They should be glossy and should stand in stiff peaks. Using a metal spoon, fold 1 tablespoon at a time of the beaten egg whites into the egg and milk mixture; be careful and gentle to ensure that you do not flatten the egg whites.

Spoon the mixture into the prepared ramekins. Bake in the middle of the oven for 15–18 minutes until well-risen and golden brown on top. Serve immediately.

THYME AND CHEESE TOMATOES

This is a lovely summer meal. If you have lemon thyme the flavour is brilliant with tomatoes, if not, garden thyme is a good substitute. Serve with a crisp green salad and dauphinoise potatoes.

Serves 6

6 large, ripe firm tomatoes
salt and freshly ground
black pepper
1 tbsp lemon thyme leaves,
finely chopped
1 tbsp parsley, finely chopped
1 garlic clove, finely sliced
1 tbsp Parmesan,
freshly grated
1 tbsp strong Cheddar,
freshly grated
2 tbsp breadcrumbs
8 tbsp olive oil

Pre-heat the oven to 180°C/350°F/gas mark 4.

Wash, dry and halve the tomatoes and gently scoop out the flesh and seeds using a teaspoon. Be careful not to break the skins and to leave enough tomato flesh to keep the shape of the fruit. Put the flesh into a bowl and the tomato halves into an ovenproof dish, cut-side up. Season with salt and black pepper.

To the bowl of tomato flesh, add the thyme, parsley and garlic, stir in the grated cheeses, the breadcrumbs and 4 tablespoons of the olive oil. Spoon the mixture into the tomato halves. Drizzle over the remaining olive oil and cook in the oven for 25 minutes or until the tomatoes are lightly golden on top.

THYME CHICKEN PARCELS

In one of Jamie Oliver's early TV series I watched him creating meals by wrapping the ingredients in foil and then baking them in the oven. I immediately thought what a brilliant idea and adapted some of my recipes to suit this method of cooking.

Here, the flavour of the thyme is enhanced by the light flavour of the leek and the white wine, which all infuse the chicken. This is a great way to cook; all the flavours are locked in and there's also minimal washing up to be done.

Serves 2

1 red or yellow pepper, seeded and sliced
1 leek, well washed and sliced
1 large glass of white wine
45 g unsalted butter, cut into little pieces
1 tbsp broad-leaved thyme leaves (or you can use compact, lemon- or orange-scented, caraway, French or common)
2 garlic cloves, finely chopped
olive oil
sea salt and freshly ground black pepper
2 skinless chicken breast fillets, lightly scored

For each chicken breast you will need 1 piece of foil 360 mm x 400 mm and 1 piece of greaseproof paper 360 mm x 400 mm

Pre-heat the oven to 170°C/325°F/gas mark 3.

Mix together the pepper, leek, wine, butter, thyme, garlic, olive oil, salt and black pepper in a bowl.

Place the pieces of foil on a work surface and on top of each place the greaseproof paper. Fold in half and then seal the two shorter sides by folding over twice, leaving the top open, thereby creating a bag. Into each bag place a chicken breast and half of the mixture you have in the bowl. Once the ingredients are in, fold over the top twice to seal the bag.

Carefully, so as not to make a hole in the bags, place them in a roasting tin and bake in the middle of the oven for 25 minutes. Do take great care when opening the bag as these will release hot steam and hot liquid. I recommend doing this at the table with any other vegetables or rice that you have prepared already plated, so you can serve the chicken direct.

BAKED LAMB STEW WITH POTATOES AND THYME

Serves 6

1 kg stewing lamb, cut into chunks,
or 12 small chops
2 large red onions,
roughly chopped
1 kg potatoes, peeled and
cut into large chunks
salt and freshly ground
black pepper
3 tbsp thyme leaves (a single
variety or a mixture of compact,
Porlock, French, common or Jekka's)
3 tbsp celery leaf, including
the stems, chopped (or use
flatleaf parsley)
125 ml water
125 ml olive oil
6 ripe large tomatoes,
cut into thick slices
50 g butter

This is a form of Irish stew that my mother regularly made from cheap cuts of lamb. The potatoes absorb the fat released from the lamb as it cooks, which in turn makes them delicious. The thyme enhances the flavour of the lamb. You can use stewing lamb or, if you wish to impress, you can use lamb chops. It is a highly aromatic, warming and nourishing all-in-one meal.

Ideally, serve with fresh crusty bread and salad or broccoli.

Pre-heat the oven to 180°C/350°F/gas mark 4.

Put the lamb, onions and potatoes into a large casserole dish or a deep baking dish and season to taste. Add the thyme, celery leaf, water and olive oil.

Mix the ingredients thoroughly with your hands, turning all the vegetables and meat over. Cover the potatoes and lamb with a single layer of sliced tomatoes, lightly salt, then dot with butter over the top. Cover with a double layer of greaseproof paper or foil and bake in the oven for 2 hours. From time to time, remove the cover and spoon some of the juices over the top of the dish. When cooked the lamb should be tender and the potatoes soft.

Remove the casserole from the oven, increase the oven temperature to 200°C/400°F/gas mark 6. Remove the greaseproof paper or foil, return the casserole to the oven and cook for a further 45 minutes. After 20 minutes gently, but thoroughly, turn the lamb, potatoes and tomatoes. This will brown the potatoes and the meat as well as reducing the cooking juices.

ORANGE-SCENTED THYME IN TREACLE AND ALMOND TART

Here is a family favourite which, when served with Cornish clotted cream, turns into a treat. Over 20 years ago I had a visitor to the herb farm who introduced me to the idea of using thyme in puddings. Once she had left I went to the cottage and immediately experimented and discovered that the sharp aromatic flavour of thyme offsets the sweetness of sugar or, in this case, treacle.

Serves 6

For the pastry

140 g unsalted butter, plus
extra for greasing
200 g plain flour, plus
extra for dusting
a pinch of salt
1 tsp finely chopped
orange-scented thyme leaves
4 egg yolks
cold water

For the filling

4 tbsp golden syrup
7 tbsp fresh brown breadcrumbs
2 tbsp peeled and flaked almonds
1 tbsp grated zest from an
unwaxed lemon
2 tbsp lemon juice
2 tsp finely chopped orange-
scented thyme leaves

Pre-heat the oven to 200°C/400°F/gas mark 6. Grease a 20-cm flan dish with butter.

Before making the pastry, weigh and wrap the butter in foil or cling film and place in the freezer to harden.

Sift the flour and salt into a large bowl. Remove the butter from the freezer, fold back the covering and grate over the flour using the coarsest side of the grater. Once you finish grating, add the thyme leaves and fold in with the butter and flour using a palette knife. Once the butter and flour are well combined and start to resemble breadcrumbs, use a fork to lightly mix in the egg yolks with a little cold water.

(I do use my hands for the last bit.)

Having made the dough, remove it from the bowl, place it in cling film or in a plastic bag and put it in the fridge for at least 2 hours, until you are ready to use it.

Roll out the prepared pastry on a lightly floured surface to about 3 mm thick. Gently lift it from the table and line the prepared flan dish. Cut off any excess pastry, and set aside – this can be used to decorate the top of the tart. Prick the base all over using a fork.

Mix together the filling ingredients and spread them gently and evenly over the base of the tart. Decorate with the remaining pastry trimmings. Bake for 25–30 minutes on the middle shelf of the oven, until golden.

Serve hot or it can be eaten cold, if you can keep it that long.

LEMON THYME APPLE SAUCE

The citrus flavour of the lemon thyme is perfect with the tartness of cooking apples. This sauce is great hot or cold and can be served with pork chops or a roast griskin. A griskin is a special pork cut which I thought was common but have since found it is rarely known outside South Gloucestershire and Bristol. It is the cut usually reserved for making back bacon and it is brilliant as there is absolutely no waste. Buy a large enough bit to do two meals.

A griskin is great roasted and almost even better cold, thinly sliced and served with this lemon thyme apple sauce, spicy red cabbage and dauphinoise potatoes.

Serves 4–6

45 g unsalted butter
2 cooking apples, peeled and cut into quarters, cored, then sliced
2 tsp lemon thyme leaves
caster sugar, to taste

Melt the butter in a small pan. Add the sliced apples and lemon thyme leaves, stir, reduce the heat to minimum, cover and cook very slowly, checking from time to time to make sure it does not stick. The apple will break down but not become totally mushy.

Check for sweetness; if you or your family has a sweet tooth, add sugar to taste and stir well. Cook for a further 2 minutes to dissolve the sugar. Serve hot or cold.

Excess thyme

As thyme is evergreen there are always leaves that can be picked to use fresh, so there is no need to dry or freeze them. However, at certain times of the year, especially during flowering, when there is a profusion of flowers, and just after flowering, when the plant is cut back, you will have a lot of leaves available.

The great thing about thyme leaves and flowers is that they are so versatile; they can be used and preserved in many ways.

Thyme leaf butter

This butter can be used with grilled fish, pushed under the skin of a chicken prior to roasting, rubbed into flour or simply put on cooked vegetables.

Makes 125 g

a handful of thyme leaves, from any of your favourites
125 g unsalted butter, slightly softened

Gently chop the thyme leaves to release the oils. Then mix the chopped leaves with the unsalted butter. (It is important to use unsalted butter because it has a mild flavour, compared to its salted counterpart, and the added herbs will provide enough flavour.) I have found that the simplest and easiest way of blending the herb and butter together is to use a fork.

When it has been thoroughly mixed, place it on some greaseproof paper, bringing the paper right over the butter, then roll the soft butter in the paper to make a sausage shape; this makes it easy to cut the required amounts.

Place this in the fridge for at least 24 hours before use. The longer you leave it, the better the flavour. Use within 2 weeks. Alternatively, it can be frozen for use within 3 months.

Thyme leaf vinegar

This is a useful vinegar to use in marinades and mayonnaise.

Makes 500 ml

thyme leaves
500 ml white wine vinegar

Fill a clean empty bottle with fresh thyme leaves. Top up with white wine vinegar and seal. (Use a plastic or plastic-lined top as vinegar corrodes metal.) Leave on a sunny windowsill for 4 weeks, shaking gently from time to time. Strain off the liquid through unbleached coffee filter paper into another clean, sterilised bottle. Put a sprig of thyme in the bottle for identification and decoration.

If you cannot wait 4 weeks for the vinegar to infuse with the herbs, try this quick method, which is good for emergencies, although the longer method produces better-flavoured vinegar: Put the herbs and vinegar into a covered, heatproof glass or china bowl and set it over, but not touching, a pan of cold water. Bring the water to the boil, remove the bowl from the pan and leave it to cool for about 2 hours before using the vinegar. Being vinegar this will keep for a number of years in a dark cupboard.

VIETNAMESE CORIANDER

(also known as Rau Ram, Laksa Plant, Vietnamese Hot Mint)
Persicaria odorata

I was given this herb by John Carter, who is one of the most erudite men I have met, he also is an extremely good plant collector specialising in water plants. He was given this herb by a nursery in Australia which was given it in turn by some Vietnamese boat people. In Australia it is called Vietnamese Hot Mint, which is a misnomer as it is not a member of the mint family but a member of the knotweed family.

Persicaria odorata is the only one of the Persicarias that is edible, so please be careful. The first time I ate its leaves I was totally taken by surprise. To begin with the taste is mild with a hint of lime and spice, then as the flavour develops it becomes hot and peppery.

Description

Vietnamese coriander is a subtropical, evergreen perennial. It has attractive creamy white flowers in summer which are rarely produced in cold climates, even when it is grown as a house plant. The highly aromatic leaves have a narrow, brown/maroon V shape near the base. In cold climates this herb happily adapts to being grown as a house plant. Position it in a window that does not get the midday sun as this will scorch the leaves. You will find that it does grow fast, so it will need repotting twice a year. In the tropics it is a rampant grower and will spread happily around the garden.

History in cooking

This native Vietnamese wild plant is considered a traditional herb in Thai, Malaysian and Vietnamese cooking, where its hot pungent flavour with a hint of lime is used to flavour soups and fish dishes.

Harvesting and uses

Leaves:

As this is an evergreen herb there is little need to preserve it, as the leaves are available all year. However, it does make good oils and vinegars and the best leaves for this are the new young leaves rather than the tougher old leaves.

Properties

Throughout the Far East Vietnamese coriander is used to treat indigestion, flatulence and stomach aches. It is reputedly eaten by Buddhist Monks to suppress sexual urges. This herb is never cooked; it is used as a fresh leaf condiment and is always added at the end of cooking. In Asia it is usually eaten raw as a salad or herb accompaniment. It combines well with meat, vegetables and fruit. It is important in Vietnamese cooking, being used copiously with noodle soups (pho), where large heaps of the leaves are dipped into the soup using chopsticks.

Different varieties

No other member of this plant family is edible, so please be careful.

MELON À L'INDIENNE WITH VIETNAMESE CORIANDER

My mother always made this first course when she was in a hurry and had a house full of people who had to be fed fast. I had no idea until I was reading my grandmother's cook books that she was the origin of this amazing dish. I have added the Vietnamese coriander to this recipe because the flavour of the leaf, with its hint of limes, heat and spice, combines so well with the cool sweetness of melon.

If you have a food processor the flavour of home-made mayonnaise is brilliant, but for speed one can buy good ready-to-eat mayonnaise from many stores. However, in case you wish to make your own, I've included here a reliable recipe. Use enough of it to coat the fruit and reserve the rest for sandwiches, potato salads or other dishes. Store in the fridge and use within 48 hours.

Warning: There can be an increased risk of salmonella poisoning when eating raw and lightly cooked eggs. Pregnant women, the elderly and young children should take particular care and such dishes are not recommended.

Serves 4–6

1 melon (I would normally choose a honeydew or similar; it doesn't work with watermelon)
2 tsp curry powder (preferably a mild korma spice blend made with coriander, cumin and turmeric)
2 Vietnamese coriander leaves, very thinly sliced, plus one left whole to decorate

For the mayonnaise
2 egg yolks
½ tsp Dijon mustard
2 tbsp white wine vinegar
275 ml olive oil
salt and freshly ground black pepper

First make the mayonnaise. Place the egg yolks and mustard in the food processor bowl with 1 teaspoon of the vinegar. Process until all is well mixed. With the machine switched on, very slowly add the olive oil in a steady stream through the feed tube until all the oil has been used up and the mayonnaise is thick and shining. With the machine still on, very slowly add the remaining vinegar.

Switch the machine off, add salt and black pepper to taste and give it a quick whiz, then place in a bowl and cover and refrigerate until needed.

Cut a thin slice off the bottom of the melon so it will stand up. Cut the top off the melon and reserve it. Remove the seeds from the centre and put them into a sieve, over a bowl, so you can save the juice. Use a serving spoon to remove the flesh from inside the melon and place this into another bowl. Go as deep as you dare, but try not to break through the bottom or the sides.

Mix the juice from the seeds in the bowl with 2 tablespoons of mayonnaise, the curry powder, sliced Vietnamese coriander and all the melon pieces. Once combined, check it for flavour.

Put the melon pieces back into the melon skin and decorate with one leaf of Vietnamese coriander. Replace the reserved top of the melon as a lid and pop it into the fridge for at least 2 hours before serving.

VIETNAMESE CORIANDER, GREEN BEAN AND MUSHROOM STIR-FRY SALAD

The pungency of the Vietnamese coriander with vegetables is excellent, as it adds another dimension to the tangy soy-based flavour of the dressing. This simple dish is lovely served with noodles as a light supper or lunch.

Serves 2

200 g French beans, topped and tailed
3 tbsp sunflower oil
100 g mushrooms, sliced
2 tbsp light soy sauce
2 tbsp white wine vinegar
salt and freshly ground black pepper
2 Vietnamese coriander leaves, finely sliced

Cook the French beans in a pan of boiling water until just tender, then drain.

Heat 2 tablespoons of oil in a deep frying pan or wok, add the mushrooms and stir fry quickly. Add the beans and fry for 1 minute.

Whisk together the remaining oil, the soy sauce and vinegar and add seasoning to taste.

Turn the cooked vegetables into a bowl, scatter over the Vietnamese coriander, and then pour over the dressing, making sure all is well coated. Serve.

SPICY FISH CAKES

Here Vietnamese coriander is in its element as it goes so well with fish and lemon grass. The wonderfully flamboyant Nancy Lam cooked this herb for me at an RHS Chelsea Flower show. She created a fish curry with it, and the memory of her calmly dominating the kitchen has stayed with me. Serve with home-made tomato sauce (see page 12) or chilli dipping sauce and plain rice.

Serves 4

1 lemon grass stalk
300 g skinless cod, bream, John Dory or sea bass fillets, chopped
1 tbsp desiccated coconut
175 ml coconut milk
1 tbsp cornflour
2 egg whites, whipped to soft peaks
1 tsp ground turmeric
3 Vietnamese coriander leaves, finely sliced
1 tsp salt
1 tsp sugar
plain flour, for dusting
butter and olive oil, for frying

Grind the lemon grass stalk in a blender or food processor. In a large bowl, mix together the fish and lemon grass, then add all the other ingredients, except the flour, butter and olive oil.

Take handfuls of the mixture and form individual little cakes. Roll the cakes in the plain flour, shaking off the excess.

Heat a little butter and oil in a large frying pan and cook the fish cakes, turning them so that both sides are cooked and golden brown. Remove from the pan and drain on kitchen paper before serving.

Excess Vietnamese coriander

Vietnamese coriander oil

The leaves of this herb are excellent for making chilli oil or vinegar, and a lot easier to use. These oils and vinegars are extremely good for use in marinades, dressings and sauces.

For more information about preserving and the risks of using herbs in oils, see page 36.

Makes 250 ml

3 good handfuls of Vietnamese coriander leaves
250 ml light olive oil or sunflower oil
2 tsp lemon juice

Wash and dry the leaves on kitchen paper. Finely chop the leaves (this can be done in a food processor), add the oil and the lemon juice and mix well. Pour into a container with a sealing lid, and pop into the fridge. Use within 5 days; shake well before use as the lemon juice will separate.

Alternatively, after 2 days strain the oil through an unbleached coffee filter, pour into a clean dry container with a sealing lid and keep in the fridge. Use within 3 days; shake well before use.

Vietnamese coriander vinegar

This vinegar is ideal for use in pungent sauces or stir-fry dishes.

Makes 400 ml

8 tbsp young Vietnamese coriander leaves, sliced
400 ml white wine vinegar

Put the leaves into a jam jar, pour over the vinegar and seal with a non-metallic top. Place on a sunny windowsill and shake the jar every so often.

After 2 or 3 weeks, test the vinegar for flavour. If satisfactory, strain through an unbleached coffee filter paper and return the vinegar to a clean bottle with a single leaf as decoration. Label and date the bottle.

This will keep happily for a year or even longer, as vinegar does not age like oil.

VIOLET

(also known as Garden Violet, Sweet Violet)
Viola odorata

This herald of spring can also be found flowering over winter, when you can catch the perfume of the flower wafting on the cold air of a crisp morning. My grandmother used these flowers to decorate food, however she was fairly scathing if they were used in profusion. To her, food was about texture, flavour and platefuls rather than being dainty, decorous and works of culinary art.

Description

The scent of the sweet-smelling white or purple flowers transports me back to my childhood. The heart-shaped leaves, which are edible, are great for early spring salads; ideal for mixing with salad burnet, sorrel and mustard leaves in particular. All violas are edible, but the small-flowering species have a far better flavour than the large ones. The best of the lot for flavour and scent are sweet violets.

Sweet violets are fully hardy and can be easily grown in a semi-shaded position. They thrive in a moderately heavy rich soil. If you have a light or gravelly soil some texture should be added; a mulch of well-rotted manure the previous autumn is a good idea, which can be dug in in spring. You can raise this plant from seed sown in early autumn, however it is much easier to propagate from the runners of an established plant removed in spring or by division of an established plant in early summer after it has finished flowering.

History in cooking

This charming herb has been much loved throughout the ages and, having been around for over 2,000 years there are many myths. The one I am particularly fond of is based on a Greek legend. Zeus fell in love with a beautiful maiden called Io and he turned her into a cow to protect her from his jealous wife, Juno. The Earth grew violets to be Io's food, and so the flower was named after her. Historically, the crystallising of the flowers dates back to the 13th century, at which time they were boiled in sugar and sold by the French apothecaries.

Harvesting and uses

Leaves:
The leaves are available all year round, but they have their best flavour in late spring. They have a mild flavour that is good in salads, but the mature leaves are tough, so it is best to use new growth.

Flowers:
Pick the flowers as they appear from late winter to mid-spring. Harvest them in the late morning when the dew has dried and the flower is fully open.

Properties Traditionally the flowers were used in cough medicine and as a breath freshener so, from a culinary point of view, sweet violet has few digestive benefits beyond fresh breath. Medicinally the flowers and leaves are used to treat various skin conditions from eczema to acne.

Different varieties All the violas are hardy perennials and all are low growing.

Wood Violet
Viola reichenbachiana
This variety has pale lilac/blue flowers in early spring and heart-shaped green leaves. The flowers have little scent.

Common Dog Violet
(also known as Blue Mice, Hedging Violet, Horse Violet, Pig Violet)
Viola riviniana
Pale blue/lilac flowers in early summer and heart-shaped green leaves.

Field Pansy
Viola arvensis
This herb has predominantly white or creamy flowers in early summer. The green leaves are oval with shallow blunt teeth.

Mountain Pansy
Viola lutea
The flowers vary in single colours from yellow, blue and violet. The green leaves are oval near the base of the stem and narrower further up.

Heartsease
Viola tricolor
This variety has attractive, small tri-colour flowers which appear in many different combinations that include yellow, violet, blue, purple and white. The green leaves are deeply lobed.

VIOLET SPRING SALAD

This is a pretty salad that is also very tasty. It can be made with any green salad leaves, and for those of you lucky enough to live in or near the countryside, you can make a true spring salad with young dandelion leaves, hawthorn shoots and primroses.

Serves 4

1 lettuce (butterhead or romaine)
115 g lamb's lettuce
1 tbsp flatleaf parsley,
finely chopped
1 tbsp chervil, finely chopped
½ cucumber, peeled and chopped
1 tbsp young sweet violet leaves,
finely chopped
10–15 each sweet violet, hearts-
ease, common dog violet flowers

salad dressing
3 tbsp olive oil
1 tbsp lemon juice or
white wine vinegar
salt and freshly ground black pepper
a pinch of caster sugar

Wash and shake dry the lettuce, discarding the outer leaves, and put into a large bowl. Add all the other ingredients, except the flowers and the dressing, and gently mix.

Make the salad dressing by combining the oil and lemon juice or vinegar in a bowl and whisking thoroughly. Season with salt and black pepper to taste and add the smallest pinch of caster sugar. Add the flowers to the salad, reserving a few to add just before serving. When you are ready to serve the salad, add the dressing, toss well and decorate with the remaining flowers.

SWEET VIOLET JELLY

This is a great way to use up the apples stored over winter. Violets make this jelly so delicious that you will treasure it, or alternatively give it to friends as a special present.

Makes 2 x 350 g jars

1 kg cooking apples,
washed, cored and chopped
900 ml water
450 g sugar
8–10 tbsp sweet violet flowers,
stems and green removed (reserve
1 tbsp to decorate, if you wish)
2 tbsp lemon juice
2 tbsp white wine vinegar

Put the apples into a large pan with a lid. Add the water and bring to the boil, then simmer until the apples become soft and pulpy. This takes anything from 20–30 minutes, depending on the variety of apple. Pour carefully into a muslin (or a jelly or cheesecloth bag) and leave for a day or overnight to drain into a large bowl.

When the draining has finished, measure the juice and add 450 g of sugar to every 600 ml of juice. Put into a large pan and bring to the boil, adding the flowers tied in a piece of muslin. Boil for about 20 minutes until setting point is reached. At this point remove the flowers in the muslin and spoon off the surface scum. Stir in the lemon juice, vinegar and 1 tablespoon of flowers, if you wish, and pour into 2 warmed, sterilised glass jars (see page 12). Seal when cool, date and label the jars.

VIOLET APPLE CAKE

This is the best pudding one can make to use up apples from the winter store. The delicate flavour the violets add is beautiful.

My father gave me a food processor in 1975; it transformed my cooking and this is one of those recipes that really benefit from being made with it.

The violet apple cake is best served warm with lots of double or, even better, clotted cream. Alternatively, you can serve it cold for tea.

Serves 6–8

675 g cooking apples (before peeling and coring)
225 g self-raising flour
1½ tsp baking powder
225 g caster sugar
2 eggs
1 tsp almond essence
125 g unsalted butter
icing sugar, for dusting
2 tbsp sweet violet flowers

Pre-heat the oven to 180°C/350°F/gas mark 4. Grease and line a 25-cm, loose-bottomed, round cake tin with baking parchment or greaseproof paper.

Peel, core and quarter the apples, then either slice by hand or use the slicing disc on a food processor. Once sliced, keep them in cold water to stop them going brown until the cake mixture is made.

Sift the flour and baking powder into a large mixing bowl, add the sugar, then beat the eggs lightly with the almond essence and add to the bowl. Melt the butter and pour into the bowl. Either beat well by hand or whiz in a food processor for roughly 10 seconds. Remove the cover, scrape down the sides of the bowl then mix for a further 5 seconds.

Put half of the cake mixture into the prepared cake tin spreading it evenly over the bottom. Drain and dry the apple slices and lay them over the cake mixture in an even layer. Scatter over 1 tablespoon of violets. Spread the rest of the cake mixture on top of the apples. This mixture is rather thick and not easy to spread, but it honestly does not matter too much if some of the apple is left showing, as it will become covered during cooking.

Bake in the oven for 1½ hours until golden brown, risen and slightly shrinking away from the sides of the tin. Turn out and serve, thickly dusted with sieved icing sugar and decorated with the remaining violet flowers.

CRYSTALLISED VIOLETS

14 wild or sweet violets (including stems), washed (do not use the African Violet, Santpaulia, which is a houseplant and not edible)
2 egg whites
caster or icing sugar

I was bribed with these delightful crystallised flowers to go to dancing classes. At the end of each class Mum used to take me to Carwadines cake shop, where I always chose a small lilac cake with a crystallised violet on top.

I have mentioned crystallising flowers before in this book (see Borage, page 55), but this is the quick method which is useful not only because of its speed but also because the ingredients are easily available. However, it does use egg whites, so I should warn that there can be an increased risk of salmonella poisoning with raw and lightly cooked eggs, so care should be taken, particularly amongst pregnant women, the elderly and young children. If you are worried about the risk, please follow the crystallising method mentioned for Borage flowers on page 55–6.

Pre-heat the oven to 120°C/250°F/gas mark ½.

Pick the flowers in late morning, choosing perfect specimens. Dip them first in water to remove any insects or dust, then dry them gently on some kitchen paper.

In a bowl, beat the egg whites with a wire whisk until just frothy. Place the sugar in another bowl. Taking one violet at a time, pick it up by the stem and dip it into the egg whites, covering all surfaces. Then gently dip it into the sugar, again being sure that all of the petals, top and bottom, are covered.

Place the coated flowers on baking sheets lined with baking parchment and snip off the stems. Using a toothpick, open the petals to their original shape. Sprinkle sugar on any uncoated areas. Use a fine, clean, artist's paint brush to remove any lumps of sugar.

Dry the flowers in the oven for 30–40 minutes or until the sugar crystallises. Gently remove the violets to a wire rack with a spatula or a two-tined fork. Sprinkle again with sugar if the violets appear syrupy. Cool.

Store in airtight containers with waxed paper between layers for up to 2 weeks.

Excess sweet violet

Sweet violet syrup

This is an excellent syrup which is useful when making fruit salads, sorbets or any pudding needing an aromatic syrup base.

Makes 350 ml

300 ml water
450 g granulated or caster sugar
8–16 tbsp sweet violet flowers

Bring the water to the boil in a pan, turn down the heat and add the sugar, stirring all the time. When the sugar has dissolved, add the flowers, stirring from time to time, and gently simmer the mixture until it turns into a syrup. This can take up to 8 minutes.

Strain the syrup through a fine sieve or some muslin (cheesecloth) if you want absolutely no flower bits left. Pour the strained syrup into a clean, sterilised (see page 12) glass jar, allow to cool, seal well and store in the fridge for up to 2 weeks.

WILD STRAWBERRY

(also known as Woodland Strawberry, Fraises des Bois, Wild European Strawberry)
Fragaria vesca

This is a herb of my childhood. I remember picking wild strawberry and wortle berry on walks in the forest on Exmoor, bringing them home carefully and then eating the delicious fruit the following morning with our cereal.

Description

Wild strawberry is a low-growing hardy perennial that can spread profusely. The flowers have four or five white petals with a yellow centre, which are followed by delectable small red fruit. The leaves are bright green and are made up of three leaflets with serrated edges.

This herb can be easily grown by breaking off a runner (a miniature form of the plant with a tiny root system on a long stem coming off the parent plant), then transplanting it.

Alternatively, it can be raised from seed, which takes longer and is a less reliable method. The seed of the strawberry is visible to all, being embedded all around the outside of the fruit. To collect your own seed, leave the fruit in the sun to dry in summer. When fully dry and shrivelled, rub off the seeds and store them in a dry place until you are ready to sow them in early spring. Wild strawberry prefers a good fertile soil that does not dry out in summer, in either full sun or shade. It grows well in woods and hedgerows and makes a marvellous ground cover plant, as it spreads quickly by means of its runners.

History in cooking

This native wild strawberry is not a direct ancestor of the modern commercial varieties but is a species in its own right. Richard Mabey, in *Flora Britannica*, says that he has seen a 16th-century recipe for a form of strawberry shortcake, made with almond flour and cooked simply by leaving the paste in the hot sun for a couple of hours. In the 17th century, the famous herbalist Nicholas Culpeper said that the fruit is 'excellent good to cool the liver or a hot choleric stomach, and to quench thirst', amongst many other attributes.

Harvesting and uses

Leaves:
The leaves can be picked throughout the growing season, however the young ones are the best and have a musky flavour and scent. The leaves can be used to make teas and infusions.

Fruits:
The strawberries can be harvested from early summer until early autumn. They are delicate when ripe and are easily bruised if gathered directly into a basket or jar, so take a tray and gently lay them out so they do not touch each other. They can be added to fruit salads, eaten on their own with cream, used in cakes, pies and

syrups or to flavour cordials. If you have enough, you can also use them to make vinegar or jam.

Properties   The strawberries are a mild diuretic and have a laxative effect that improves digestive functions. The leaves are included in many blended herbal teas; they were traditionally used to treat stomach upsets. Please note this does not apply to the cultivated form of strawberry, which is why this plant is a herb.

Different varieties   Alpine Strawberry
Fragaria vesca 'Semperflorens'
This hardy perennial looks identical to the wild form, with the exception that it does not produce runners so it has to be propagated from seed.

WILD STRAWBERRY SHORTCAKE

I make no apology for this recipe, it is gorgeous, and made even more so using these delightful wild strawberries with their unique sweet aromatic flavour.

Serves 6–8

75 g unsalted butter, cut into small pieces, plus extra for greasing
250 g self-raising flour, plus extra for dusting
1 tsp baking powder
3 tbsp caster sugar, plus extra to serve
1 egg, beaten
4 tbsp semi-skimmed milk
½ tsp pure vanilla extract
90 ml whipping cream
85 g Greek-style yoghurt
1 tsp icing sugar
340 g wild strawberries

Preheat the oven to 220°C/425°F/gas mark 7. Grease a baking sheet with a little butter.

Sift the flour and baking powder into a bowl. Rub in the butter with your fingertips until the mixture resembles fine breadcrumbs. Stir in the caster sugar and make a well in the centre.

Mix together the egg, milk and vanilla extract, and pour into the dry ingredients. Gradually stir the dry ingredients into the liquid, then bring the mixture together with your hands to form a soft dough. Gently pat the dough into a smooth ball and turn it out onto a floured surface.

Roll out the dough into a 19-cm round. Transfer it to the prepared baking sheet and bake for 10–15 minutes or until well risen, firm, and browned on top. Slide the shortcake onto a wire rack and leave to cool.

Using a large serrated knife, slice the shortcake horizontally in half. With a large fish slice, lift off the top layer, place it on a board and cut into 8 equal wedges. Set aside. (If you like, for an attractive finish, trim a fraction off each cut so that the wedges are slightly smaller.) Place the bottom layer on a serving plate.

Whip the cream to soft peaks then fold in the yoghurt and the icing sugar, followed by three-quarters of the strawberries. Spoon the cream over the shortcake base. Place the 8 wedges on top, sprinkle lightly with a little caster sugar and the remaining strawberries. Serve.

WILD STRAWBERRIES WITH STRAWBERRY-LEAF SABAYON

This is a delicate summer dish. There is something magical about these small wild delights that makes this pudding so special.

Serves 6

250 g wild strawberries, reserve 6 for decoration

For the sabayon
10 strawberry leaves
50 ml water, boiled and allowed to sit for a couple of minutes
3 egg yolks
100 g caster sugar
150 ml white wine

Infuse the strawberry leaves in the boiled water until it is cold, about 40 minutes, then strain and reserve the water.

Whisk the egg yolks and sugar together in a large bowl until thick and pale. Put the bowl over a pan of hot, but not boiling water, so that the bottom of the bowl is immersed in the hot water. Keep whisking and add the wine. After more whisking the mixture should become frothy and mousse-like. Make sure that during all the whisking the water does not boil; this is critical as the mixture will separate.

Remove from the heat once you achieve mousse texture, then whisk in the strawberry leaf water. Set the bowl over a bowl of ice cubes and continue whisking until the mixture is cold.

Serve by placing the strawberries in 6 small individual bowls, add 1 tablespoon of sabayon over the fruit, then decorate each with one of the reserved strawberries.

WILD STRAWBERRIES WITH BALSAMIC VINEGAR

The first time I ate this I could not believe how simple it was. My mother found the recipe in Tuscany and I have reproduced it. It is essential to get the best thick balsamic vinegar for puddings or for eating with bread, not the one used for salad dressing.

This pudding is delightful served with vanilla biscuits. I have included the biscuit recipe (see page 346) as it is worth the effort; alternatively, if you do not have the time, serve it with vanilla ice cream.

Serves 4

125 ml red wine
125 ml water
500 g wild strawberries, rinsed and allowed to drain
75 g caster sugar
1 tbsp balsamic vinegar

Put the wine and water into a glass or china bowl, add the strawberries, and sprinkle with the sugar and balsamic vinegar. Mix gently, then put into the fridge for at least 45 minutes before serving.

VANILLA BISCUITS

Makes approx. 30 biscuits

120 g unsalted butter, softened
150 g caster sugar
1 tsp vanilla essence
2 eggs
250 g plain flour, sifted,
plus extra for dusting

Pre-heat the oven to 180°C/350°F/gas mark 4.

In a large bowl, mix the butter with the sugar and vanilla essence until it is light and fluffy, then add the eggs one at a time and beat well. Add the flour using a wooden spoon to make a soft sticky dough.

Remove the dough from the bowl and place on a sheet of cling film. Wrap it up and place it in the fridge for at least 1 hour.

Lightly flour the work surface and your hands, remove the dough from the fridge and roll it out to about 5 mm thick using a floured rolling pin. If necessary add extra flour, but not too much as this will make the biscuits hard.

Cut shapes, stars, rounds – whatever takes your fancy – and using a flat knife lift the biscuits onto a greased baking sheet or one that is lined with non-stick baking parchment. Leave a small space between each one to allow for spreading. Bake in the oven for about 10 minutes until they are lightly golden.

Remove and cool on a wire rack before storing in an airtight container.

Excess wild strawberry

Wild strawberry vinegar

I doubt that you will ever have a glut of this herb, but if you do ever have too many, wild strawberry vinegar is a must. You can use this with fruit, in salad dressings, sauces and marinades.

Makes 500 ml

500 g wild strawberries, washed
500 ml white wine vinegar
2 tbsp caster sugar

In a glass or china bowl, add all the ingredients, stir well, cover, and allow to infuse for 2–3 days.

Strain first through a colander to remove the strawberries, then through an unbleached coffee filter paper. Pour into clean, sterilised (see page 12) bottles with non-metallic lids.

This vinegar will keep well for a number of years.

GLOSSARY

BOTANICAL

Acid soil
A soil with a pH value of below 7 – from 1 to 7 on the pH scale.

Alkaline soil
A soil with a pH value above 7 – from 7 to 14 on the pH scale.

Annual
A plant that completes its life cycle in one year.

Aromatic
A plant with high levels of volatile oil.

Biennial
A plant that completes its life cycle in two years; in general it produces leaf in the first year and flower and seed in the second year.

Bulbils
Small bulb-like structures which form in the flower heads, such as inchives.

Crown
The upper part of the rootstock from which the roots arise, at or just below soil level, such aschicory and horseradish.

Deciduous
A plant that drops its leaves in the winter/cold months.

Evergreen
A plant that bears leaves all year round.

Frost hardy
A plant that needs protection when temperatures fall below -5°C (23°F).

Half-hardy
A plant that needs protection when temperatures fall below 0°C (32°F).

Hardy
A plant that needs protection when temperatures fall below -15°C (5°F).

Herbaceous
A perennial plant that dies down at the end of each growing season, reappearing in the spring.

Monocarpic
A plant that only flowers once, produces seed, then dies. This can take 3 or more years, such as Angelica.

Perennial
A plant that lives for at least three growing seasons.

pH value
This is the number that describes how acid or alkaline your soil is. A pH of 7 is considered neutral; an acid soil has a pH value below 7, whereasat above 7 the soil is alkaline.

Rhizome
Swollen underground stems. As the rhizome grows it often develops segments with buds that break into growth. Mint is a classic example of a rhizamous plant.

Tender
A plant that needs protection when temperatures fall below 5°C (41°F).

Umbel
These are umbrella-like cluster of flowers with all flowering stems arising from the same point, such as from a single stem.

MEDICINAL

Antifungal
A substance that combats fungal infections.

Antioxidant
A substance thatprevents oxidation and the breakdown of tissues.

Antiseptic
A substance thatdestroys or inhibitsmicro-organisms that cause infection.

Antispasmodic
A substance that relieves muscle spasm or reduces muscle tone.

Carminative
A substance that relieves digestive gas (wind) and indigestion.

Decoction
A water-based preparation of bark, roots, berries or seeds that has been simmered in boiling water.

Infusion
A water-based preparation in which any of the following are brewed in a similar way to tea: flowers, leaves, stems or bark.

Stomachic
A substance that eases stomach pain or increases stomach activity.

Topical
The application of an herbal remedy to a specific place on the body surface.

Vermifuge
A substance that expels intestinal worms.

Vulnerary
A substance that heals wounds.

ACKNOWLEDGEMENTS

There are so many people I wish to thank for helping me create this beautiful book. My family – past and present – especially my husband Mac, my son Alistair and my daughter Hannah for her enthusiasm and beautiful illustrations. My friends, for their contributions, either from eating and commenting or from letting me use their recipes. And a big thank you to Jamie for finding the time in his hectic life to write the glowing foreword to the book – he is always an inspiration.

Thank you to all the Ebury team, especially Imogen, who has magic eyes for seeing the missing link; to the wonderful team at Jekka's Herb Farm who kept going whatever the weather; to Will for creating a beautiful book; and to my agent Martine, for making sure all the dots were in the right place. And finally to my dog Hampton for making sure the bin got emptied.